Long-Forgotten Events
from Imperial Austria

Studies in Austrian Literature, Culture, and Thought
Biography, Autobiography. Memoirs Series

General Editors:

Jorun B. Johns
Richard H. Lawson

Jakob Ludwig Heller
(1842-1921)

Long Forgotten Events from Imperial Austria

Memoirs

*Told with Wisdom
and Jewish Humor*

Published and Annotated by his Granddaughter
Antonie Neumann
Translated by his Grandson Otto Neumann

English Text Edited by Lowell A. Bangerter

ARIADNE PRESS
Riverside, California

Ariadne Press would like to express its appreciation to the Bundeskanzleramt - Sektion Kunst, Vienna for assistance in publishing this book.

.KUNST

Translated from the German
Längst vergessene Begebenheiten aus Alt-Österreich
© 2001 novum Verlag Horitschon

Library of Congress Cataloging-in-Publication Data
Heller, Jakob Ludwig, 1842-1921.
[Längst vergessene Begebenheiten aus Alt-Österreich. English]
Long forgotten events from Imperial Austria / Jakob Ludwig Heller ; published and annotated by Antonie Neumann ; translated by Otto Neumann ; English text edited by Lowell A. Bangerter.
  p.   cm. -- (Studies in Austrian literature, culture, and thought. Translation series)
ISBN 1-57241-144-9
1. Heller, Jakob Ludwig, 1842-1921. 2. Jews—Austria—Biography. 3. Teplice (Czech Republic)—Biography. I. Neumann, Antonie, 1917- II. Neumann, Otto. III. Bangerter, Lowell A., 1941- IV. Title. V. Series.

DS135.AS93H52 2005
943.6'004924'0092—dc22

2005046976

Cover Design
Art Director: George McGinnis

Copyright ©2005
by Ariadne Press
270 Goins Court
Riverside, CA 92507

All rights reserved.
No part of this publication may be reproduced or transmitted in any form or by any means without formal permission.
Printed in the United States of America.
ISBN 1-57241-144-9 (original trade paperback)

In Memory of Our Parents

Dr. Alfred Neumann
(1872 Bielitz - 1944 Theresienstadt - Auschwitz)

"...The great doctor of the old school...a grand seigneur... and so modest..." That is how the famous Viennese neurologist and psychoanalyst, the late Professor Viktor Frankl (1905-1997), remembered our father. They both participated in the very active Jewish cultural life in the Theresienstadt concentration camp, the "penultimate stop," which actually continued in large measure - as long as it was possible - in the camp of the "intelligentsia."

The cultural activities were an attempt - out of sheer necessity - to maintain the inner strength and composure of the prisoners and to preserve their human dignity through participation in any possible intellectual or artistic diversion.

We, his children, knew him as the kindest father, a true gentleman, and a universally revered physician.

Agnes Neumann née Heller
(1887 Vienna - 1944 Theresienstadt - Auschwitz)

Unfortunately, we do not have any records of our mother's demeanor in the camp. We can therefore only draw conclusions from what we knew about her. She had an extremely courageous, energetic, and active personality that became especially evident in the last years before she was taken to the concentration camp. She was one of those people who never give up and who strive throughout life to achieve the very best in every area.

Her broad education, combined with the religious searching that led her to embrace Catholicism, as well as a deep desire to help those who were in need, may well have helped numerous fellow-sufferers.

To us children, she was a gentle, far-sighted mother who opened our eyes to the precious things in life. The sometimes strict manner in which she raised us left its mark on our lives, and for that we owe a great debt of gratitude. We have strived to lead lives worthy of such parents.

TABLE OF CONTENTS

Preface · 13

Childhood and Youth · 23
According to Father and Mother...- School Years - Our Home - Mother's Birthday - First Journey and First Drunkenness - Tinerl (Leontine)-My Little Sister - Painful Final Farewell to Mother, My Childhood Ends - Everyday Occurrences in Teplitz - Teplitz: World History in the Making - My Father and Uncle Joachim Become Merchants - Comparisons between My Own Family and That of Uncle Birnbaum

Grandparents · 53
My Paternal Grandmother, the "Leeser Woman" - My Maternal Grandfather, Jakob Herschmann Jeiteles - My Maternal Grandmother, Rebekka Jeiteles - Koppelmann Foges

My First Business Trips · 63
First Experiences at the Markets (1853 to 1855) - An Arrest - The Prestige of the Markets at Brünn and Their Gradual Decline After 1854 - Youthful Attempts at Independence and More Amusing Events

European Business Travels · 77
First Journey to London and Paris (1862-63) - Our Subsidiary Factory in Dresden (1864-66) - Journey to London in November of 1865 - Travels in 1866, Political Tensions Notwithstanding - A Problematic Journey to Dresden in 1866 - Journey to Vienna in 1866 - A Lost War with Positive Consequences, 1866 - Stock Market Fever

Work and Leisure · 101
The Trade Fairs in Leipzig - Freemason Lodge, 1869 - My Teplitz Circle of Friends

The Immediate Family · 111
My Brother Heinrich - My Brother Julius - The Jeiteles Family: Cousin George's Childhood - Purchased Release from Military Service - Uncle Joseph and Aunt Rosa Jeiteles - Gablonz - The Difficulties and Worries of a Successful Businessman - Uncle Joseph Jeiteles - Aunt Rosa Jeiteles - Cousin Auguste Becomes My Wife - My Severe Illness - Brother Julius: The Horse-Coach Accident - December 1881, Fire at the Ringtheater in Vienna - My Brother Leopold - My Sister-in-Law Pauline - The First Prize - Uncle Joseph Heller and Aunt Regie

Character Studies · 151
Uncle Joachim Heller - Uncle Schmule Heller - Cousin Heinrich Heller - Cousin Karl Heller and His Family - Uncle Israel (Ignaz) Jeiteles, 1811-1886 - Lori Jeiteles - Uncle Hermann - Uncle Jacques Foges ("The Peasant Foges") - Klara Schwarz (née Foges) - My Cousin Johanna - My Cousin Adolph - My Cousin Oskar

Looking Back · 177
George Jeiteles - Max Jeiteles: An Obituary - Auguste: A Very Personal Depiction of a Broken Marriage

Great Worries…Small Pleasures · 193
The Brioni Project - My Grandson Otto - Changing Moods - "Jour Fixe"

Written during the First World War · 203
Dated Writings - The Operation - A Strange Coincidence - May 9, 1917, My 75th Birthday - Heller & Thewett Exports

The Doctorate of Dr. Jonas Jeitteles at Prague University · 227

Epilogue · 231

Appendix · 233
*Memories of Inexplicable Events ·235 - Annotations · 251
Family Trees - Excerpts from the Jewish Encyclopedia - Acknowledgements - Biographies of the Editor and the Translator - Commentaries - Bibliography*

How much patience and energy, what will to survive must have been stored up in these writings for them to lie dormant for decades, seemingly dead, yet still so much alive that they tried again and again to jolt me into action.

Antonie Neumann

November 15, 1913

I ended my business activities at the beginning
of this year and have not yet become accustomed
to the idleness; I hope to create a pastime for myself
by writing here things that I have experienced and felt,
thoughts, and impressions:…

PREFACE

How this Book Came to Be

I can see Grandfather vividly before me, because my actual memories mingle with the pictures that we have of him. He was a handsome old gentleman with thick white hair and a beard, expressive eyes, and a face that mirrored his noble way of thinking. He had led a long life in which work, duty, and honor came first, but in which heart and common sense played equally important roles.

We find that same balance in his writings, which came into our possession under almost miraculous circumstances, and which we do not want to keep to ourselves.

He was born in Teplitz, Northern Bohemia, in 1842, and died after a long and fulfilled life in the house of our parents, Dr. Alfred and Agnes Neumann, in Gainfarn near Bad Vöslau, Lower Austria, in 1921.

For us grandchildren it is important to bridge the gap caused by the disappearance of our parents' generation in Auschwitz, and in so doing to permit this man to speak, a man who not only gives us an overview of his own long life, but also looks back much further into the time of his parents and grandparents.[1] He records history in his own way, history that he himself experienced.

As a child, he experienced the revolution year of 1848, and as a young man the conflict of 1866, which was of great importance for Austria. During his honeymoon the Franco-Prussian War of 1870 broke out, and as an old man he had to suffer the hardships of the cataclysm of the First World War.

The origin of his writings lies within the framework of his Jewish family, in the Jewish quarter of a small provincial town in what

---

[1] Our grandfather takes us back to *those* days and *those* people whose lives date back to the 18th century and for whom the Napoleonic Wars, with all their hardships, were part of daily existence. They literally lived close to where wars had taken place: Kulm, Austerlitz, Dresden, and Leipzig.

When the Emperor of France demonstrated an enlightened and tolerant attitude toward the Jews, it excited great hopes among them. It also aroused a special interest in France generally, which is clearly evident in our family.

was then the great Austrian Empire. Yet his perspective slowly broadened through his contact with the outside world. He observed with a positive but critical eye the revolutionary changes, the progress and modernization that took place during his long life.

In his parents' business, he learned how to be a merchant from the ground up. It seems worth mentioning that within only two generations a small peddler's business was transformed into a respected international export and import enterprise.

Finally, I would like to add that Grandfather only went to school until the age of eleven, and that his broader education was only the result of his unquenchable thirst for knowledge.

In 1913 Grandfather is seventy-one years old. He has been retired from his business for a year now. For quite a while he has been considering how he might find a fulfilling use for the leisure time to which he is still unaccustomed, since his entire life has been full of activity. He now lacks a regular occupation. So he finally sits down at his desk. He is going to tell his children about his life. He decides to write down his recollections, just as they come to him. He has really experienced so much, and his children know nothing at all about some of it.

The pastime becomes an interesting occupation for him as well, for as he writes, more and more lively images come to his mind. He becomes aware that he needs to give his story some sort of structure. So he starts over again. That is why some sections are more devoted to his parents and close relatives and the paths that their lives have taken, while others deal with contemporary events. These two areas of focus complement each other, of course, since the life of a family is always rooted in circumstances such as time and place.[2] Grandfather not only reports events, but also adds in a natural way his own experiences, his world view, and sometimes even advice, as only a caring person can. There is not one bitter word to be found anywhere in his account. If he has to criticize for the sake of truth, he balances his criticism with well-meaning or humorous comments. Grandfather wrote only for his family and never thought that his memories would be of wider interest. But

---

[2] This makes it difficult to write the book in a way that allows the reader to keep an orderly overview.

would it not be regrettable to let his writings simply gather dust in the archives of some history department?

That could have easily happened, if not for....

...well if not for some strange occurrences!

Who has not experienced events, so-called coincidences that are not as "insignificant" as they may seem at the time, but rather turn out to be signals. It is often only much later that the truth is realized, especially when such apparently "independent" events occur over a number of years and suddenly become linked in an unexpected manner. Then we prick up our ears and wonder if something strange is going on, something that has been beyond our control up to now. This book owes much to a series of such "coincidences."

Alone the fact that in 1939, that year of tumultuous outcomes, our mother's most prized possession, her father's irreplaceable handwritten memoirs, escaped the persecutors and reached my brother in Australia, where he alone had found refuge[3] - that in itself seems like a miracle, a destiny that was unfortunately denied our parents. The books of writings, however, were destined to survive!

More than two decades later, my brother brought them to me in Paris. For both of us, reading them was an exciting experience. It was evident to us that the contents went far beyond our own family saga. But what could we do at that time?

---

[3] My brother left Austria in the autumn of 1938, first for Holland, then for England, to wait anxiously for an immigration visa to Australia. It was our hope that our parents would follow him to Australia.

A small part of our furniture and our "most personal treasures," i.e., a little chest with family photos and the handwritten memoirs of our grandfather, were in a container on the very last ship that was able to dock in Sydney before WW II started.

It is not necessary to emphasize in particular the acute danger associated with sending such things under those circumstances. Our parents received their immigration visas on the same day that the borders of Germany were sealed.

The books of writings were written in the old German script, a handwriting style that even then had been almost completely forgotten. Furthermore, my brother's home was now in Australia, mine in Paris. Our occupations did not allow us to copy the long handwritten text in a leisurely fashion. We had neither the time nor the financial resources to work on the manuscripts. They therefore "slumbered" for many years at my home.

I must now go even further back into the past. One of my mother's favorite books (at home in Vienna) was *Jugenderinnerungen eines alten Mannes* [An Old Man's Memoirs of His Youth] by Wilhelm von Kügelgen. Her copy of that 19th-century book got lost with "many other things." By a pleasant "coincidence," I found a copy of it in a second-hand bookshop here in Paris in the 1970s. I recognized it immediately: the same dark red binding with the green trim, the yellowed pages, the Gothic type... I bought it with my heart pounding. I did not want to read it immediately, however. Rather, I wanted to save it for later, when I would have the time to immerse myself in it. That book waited for more than twenty years for me to read it! Every time I saw its spine on the shelf, I thought: "Soon!" My anticipation grew, but it was not yet quite the right time.

Then in 1980, while traveling in Austria, in Salzburg I became acquainted with a young woman, Ingrid Wagner, whose spare room I rented for a few days' vacation there. Who could have anticipated in 1980 that very shortly Ingrid would become one of my dearest and truest friends? That she would create an extremely strong link between me and my homeland? That it would be she who would suggest to me a few years ago to dictate the books onto cassettes...who would cheerfully take it upon herself to type the many long texts on her computer? An enormous job! And yet without her willingness such an undertaking would have been simply inconceivable! I want to express here how deeply grateful I am to her.

Once again years passed by.
In the spring of 1994, I made a short trip to Vienna to attend a discussion on Austrian architectural monuments. I engaged in conversation with a friendly gentleman who was sitting at the same

table, Dr. H. Douffet from Dresden, whom I did not know at all. During our conversation, he invited me to Dresden to visit the city's sights and its beautiful surroundings. During the following summer, that highly unexpected suggestion became a very pleasant reality.

Two strange surprises awaited me in Dresden: First, it turned out that like my grandfather, my dear host was actually born in Teplitz and that he possessed a treasure of historical documents relating to that town. Second, while taking a stroll through what remains of historic Dresden, I came across the family home of the painter Wilhelm von Kügelgen, the author of the aforementioned book. At that moment I knew for certain that the first thing I would do when I got home would be to read the book! Now it was time!

Another surprising event occurred several months later. One evening at home, while leafing through a biography on Beethoven,[4] I suddenly found myself confronted with the most astonishing and most welcome illustration, one that I had never noticed before! It seemed unbelievable! It showed a street scene in Teplitz. In the very middle of the picture was Grandfather's birthplace, the house *Zur Eiche* [Oak House], which was demolished long ago. Next to it was the house *Zum Tempel* [Temple House], which then belonged to his closest relatives, the Birnbaum family. That book had been in my possession for years, but only then, at the right moment, did I open it to exactly the right page.

How strange! Was all this purely coincidental?

Were my parents and my grandparents supporting me in my intentions? I hoped so. For I certainly no longer believed in coincidences! I viewed it as a sign that I should publish Grandfather Heller's memoirs out of admiration for him and as an expression of my gratitude for his love and that of our parents.

One might ask why Kügelgen's book plays such an important role in my project. Although it was written by a real artist, precedes Grandfather's notes by half a century, and describes a significantly different social class, it reflects similar attitudes: "...refreshing liveliness...humor and the belief in a higher power that determines our

---

[4] L. van Beethoven, *Collection Génies et Réalité*, Paris, Hachette, 1961.

destinies...."[5] Kügelgen's recollections of his youth paint a picture of the cultural life of the upper classes in the formerly influential city of Dresden. Grandfather, on the other hand, unknowingly drew a parallel to it by showing us, through the eyes of his own *Jewish family*, daily life in a coquettish, bourgeois, provincial town, a popular spa, and an active trade center near Dresden, not far from the border of Saxony. But there is another special reason why it is important to me: I subsequently discovered some principles and thoughts that are expressed by Kügelgen in his book[6] - concerning biographies in general - which seem to confirm my own way of thinking.

Could it be one more "coincidence" that of all books mother's favorite one subconsciously led me to awaken Grandfather's "mind and heart"?

Paris, September 2001

Antonie Neumann

---

[5] From the preface of W. v. Kügelgen, *Jugenderinnerungen eines alten Mannes*, 1900.

[6] To quote from Kügelgen:

"If people live with heart and soul, anybody's life is interesting. The right to a biography is not solely reserved for historical persons."

"...I have found that even the simplest things become interesting if only they are given proper expression."

"...one should not do *loved and honored people* the injustice of publishing 'drafts' written by them, that were not meant for publication and which they themselves would have rewritten ten times beforehand, had they known!"

"...by the way, the greatest mistake one can make in writing a biography is to put too much order and clarification into it. I tell everything in a mixed-up way, which of course makes it difficult to connect the various subjects. But it means that the entire picture looks so much more like the colorful, speckled image of reality."

The older I get, the more quickly I forget events of recent times!
In order that in my later years I may more easily remember events of the past, from now on I intend to write down everything that I think worthy of not being wholly forgotten.

Vienna, December 10, 1913.

Jakob Ludwig Heller

The publisher has allowed herself to make slight, respectful corrections. These changes were carefully considered, so as not to interfere with the original style of her grandfather's writing.

The translation of the German text into English was carried out by Otto Neumann, the author's grandson.

In order not to disrupt the reading of the main text with numerous footnotes, annotated portions have been marked with asterisks. The corresponding references are given by page and introduced with key words in the "Annotations" section of the Appendix.

"What I have experienced in years previous
Many a thing both happy and serious,
Faithfully, I'll write it down,
To banish boredom, not for renown.
Enjoyment it shall bring to you
And smiles on your faces, too
And may this old man's reflection
Always show his true affection."

CHILDHOOD AND YOUTH

According to Father and Mother...

I was born on May 8, 1842 in Teplitz (Teplice in Czech), Northern Bohemia. A few weeks prior to my birth, my grandfather - mother's father - died, and I, as was the tradition, was given the name Jakob to honor his memory. That name probably did not seem sufficiently charming for a baby and therefore the sweet nickname "Kobi" was bestowed upon me, and I will probably have to live with it until my dying day.

Before my birth, it had originally been decided that I would be called Ludwig, which was my paternal grandfather's name. But due to the death of my grandfather, Jakob H. Jeiteles, it was decided that the name Jakob would be used as the first of my given names, and thus at official functions my name is "Jakob Ludwig Heller," which does sound nicer than "Kobi"!

My dear mother told me that before I was born, several of my brothers and sisters died very young, but none of them had been named after my mother's father. That is why I was to bear his name, and my family hoped that in so doing I would be blessed with a longer life. That wish was granted!

What I am going to write about my dear father, I owe to his own accounts. He was born the son of penniless parents on February 16, 1809. His father, Leeser* Heller, was a Jewish teacher, and his mother was a peddler.

The infant child was given the Jewish name "Beerl," which his parents also recorded when registering his birth at the civil registry.

At that time those authorities could do as they wished, and thus the certificate was returned with the comment that the Jewish boy must not be called "Beerl," but "Balduin" instead. Such "jokes"* were then quite normal. This willful behavior of the officials certainly turned out to be advantageous for my father, for it surely must have been better to be called Balduin than Beerl.

My dear father also told me that he was seven years old when his own father died in 1816. Grandfather did not leave a fortune to his widow, but he did leave seven children who were not provided for, specifically: Joachim, Minke, Beerl (Balduin), Lotti, Leni, Josef, and Schmule (Samuel). Rachel Heller, his widow, supported herself and her family wretchedly but honestly by peddling. She delivered goods to some aristocrats who lived in Teplitz, as well as to members of the nobility who spent only the summer months there. Grandmother was one of those entrepreneurs who were then known as "house Jews," and she was called "the Leeser woman," because her husband's name was Leeser and she was well liked by the ladies of high society.

Despite her poverty, she did achieve her goal after a number of years, in that all of her sons and daughters - with the exception of her son "Schmule,"* who died penniless in America - lived in favorable social circumstances. That occurred on the one hand as a result of the good example that she set for them through her untiring diligence and earnestness, and on the other hand because of the conscientiousness and abilities that were displayed by her children.

Now I want to tell you how my dear father came to embrace his business career! His mother promised him that he could attend the wedding of his eldest sister, Minka, who was to marry a Mr. Patek in Raudnitz. However, a few days before the planned departure, my father had to content himself instead with five gilders in Viennese currency as compensation, because the cost of the trip to Raudnitz would have been too high after all.

Those five gilders* in Viennese currency, or four crowns twenty, constituted my father's business capital, and with that money he started a peddling business in Teplitz as a ten-year-old boy, a business that brought him some success, albeit minor, especially during the summer when Teplitz was visited by many rich visitors. But little by little he progressed, and through his diligence and thriftiness, by the age of twenty my father had accrued some capital, with which he was able to open his own modest, but well-stocked shop.

He then went into business with his eldest brother, Joachim, and with Moritz Birnbaum, who was engaged to Father's youngest sister, Leni. Marriage was out of the question, however, because they lacked funds to ensure them a reasonably secure livelihood. So my father made it possible, but that did not earn him any gratitude from either his sister or his brother-in-law. The partners became the fiercest competitors. Only during the last years of their lives, long after their wives had died, did they become closer friends.

I cannot remember that my parents ever visited the Birnbaums, or vice versa, except on special occasions. If they met by chance, the usual polite phrases were exchanged, but their relationship was never congenial. That did not mean, however, that either our parents or theirs were unhappy about the friendly contact between their children. So Johanna, Friedrich Birnbaum, and I were very good friends. We used to walk to school and back together, and since we lived next door to each other, they in the house *Zum Tempel* on *Lange Gasse* and we in the house *Zur Eiche* on *Lange Gasse*, we had no trouble finding each other in our spare time.

I have only a few memories of my very first years. I must have been an ugly boy, because I often heard people say: "His eyes are his most beautiful feature." Therefore I often looked in the mirror, but did not derive any satisfaction from it. I also remember that I regretfully found that other children were dressed in better clothes than I, but unfortunately I could not change that, either.

I spent most of my time in the big kitchen or in my parents' shop. Apartment and shop were in the same building, in *Zur Eiche* on *Lange Gasse* in Teplitz. Since I had neither a governess nor any other person supervising me, as is the custom today, nobody stopped me from playing with the other boys in the street - come rain or shine. That continued until my sixth birthday, when I had to start school!

School Years

In those days children started school a year earlier than they do today (1913). I had to attend the Jewish public elementary school.

Its principal was the teacher, Mr. David Sohr. The rest of the time I spent at Mr. Deutsch's Jewish private school, which was located on the second floor of the building in which we lived. It was a very pleasant school indeed. All of the Jewish children in Teplitz between the ages of five and twelve, boys and girls, sat peaceably side by side in two not very large rooms. A lesser number of pupils who were on the same "educational level" were taught in a third small room. All the others could choose for themselves what to do with their time. In other words, it was truly a very easy-going school!

Mr. Deutsch, a former businessman who had gone bankrupt, had not become a teacher until the age of fifty. Since there was no other or better school in those days, the children were entrusted to him for a monthly fee of two gilders in convention currency, i.e., four crowns twenty.

Work was taken much more seriously in the Jewish public elementary school! Mr. Sohr knew how to inspire his pupils with the pleasure of learning, but he had a difficult task! The school was allowed to teach only the first and second years of elementary classes, but each pupil had to attend them for at least six years in order to obtain a completion certificate. Thus there were several subdivisions for each class. The number of pupils per class was seventy to eighty boys and girls, and the lessons were held between 8:00 a.m. and 10:00 a.m., and between 1:00 p.m. and 3:00 p.m. How Mr. Sohr managed this task alone, without any help, is a mystery to me. Nevertheless, I must point out that any child who really wanted to learn something had done so by the time he or she left school.

Fortunately, since the beginning of the 1850s, a tremendous change and improvement in the entire school system has taken place. I wish to describe here, however, what the Teplitz Jewish public elementary school was like until then.

On the *Zigeuner Gasse*, or, as it was usually called, the *Hintere Gasse*, stood the Jewish community house. The school caretaker and the beadle lived on the ground floor with their two large families. The building also housed the *Sholethhaus** and the oven for the *Mazes*,* the unleavened bread. A large number of rats had also set up their quarters there. On the second floor was the *Hekdisch*, the home for poor, sick, and elderly members of the Jewish community. On the third floor was the large school room for the many children, and next to it were some more rooms for poor married couples.

It was typical for the era that the school and children were housed in the same building that served so many other purposes, but which certainly did not meet the hygienic requirements. Nevertheless, I cannot remember even one occasion during all my school years when lessons were interrupted because of illness.

It was the caretaker's duty to clean the school premises, but he did not do it very well. We feared the man very much, however, because he denounced us to the teacher wherever and whenever he could. Mr. Sohr often had reason to dispense corporal punishment, and he called it "dishing out the straps," which were administered either to the back of the hand or to that other well-known part of the body. And the dear caretaker, whose task it was to carry out such "sentences," fulfilled them by making use of a "Spanish cane," more to his own satisfaction and that of the teacher than to the pleasure of the "clients"!

I am happy to say that I never received "the straps," but was *once* quite unjustifiably given two hours of detention by Mr. Sohr. But my cousin Johanna helped me. Right after school she went to see Uncle Balduin and told him about the injustice to which I was being subjected. Half an hour later my father rescued me from custody. I will never forget what Johanna did for me!

During the winter, Mr. Sohr also gave private evening classes for boys and girls, which I also attended. I was not among the worst pupils. In the elementary school I was even the class prefect and carried out my responsibilities rather strictly, but only until I was moved to adopt a somewhat milder approach after I was beaten up by some classmates whom I had reported.

As I mentioned earlier, in our schools boys and girls were together in the classes, and I am of the opinion that it was quite advantageous. Among the seven and eight-year-old boys and girls friendships were already forming. After the morning classes - as well as in the evenings - we went home in pairs, making smart remarks, criticizing the carelessness of other pupils, and enjoying comments such as: "You were very good today..." Thus, the enthusiasm and eagerness to learn increased for both. But I think that it is also good in another respect for boys and girls to have contact with one another at an early age, because in so doing they become more uninhibited and better able to make judgments later on. By the way, many a tender affection that began back then in the schoolroom led to a marriage in later life!

Our Home

I now want to describe my home and what our life was like there.

The situation in the home was very different from what it is today (1913), and the relationship between the employees and employers was also completely different. The cook usually worked in the house for many years, quite often until she married, and was, so to speak, a part of the family. It was the custom in those days that Jewish cooks were employed for at least six months, and changes could take place only at *Pessach* (Easter) or at *Roschhaschono* (New Year), and that arrangement endured because the mutual feeling of being bound to an agreement made it easier for them to get along with each other. In spite of the fact that there was no "formal curtsey" or "hand-kiss" back then, the lady of the house was treated with the respect that she deserved, and the employees were treated well and affectionately.

In my parents' house affairs were conducted in a "pious" manner. My dear mother set great store by that. We had separate crockery and cutlery for meat dishes and for food that contained milk. Whenever a knife was used improperly, it had to be stuck as deeply as possible into a gap in the floorboards so that only the handle was visible. After it had been there for twenty-four hours, it could be returned to its previous use! We even had separate "milk" and "meat" utensils for Easter, the "Feast of Unleavened Bread," which was observed very strictly in general.

There were many things that had to be observed until approximately the 1850s, things that are now considered to be antiquated, and with good reason. But many things have been gradually lost in giving up those small formalities. On Friday evenings the business was closed earlier than usual. My mother put on a formal dress and solemnly began the Sabbath by praying in front of two candles, after forming a semicircle above them with both hands. The table was set festively. Four elegant silver candlesticks lit the table, and at the head of the table, in front of my father's seat, a large *Barches*, a kind of plaited brioche with poppy seeds, lay on a flat dish. It was made, however, in such a way that it could be eaten with both meat and desserts. My father blessed this *Barches* before beginning the meal, cut it, took a bite for himself, and then gave a piece to everyone at the table. Afterward it was served in larger pieces for general consumption. It was that way every Friday evening.

On high feast days it was even more ceremonial. I will never forget the impression that it made on me, when, on the evening before such a feast, Father and Mother embraced, kissed, and congratulated each other, and how they blessed each child afterward, first Father and then Mother, by placing their hands on the child's head. The child then solemnly expressed gratitude and love with a warm kiss.

I often feel sorry for the youth of today, for although they receive more expressions of love and care now than they did in the old days, they do not come to know the deep feeling of togetherness that was formerly prevalent in Jewish families. What does a child receive today as a replacement for the old contemplative ceremonies that, in those days, remained unforgettable for the young and had a better educational effect than the methods used today? Nowadays, the Jewish feast days are completely ignored. They are just considered to be "free time," because the children are not sent to school. They are not really festive anymore, and parents who do not downplay the value of Jewish feasts in the eyes of their inexperienced children are very rare today!

It was different in my childhood! As early as when we were five or six years old, we boys all went to the synagogue every Friday evening and Saturday morning, both in summer and in winter. The service was beautiful and ceremonial. The organ and the beautiful singing made a deep impression on a child's mind, and in a quietly reverent manner we listened to the singing of the prayer leader* and the choir. Memories of those Friday evenings at the synagogue will always remain vivid within me.

Grandfather's birthplace, "Oak House"

Fifty years later, when I visited the synagogue on the *Rue de la Victoire* in Paris on a Friday evening, to attend the service on the anniversary of my mother's death, and heard the *"Lechau Daudi"* sung to the same melody as fifty years earlier in our Teplitz synagogue, my eyes filled with tears.

There is something very special, I would say, something indescribably beautiful about memories of youth, and that is especially true when they are combined with religious feelings. It is true that in my childhood I was brought up to be pious, and that I remained so for quite a long time, but it is equally true that I assumed a more liberal view of things as a result of experience, serious thinking, and inner turmoil. I will always be grateful to my mother, however, for raising me in a religious manner, because I would not want to do without the foundation for the feelings that I had at that time, which still exists today. Those sentiments have influenced my life and my actions, maybe more than I can imagine, because modern times demand more action than compassion, more recklessness than warm feelings.

But are people happier now that they are free from any religious impulse? Will the rising generation really be happier and more satisfied on the basis of material success alone? I fear that such is not the case! That is why I wish things were different!

Listen to the opinions of an old man who spent his youth in a truly antiquated era and in a very different environment, but who also tried to adapt to modern times: Set the greatest store in developing your children's hearts and minds. Observe feast days that will remain in your children's memories. Have family celebrations that tie you closely to your children. Make sure that you teach them love, respect, and gratitude, and regarding religion, do not portray it to your children as something unimportant, and act in such away that in later years they can fight "without bias" the battle within themselves that every thinking person must fight.

Now I want to return to telling you about my home and my dear parents.

My mother, Sophie Jeiteles, who was born on September 18, 1813, was the daughter of well-to-do parents who had a rather large wholesale haberdashery business in Prague. As was then customary, she worked in her parents' store after finishing school. That was how she got to know and love my father, who had many business dealings with her parents. The wedding occurred in 1834. All of my memories indicate that my parents had a very harmonious relationship, and that they were full of love and consideration for each other. Mother was a kind-hearted but serious woman, who was usually happiest within the circle of her closest family and at work, but who made few demands of the world. She also worked incessantly in her husband's business. My father was often away on business for long periods of time, and so my mother had to manage the rather extensive enterprise, which often employed more than twenty workers.

Not many social functions took place in our home. My father's brothers and brothers-in-law, who remained his business partners even after he was married, became his competitors, and his sisters and sisters-in-law were jealous of my mother because she came from a wealthy family. Besides that, my father's old mother was always on *her* own family's side, and thus friendly relations could not be established. Outside of the family, social dealings were rare and loose. Leisure hours on Saturdays and holidays were used for walks and excursions, and I was included in them. I still remember how much I enjoyed going for walks with my parents.

For a long time I was the "only" child in the house, because my brother Heinrich, who was seven years my senior, studied in Prague, lived at the house of my grandmother, Mrs. Rebekka Jeiteles, and came home only during the holidays. However, in 1846 my little sister Leontine was born. I will describe her sad fate later. My brother Julius was born in 1848 and my brother Leopold in 1851.

The only relative who came to see us often and to whom we were very close was Uncle Josef, one of my father's younger brothers. He was the only one of them who had studied at a university. He was a chemist and worked for many years as a colorist in one of the largest calico mills in Vienna. In 1844 my father opened a metal button and fashion accessories factory in Teplitz, and Uncle Josef went into business with him. He came to see us very often and regularly spent Friday evenings at our house. He always had hilarious stories to tell. He played funny games with me, and I really liked him.

As often as possible I visited him in the so-called *Posthof*, the building where his factory was situated. It was only ten minutes away from our apartment, and I was usually drawn to the laboratory. There I watched in amazement how raw and dirty brassware caused hissing and roaring sounds when it was immersed in a container of nitric acid, and how it came out clean and beautiful after a few seconds. It was also fascinating to watch how a ducat could be chemically dissolved and turned into a brown, dirty, fluid mass. It was even more surprising that this same mass could produce a beautiful, shiny, golden coating on brassware when treated correctly. All of those things interested me a great deal. I found the work at the presses and drop hammers no less interesting to watch, and I remember having worked "properly" for a few minutes at a small press under Uncle Josef's supervision! That was all very entertaining to me, but I also enjoyed playing with Diana, my uncle's favorite dog.

The 19th of March, St. Joseph's Day, was always a special holiday in the factory, because it was my uncle's name day. Then the workers - although Uncle Josef was a Jew - arranged for a number of musicians to come in the afternoon. First they serenaded my uncle, after which they were led to a room in the factory that had been emptied for the occasion. Uncle Josef graciously bought everyone lots of beer, wine, sausages, and God knows what else. The cheers for my uncle went on and on, and people danced and drank until late at night. I was always sorry that I was not allowed to watch those merry activities for more than a short time, but today I believe that it was for the best! Uncle Josef will appear in my writings in many other places.

For now I will continue with my experiences up to my tenth or eleventh year. I had a good time at school. Besides the instruction there I also received very good private lessons. Our friends, the Jakob Spitz family, engaged a private tutor for their children, and I also attended his lessons regularly. I also learned eagerly in Mr. Sohr's classes in elementary school and was always a prefect. During examinations it was I who had to memorize and then recite the address to the dean and to all those who "promote the school and science." I also had to recite poems and, in a nutshell, I was the teacher's pet. I was popular with the other boys at school, even more so with the girls, and all in all I was rather satisfied with my life! But I was not too strict anymore, for I learned that beatings are painful, even when they come from schoolmates!

But there were some really bad boys in my class, especially one about whom I want to write briefly here. He got into all kinds of mischief in school, made fun of the teachers and religion tutors, and was not afraid of the school's caretaker, the one whom everybody else hated and who was very good at applying "the straps" to various parts of the body with his Spanish cane. In a word, that rascal seemed incorrigible, and he received the worst marks.

That boy's name was Willibald Horwitz. He was the son of poor Jews from Teplitz and lived as a vagabond until he was fourteen or fifteen years old. Then a change took place. He left Teplitz, and nobody knew where he had gone; but he studied music with such enthusiasm and diligence that, with the help of his extraordinary talent, he learned to play several instruments and was even trained to be an opera singer. He became a valued member of the Vienna Court Opera and enjoyed numerous successes. During that time I often had the opportunity to meet with him and exchange memories of our school days. He married and had a lovely house, but died very young, barely fifty years old.

Pauline Lucca was engaged at the Vienna Court Opera at the same time as Willibald Horwitz. She had such high regard for him that he alone was her accompanist, advisor, and evaluator during all of her rehearsals!

Willibald Horwitz is a prime example of the fact that one should not be rash in judging a young, high-spirited, and audacious boy.

Mother's Birthday

Although my mother did not have much time to devote to me, she showed me her tenderness and took every opportunity to praise me whenever I deserved it. She also reprimanded me when I had done something wrong, and I tried not to give her any reason to complain. I loved her very much and always looked for any occasion to show it to her. I never came back from a walk without bringing her flowers that I had picked along the way, but I also remember one time when I wanted to give her a bigger surprise. For that she slapped me twice in the face and then rewarded me with kisses.

My mother's birthday was in the autumn. It was not celebrated according to the German calendar date, but according to the Jewish one, on the second day of New Year. For that occasion, I wanted to surprise her by giving her two pots of flowers as a present. As a seven-year-old boy, I had no money to buy them, of course, but I hoped that I would be able to get them free of charge from one of our suppliers who lived in Mariaschein, which was an hour and a half from Teplitz. He had a very large garden and often brought us strawberries, flowers, and fruit. But where would I find the time to remain away from home for that long?

Suddenly I thought of the Teplitz Fair, for which we had a day off from school. Without saying a word to anybody, I left the house at nine o'clock, believing that I would be back home by twelve o'clock, at which time we always punctually ate lunch. I walked briskly, and when I wearily arrived at the house of Mr. Fischer (our supplier) in Mariaschein and anxiously presented my request to him, I was first given a good meal and was also promised two very nice potted flowers. I firmly declined Mr. Fischer's offer to bring them to Teplitz with his next delivery - *I* wanted to carry them home *myself*. And that is the way it happened. I started my journey home with two rather heavy pots and with the sinking feeling that I would probably never arrive home in time.

At around half past one, the poor sinner crept into the kitchen, told the cook his secret, and asked her to hide the flower pots until my mother's birthday. I also learned that my dear mother was extremely worried about me, that she had people looking for me everywhere, and that she was upset that I had left the house without telling anybody!

When she saw me a short while later, I received two hard slaps in the face, which, however, did not upset me at all. When Mother asked me where I had been all that time, I gave her all kinds of muddled answers. While I had lunch, the cook apparently talked to Mother, but she did not let on and did not reproach me again!

On the day of my mother's birthday, I looked proudly at the two beautiful potted flowers on the table, and when Mother kissed me lovingly, thanked me, and said that she knew the story behind the flowers, I would not have exchanged places with a king!

First Journey and First Drunkenness

I was extremely excited when my parents promised me that I could attend the wedding of my cousin Fanni Glogau from Schokau to Alexander Stern from Vienna, which was to take place in Lobositz. At the age of eight it put me into cheerful agitation weeks ahead of time. After all, it was to be my *first* journey. Moreover, I was to *see and travel on a train for the first time*, to an *unfamiliar town*, and on top of all that, I was to attend a *wedding*!

I could not believe that this would actually happen until - about two weeks before the wedding - I was measured for a new suit and provided with a whole new wardrobe! I was very proud when I looked at myself in the mirror in all my glory, and considered myself truly worthy to represent my family.

Exactly *how* I behaved as a representative of my family, I will report later. And also how I heeded my dear mother's lessons, advice, and admonitions: "Be friendly and modest. Congratulate the newlyweds nicely but not insistently. Take care of your new clothes and, above all, eat and drink in moderation." Those were Mother's words. I must have paid little attention to them, but nevertheless loudly promised to take them to heart. But on that day I really had only one wish - "Why can't it be evening already?" - because at about eight o'clock in the evening the stage coach was leaving Teplitz for Aussig.

Father and Mother could not attend the wedding, and thus I was entrusted to Uncle Josef. After the day's excitement, I quickly fell asleep at his side, and at just before eleven o'clock he awakened me. We had arrived in Aussig, and I sleepily climbed the stairs to the station with him. The anticipation and the excitement quickly woke me up, and suddenly I saw two enormous fiery eyes appear out of the dark night. I saw a monster spraying showers of sparks, heard the deafening roar of the engine, and thought that I was seeing hell and the devil rushing toward me!

I will never forget the overwhelming impression of that moment. It took my breath away, and I stood there as though rooted to the spot. I think that every child will have felt that way when seeing a train approaching for the first time, especially at night.

I snapped out of my daze when Uncle Josef vigorously pushed me into a compartment, where I immediately went back to sleep. I awoke in a bed in Lobositz, and I have no idea how that happened. Two of my cousins, Friedrich Birnbaum and Moritz Heller, had already arrived the previous night. We spent a jolly morning together. At midday the wedding ceremony took place in the hotel's large hall, with the banquet following afterward. We children found an extra table set for twelve in the adjacent room and soon became acquainted with the groom's relatives who were about our age, both boys and girls, and were very cheerful and happy. We had our own waitress, who kindly invited us to eat and drink, which we did. We especially enjoyed the wine very much! At home we were only rarely allowed to take a sip of it, but here we were provided with an endless supply. We toasted the bride and groom, drank to close friendship with our new friends, and had such fun until...well, I do not know what became of the bride and groom and their guests, or even me. And I know just as little about how I got from Lobositz to Teplitz and into my bed.

I did not regain consciousness until the following day, late in the evening, when my mother read me the riot act. She told me off and assured me that she would never again buy me nice clothes, because I had returned with my wedding suit covered with stains. She called me an awful drunkard who brought her disgrace rather than joy, etc., etc.... I grimaced with my hangover and went back to sleep. My head was much too heavy to take all of those accusations to heart, and the next day my mother seemed to have forgotten all about it, as had I! And that was the end of my first journey and my first inebriation. The latter was followed by many more sweet occasions of tipsiness, but none of them caused me to suffer such a bad hangover.

Tinerl (Leontine) - My Little Sister

In 1846, on the 21st of June, I got a little sister. Leontine, or Tinerl, as we called her, was a dear and lovely child, and when she was a bit older I was often allowed to play with her. Until then I had been the only child in the house, and even though my little sister was four years my junior, I enjoyed playing with her. Our room was next to the large kitchen and we spent a lot of time there.

Our cook, who had worked for us for many years, was very kind to us. I always got my ten-o'clock sandwich and my afternoon snack in the kitchen. Our cook was very busy, because my parents had many employees - bookkeepers, assistants, and apprentices - and they all lived and had their meals in the house. Since my parents always had lunch with the employees, there were usually twenty to twenty-five people around the lunch table. As far as I can remember, quantity was stressed over quality because the young people were always hungry. In the afternoon the employees were served coffee at their desks, and I can still see the enormous black tray before me, with all the glasses of coffee on it. I can also still hear the employees' complaints about the quality of the coffee, complaints that were probably justified. The coffee was made in a big earthenware pot, and I would not have remembered that detail so well, if a very painful event had not embedded it in my mind forever.

Upon returning home from school one late-autumn afternoon, I found Mother and everybody in the house in great distress! Tinerl had been in the kitchen as usual. The cook had taken the big pot of boiling coffee from the stove, and Tinerl had been right in front of her. At that moment the pot had burst, and its boiling contents had poured out over the poor child. I cannot describe the shock, the wailing, and the affliction of my poor mother - Father was out of town - and everyone who was present in the house, which became all the greater when the summoned doctors declared that it was a very severe case!

Everything imaginable was tried in an effort to ease the poor child's great sufferings, and after weeks and months of devoted care it seemed that a change for the better might be expected. But all of a sudden the healing wounds burst open again and the poor child was released from her pain on Christmas Eve of 1849!

I will never forget that evening! That sad event was certainly the main reason why my dear mother's health grew worse. After the tragedy she continued working in the shop from morning until night, and perhaps the hard work kept her from dwelling on those sad thoughts. Nevertheless, I do not remember ever seeing Mother really happy again after Leontine's death.

In the meantime, my family had grown slightly larger with the birth of my brother Julius on November 16, 1848. I will talk about him in more detail later. I want to mention here, however, that in the summer of 1851 another brother, Leopold, was born. Both children were weak and therefore enjoyed Mother's particular care and attention, but unfortunately not long enough!

Painful Final Farewell to Mother, My Childhood Ends

I was not even eleven years old when I again had to suffer a very painful and irreplaceable loss. On March 25, 1853 my faithful, unforgettable mother was taken from us after a long illness. We all experienced indescribable grief. I could not grasp the idea of not having our cherished mother anymore. The feelings of emptiness and deep sadness were amplified even more by my father's bitter expression of sorrow.

On Palm Sunday, March 27, 1853, my mother was buried. She was taken from her loved ones without even having reached the age of forty. Our house was empty, and oppressive worries of all kinds troubled my dear father, not the least of which was the one that two weak little children - Julius, who was four, and Leopold, who was not quite two - needed a lot of care.

During my mother's illness, her sister, Aunt Marie Wiener, had come to Teplitz to look after us, and a few hours before Mother's death my grandmother also arrived. When the funeral was over, it was decided that Grandmother would send us a suitable person to raise the two little ones and run the large household. Then both Grandmother and Aunt Marie returned home.

My father had to leave a few days after the funeral to attend to business matters in Linz. My brother Heinrich had arrived there a week earlier with some members of the staff, because the Linz market, to which we regularly sent between a hundred and a hundred and fifty boxes of goods, was of great importance.

The only halfway "adult" family member who remained in the house was I, and I was not even eleven years old. My father handed *me* the key to the till. He ordered me to write down exactly how much money went out and came in, to open all arriving mail, to supervise the personnel, and I don't know what else, and then he said: "If there is something that you don't know, then ask Uncle Josef, who will come by every night." Finally my father announced to me that I would no longer attend school, but would remain in the shop. Then he told me to pull myself together in order to become efficient quickly!

To be honest, I was not upset about *that* announcement. I enjoyed studying, but the obligation to attend school is unpleasant for everybody. Moreover, the business did not seem completely alien to me, because I was there every day and thought that I had a rough idea about it. In fact, I was flattered by the awareness that I was entering into it as a deputy to the principal and taking on a position superior to that of all the employees. And when my father returned home, after checking the main transactions he told me that he was not dissatisfied with me.

My brother Heinrich, who had suffered from pneumonia in the summer of 1852, was supposed to interrupt his studies for a year because of his poor health, but in fact he spent that time in my father's establishment. After Mother's death, at Father's request he gave up his studies and remained in the business, which made up in part for the loss of my mother's tireless work.

I will never forget the first *Passah* evening after Mother's death. We went to the synagogue before dinner as usual, and upon our return each of us found a quiet corner to drive the pain from our hearts by shedding tears. It was the first feast day without Mother, and we could not believe it.

Again and again we were overcome by grief, but time, work, and - last but not least - recognition that we could not alter anything finally made many things bearable and even the worst things took on a milder form!

The housekeeper whom my grandmother sent us did not manage to bring happiness to the house. Her name was Minna Frankl, and she was a weak, sickly person who constantly mourned the loss of her father, a rabbi, and that of her fiancé, who had died too young. She could tell wonderful stories from her youth and her past, suffered from *Weltschmerz*, and was very pious and decent. As experts pointed out, she knew absolutely nothing about housekeeping, but she spoiled and caressed my two brothers in an alarming manner. Nevertheless, she remained in the house for many years, until Julius was sent to the boarding school in Dresden and a new person had to be found to look after Leopold.

As soon as possible, my father did his best to move out of the house where our dear mother had died. It was not even a year later that we moved to a comfortable apartment across from our old one. Miss Minna kept the house as well as she could and continued to pamper my younger brothers, but I freed myself completely from her influence.

When Father was not at home, I was my own master. However, I can honestly say that I made good use of my time and tried to teach myself. I studied and read a lot, but also spent many hours enjoying myself. I often spent the evenings at the Birnbaums' house, chatting with Friedrich and Johanna, and when my aunt or my older cousins were looking after me I was happy.

Our day off was Saturday, and we made the most of it. We went on trips in the mornings and the afternoons. As we became older, some girls joined us, and when the weather was bad, we spent the afternoons at Uncle and Aunt Glogau's place,* where there were usually some young girls around. The daughter of the house, Fanni, or one of the other young people played the piano, and we danced and spent some pleasant hours.

Everyday Occurrences in Teplitz

Here are some more of my early recollections.

At the beginning of the 1850s, Teplitz* was a very popular and busy summer resort. It was well known and highly regarded for its medicinal mineral springs and because the magnificent surroundings offered people from the upper and highest classes of society the prospect of a pleasant extended stay.*

All of the Bohemian aristocrats and many members of the Austrian nobility came together there in the summer and displayed luxury worthy of admiration in everything, but especially in their elegant carriages. Usually they organized afternoon excursions to one of the beautiful estates that belonged to Prince Clary and Prince Lobkowitz, and thus toward evening we often saw thirty or forty of the magnificent horse-drawn carriages pass through *Lange Gasse** on the way back!

In the evenings there was usually another form of entertainment for the audience. It was customary for the local orchestra to play several serenades for the more prominent visitors. These presentations usually lasted from eight until nine o'clock and attracted the townspeople. During the high season, such evening concerts took place three or four times a week and brought pleasant distraction for the working population. They provided a meeting place for young and old.

I remember one other custom, however, that was abolished in the second half of the nineteenth century. Every spa visitor who arrived in Teplitz was given a "salute" from the tower of the town church on the day after his or her arrival. Yes indeed, that is what it was called!

They were liberal with respect to the paying guests, for even the Jewish visitors were "saluted." For a quarter of an hour, drums, trumpets, and bugles sounded from the church tower to proclaim a guest's arrival. When the spa tax was calculated, of course, a certain amount was included for "health resort and welcoming music"! In addition, all paying guests were given a dawn serenade in front of their house on one morning during their stay. For that, however, they had to pay an extra fee, the amount of which was left up to the individual involved. All that ceased in later years, when they were offered a good concert every day from eleven to one o'clock, as well as every evening, either in the public garden or on the castle grounds.

Another institution comes to mind, the abolition of which deprived the Teplitz youth of many joyful hours. There were no local newspapers yet, but since it was necessary to inform the population about everything worth knowing, there was a town crier. I remember him to this day, in his military-style uniform with the large drum. He had a red drinker's nose and was always a little tipsy. He solemnly positioned himself in the middle of the street while beating his drum in a lively manner. Then when a large enough audience had congregated, he casually started as follows: "Tomorrow afternoon, between three and four o'clock, a silver lady's watch with a chain will get lost on the way from the castle square to the marketplace. The honest finder is kindly asked to turn it over to the police for an appropriate reward." That brought a great uproar! "Kroh, when will the watch get lost?" - "Shut up, you stupid boys!

You well know that it was lost yesterday, but I'll tell you again." He drummed again with all his might and announced: "It will not get lost tomorrow, but it was already lost yesterday. Now pipe down, you damned rascals!" There were such antics almost daily. It was a lot of fun!

My grandmother, Mrs. Rebekka Jeiteles, who was a very well-to-do woman, spent a few months every summer taking the cure in Schönau near Teplitz and *tried* to provide my mother with some relaxation and amusement. But to no avail! Mother's conscientiousness did not permit her to leave the business for even one hour, and she could not be convinced to participate in an afternoon walk or a leisurely drive. Although she did visit Grandmother sometimes on Saturday afternoons, every evening without fail she walked to Schönau to see her, often late at night, and I always accompanied her.

Grandma apparently liked me, and when I was not at school I was permitted to join her on her drives and walks. I enjoyed that very much. In that way, at a very early age I became well acquainted with Teplitz and its surroundings. We drove to Bilin to the well-known mineral spring and to Dux, where we visited the Waldstein* Gardens and the castle. There, according to the attendant, the *actual* helmet, the *actual* sword, and the *actual* warhorse - now stuffed, of course - of the great field marshal Wallenstein were on display. One time we drove to Ossegg and admired the magnificent cloister and the beautiful local church, and gradually I got to know the area quite well.

Teplitz: World History in the Making

The memorable year 1848 came, and the popular revolt had its repercussions in Teplitz as well, in spite of its remoteness from the great centers of the revolution. A national militia was established and all men of the appropriate service age enlisted with enthusiasm. In no time an army corps was raised. It consisted of six companies of one hundred men each. The uniform and full equipment, with all the military paraphernalia, gave each individual guardsman an aura of heroism and pride.

The commanding officer was Colonel Prince Edmund von Clary-Aldringen, and the major was Mr. Siegmund, a businessman. A large number of Teplitz citizens were made officers, but military skill was not the decisive qualification. Rather, it was the material possessions of the men concerned. There were also many Jews who volunteered for the national militia, but to their great disappointment they soon realized that none of them could advance further than sergeant, in spite of their great assets.

Military training was vigorous, and two retired soldiers, Hackschmidt and Hafenbrettl, acquired celebrity status in a short time. They had been engaged as military instructors, and to avoid public ridicule most Jewish militia members hired them at a high price for private lessons. Many funny little episodes occurred in that context, but I shall restrict myself to one. An otherwise respected but clumsy man called his wife to the window to watch him practice, and after a while he joyously exclaimed, "Lotti, my love, just look at how well I shot!"

Most of the military displays took place in front of Major Siegmund's house, which was right across from our own. They were anything but bloody affairs and therefore provided me and all the other schoolboys with great entertainment. That was the case until one time when things appeared to get really serious.

One night a rumor spread that railway workers were planning to come from Aussig to Teplitz to loot the town. That was at the time when the Lobositz-Bodenbach railway line was under construction. Shortly before nine o'clock the national militia raised the alarm. That caused considerable agitation. Within minutes the militia was standing in formation, lined up in *Lange Gasse* in front of the major's house. And there they stood for an hour or two with their guns loaded, ready for action. But what happened? Well...nothing at all!

But over time even the greatest heroes work up an unquenchable thirst. Fortunately, the *Blue Grape* and the *Black Eagle* taverns were located near the warriors, giving them ample opportunity to sacrifice a great many pints of beer to the god of war.

In the local homes the mood was not quite as relaxed. Wives were anxious about their warrior-to-be husbands, children were *not* put to bed, and apprehension had taken hold of the city. My dear father had his guard post near our apartment, which enabled him to see my mother every now and then and to soothe her fears. At about eleven he came home and said, "Sophie, do put the children to bed. I think that it is nothing more than a false alarm." And that is what it really was. At about midnight the militiamen who had been sent off on reconnaissance reported back that there was no sign of enemy forces. The guardsmen subsequently retired to their usual haunts, where they greeted the new morning with the clear consciences of men who had cared for, guarded, and had a good drink to the welfare of their home town.

But the military games soon came to an end. The national militia was dissolved and left in its wake a lot of poverty and suffering for the citizens of Teplitz. Many of the volunteers had neglected their professions and their trades and devoted themselves to drink, gambling, and general idleness. They simply could not or would not return to a normal way of life. I could name a fair number of people whose lives were destroyed in those days.

Many businesses in health resort towns depend on the income from the summer season. Since the year 1848 did not bring any guests to Teplitz, it turned into a year of double disaster. To make matters worse, the citizens frequently had to put up with having soldiers billeted with them. I remember a couple of occasions when we had soldiers at home: once a unit of infantrymen with enormous black bearskin hats, and another time six military musicians who occasionally gave us "concerts" and liked to play with us children. There was certainly a lot of distraction.

I also remember well the subsequent money crisis.* Most smaller silver and copper coins disappeared from circulation. That was extremely troublesome. At first the attempt was made to deal with it by cutting the official one-gilder notes into halves and quarters. That did not prove to be sufficient for the need, however, and another measure was taken: Some merchants and private individuals produced their own paper money in six, ten, and twenty kreutzer denominations and circulated it. They promised that they would exchange it later for real money. Many people had their doubts as to whether those "currencies" had any value at all, but there was no way around accepting those notes. Occasionally, in cases where the trust between parties was not solid enough, they were rejected, and that caused a great deal of conflict.

Then there was the agitation when the express mail coach that normally arrived daily from Prague did not come for several days. Everybody knew that the revolution had reached Prague. There was a lot of fretting and worrying because of the close family and business ties between Prague and Teplitz. After four long days the mail coach eventually arrived with a white flag flying from the top, indicating that calm had returned to Prague. Half of the inhabitants of Teplitz hurried to the post office to hear the news brought by the coach driver.

There was one more exciting incident. One morning the news spread that Prince Metternich* and his retinue had escaped from Vienna and had managed to reach Teplitz the previous night. Within minutes a large crowd gathered in front of the hotel where they were supposed to be lodging. While the people were heatedly discussing whether the refugees should be detained or let go, Metternich and his followers left the hotel through the rear entrance, and the arguments were all in vain.

My Father and Uncle Joachim Become Merchants

To tell my story properly, I must go back in time many years to a period when my Uncle Joachim and my father were ten and eleven years old. I have already mentioned that instead of traveling to his sister Minka's wedding in Raudnitz, my father received compensation in the form of five Viennese gilders. That "capital" formed the foundation for all of my father's subsequent business enterprises.

Uncle Joachim apparently had funds in about the same amount, and both boys started knocking on doors, selling knives, wallets, combs, soaps, and other similar items, each of them separately. My father was successful and made a small profit, but Uncle Joachim did not do as well. While my father stored and offered his goods in neat little boxes and packages, keeping everything nice and clean, my uncle kept his "stock" in his cap, and any potential client found it difficult to purchase any of those neglected-looking goods.

The end result was that Uncle Joachim was left without any merchandise and without money and did not know what to do. My father then rushed to his aid and asked permission to set up a small table outside the cantor's house on *Judengasse*, where he laid out some items for sale. He placed Uncle Joachim there as the salesman and continued his own activities as a door-to-door peddler, while keeping strict control over the neatness and tidiness of the goods. Before too long they were both successful. Following his brother's instructions, Uncle Joachim became my father's business partner, and after about ten years (1830) the company *Heller Brothers* had its own little shop and even a small fortune.

That brings me up to the time when the two brothers were planning to make certain that Leni would be able to marry in the foreseeable future. She was her mother's favorite and a very pretty girl. But the family's poverty precluded any prospects of marriage, because the material circumstances of Moritz Birnbaum, a poor butcher's son, were even more precarious. Nevertheless, Joachim and my father set themselves the task of finding ways and means for the two lovers to wed as soon as possible. They decided to employ Moritz Birnbaum in their company as a temporary assistant. The business flourished. By then they already had a fairly large shop and were participating in the markets at Saatz, Brüx, Kommotan, Leitmeritz, and other places.

They already owned a few horses and a freight cart that they loaded with a number of boxes. They left Teplitz in the evening and traveled through the night, while my father and his companion sat or lay on top of the boxes, asleep or awake. The next morning they unpacked the goods at a stall in the market square. They made their return trips in the same manner, either on the same or the following night.

My father told me the story of one such nocturnal journey, where he awoke from a short nap and realized with horror that his companion, Alexander L. from Teplitz, had disappeared! Of course, the driver had to turn back immediately, and after half an hour they found the missing man, unharmed, but fast asleep on the road. Many times my father found reason to say to me: "You sleep as soundly as Alexander!"

They worked hard and sensibly and continued to make progress. They had already begun traveling to Leipzig to the trade fairs to make purchases. As they were located in Teplitz, so close to the border of Saxony, they found it easy to buy "foreign" goods, and soon the company *Heller Brothers* was able to do business with large companies in Prague, trading in haberdashery goods and fashion accessories.

Around that time, in the year 1833, my father became engaged to Sophie, the daughter of Jakob H. Jeiteles, a rather affluent merchant from Prague. He was promised a dowry of 4,000 gilders in coins (8,400 crowns). Even at that time, it was a very large sum and caused a fair amount of envy on the part of my father's siblings and his prospective brother-in-law.

During one of their nightly journeys to the market at Brüx on top of a fully laden truck, Moritz Birnbaum, with whom my father was traveling, compelled my father, almost by brute force, to pledge to him a dowry as well as a partnership in the company. At least that meant that there were no more obstacles in the way of Aunt Leni's marriage.

The wedding took place, the company consisted of three partners, and Mother and Aunt Leni were also working in the business. But it did not last. Fits of jealousy and vanity caused the partners to go their separate ways, and three comrades became three competitors.

Comparisons between My Own Family and that of Uncle Birnbaum

So far I have written stories that were told to me by my father. Now I want to talk about my own impressions of Uncle and Aunt Birnbaum at the time.

I was well aware of the tensions between my parents and the Birnbaum family. They did not come together very often. Nevertheless, I really liked Uncle and Aunt Birnbaum. My aunt's manners were refined and distinguished. She was a beautiful woman with a winning demeanor. She was always friendly and treated me kindly, and although I did not see her very often, I was always left with a pleasant impression after each encounter.

My best friends were my cousins Johanna and Friedrich Birnbaum, and we were always together in our spare time. We rolled hoops, ran races, and played ball and all sorts of other games in the large courtyard of their house. Often we were called into the living room, where Aunt Leni gave us little goodies such as fruit, pieces of cake, or other sweets. It is a curious thing that although I knew that my parents did not get along well with the Birnbaum family, I nevertheless felt attracted to them.

There were also other factors that might have influenced the way I felt. The atmosphere in the Birnbaum home was always serene and sociable. The parents were both cheerful people who took their work very seriously, but did not think of it as their unique and sole purpose in life. They permitted themselves enjoyable evenings with their friends and were really happy to be able to afford their children little pleasures as well. The older daughters in the family all played the piano, and I remember being invited over quite often, particularly for Purim* and Hanukkah,* but also on other occasions. We involved ourselves in all sorts of nonsense and had a very joyful time with all the music and dancing.

From what I can still sense today, there was a big difference between the way of life of my dear parents and that of the Birnbaums. In the Birnbaum home there were nine children of varying ages. At our house, during the time that I am talking about, I was alone, a little boy of seven or eight. Heinrich, who was seven years my senior, was already at school in Prague, and Julius was born much later. It is therefore quite understandable that I was very much taken by the pleasant domesticity of the Birnbaums.

Furthermore, my parents' financial circumstances did not seem to be very favorable in those days. Their lives revolved entirely around their business, and they experienced an uninterrupted string of worries in their work. My father was certainly a competent and experienced businessman, but perhaps a little too eager for success. He expanded the business to a point where he was no longer able to keep an eye on everything.

Each year he went to four markets in Brünn, three in Altbrünn, and two in Linz, taking with him a huge collection of stock. This activity alone took up more than half a year. On top of that there were trips to three annual fairs in Leipzig and various other buying and selling trips. Where could tranquility and contentment come from under those conditions? The periods between one market and the next, between trips, were hectic and very demanding. And my mother was always a part of all that.

During my father's frequent and protracted absences, Mother was in charge of all operations, while presiding over the large household as well. As I mentioned earlier, she had worked in Father's business since their wedding, and over time it had grown to be very large. We had up to twenty-five employees, assistants, and apprentices who had room and board in our home, as well as a number of servant girls. That left her with little time for rest or amusement. Whenever Papa returned from a journey, he brought so much work back with him that there was very little time for Mama and him to be together. Thus their lives were always filled with work, and I think there were also serious worries!

Saturday was the obligatory day of rest, but everyone worked until lunchtime behind closed shutters. Sunday was a normal working day, because the law required only that the business remain closed between the hours of nine and eleven in the morning, and since Teplitz was a spa, even that rule was not rigidly enforced!

My parents certainly believed that there was no other way, although their material success was not in proportion to their hard work and effort. Real success came to my father's business only when a quieter, more focused pace was introduced. Unfortunately, my mother did not live to see it, and I remember the evenings when she returned from work at a very late hour, had her supper, and went straight to bed, physically and mentally exhausted.

Father and Mother were both proud people in a positive sense of the word. It was not that they behaved in a condescending manner toward others, but they expected to be treated - always and by everyone - in a way that confirmed their well justified sense of worth.

In small towns - and Teplitz was definitely one - there are always cliques that you have to join in order to avoid the risk of being treated as an outsider. In those days, the custom was for the men to go to the inn after the close of business, or after dinner, to drink beer or to play cards - and on some evenings their wives also accompanied them. My parents found no pleasure in that and thus became estranged from society and ended up without any social life at all!

At the Birnbaums' house things were different. They, too, pursued their business eagerly and diligently, and even successfully, but they still found time for other things. They had a lighter, happier nature. They mixed with everybody and loved company inside and outside their home! That is what set my parents' house apart from my uncle's, and I believe that I discovered that difference at a very early age. That is what I liked about the Birnbaums!

While describing the two homes I must also touch on a point that seems most remarkable to me. As I mentioned earlier, my father and Uncle and Aunt Birnbaum all came from a very poor background. It was the beginning of the nineteenth century. The world was still traumatized by the Napoleonic Wars, and in those days - and even later - hardly any or very little effort was made in educating the minds of young people. That was especially so in poor Jewish families in small towns. They learned only reading, writing, and arithmetic! Therefore, it is all the more remarkable and indicative of people's thirst for knowledge and refinement, when, despite unfavorable conditions, they develop into full members of society, people who are well received everywhere because of their behavior, their knowledge, and their intelligence, and who also fulfill their roles in public life.

I am thinking here not only of Father and the Birnbaums, but also of a large number of Jews from Teplitz whom I remember from my youth. I mentally compare them to many people in today's world who have spent a fortune on their knowledge and education, and I find that *these* people do not live up to *those* standards, as far as finesse, morals, and ability are concerned. How often we have occasion to feel embarrassed by the loud and ignorant talk of our fellow Jews today. How ugly, in contrast to those days, is the manner of well-dressed men and elegant women covered with jewelry, when they express themselves in Yiddish slang.

Neither my father nor Uncle Birnbaum, nor most other Jews in Teplitz in those days, had any typically Jewish traits, not in the way they spoke nor in their behavior. It was simply because of their intelligence and their adaptability that they became widely respected people and well-to-do industrialists!

GRANDPARENTS

My Paternal Grandmother, the "Leeser Woman"

I now want to write a few lines about my grandmother Rachel Heller, known as the "Leeser woman."* She lived to the age of eighty-seven and enjoyed a quiet, carefree existence for a long time, because her children provided most generously for her needs! She died in the same apartment where she had lived for sixty years, in a house on *Judengasse*. It was very near the old temple that we attended each Friday evening and Saturday morning. Every Saturday after the worship services, we children all went to see Granny!

Even today I remember exactly how Grandmother's large living room looked. On the walls hung four pictures in black frames that Uncle Josef had painted when he was a student. Two of them depicted fruit baskets, the other two portrayed animals. The wooden floor was freshly scrubbed and covered with white sand.* There was a large, heavy sofa in one corner, covered in a rather faded floral material. The cover of an armchair by the window matched that of the sofa. In the center of the room there was a large, old-fashioned table with a number of chairs, and two small cupboards stood along the wall. One of them had glass doors and contained old souvenirs.

Grandma usually sat in the armchair. I can still see her before my eyes: a short, rather stout woman with dark, knowing eyes and a face that was quite dark and wrinkled. She always wore a black velvet ribbon on her forehead and a white bonnet on her head, which hid her hair completely. Her mouth moved constantly, and she often hummed softly to herself.

We children could hardly wait for the end of the worship service to go to Grandmother's place. First of all, there were often ten or twelve of us cousins together at her house, and that was great fun. In addition, there were always *Buchteln** at Grandmother's house on Saturdays. Every time one of us came, she got up, went to the little room to the left of the large living room, and got two *Buchteln* out of the chest of drawers. Before doing so, however, she always asked: "*Powidl* or *Zworoch?*" [Plum jam or cream cheese?],

53

and then brought them out. This procedure was repeated countless times on any one Saturday morning. She seemed to have figured out that it was not a good idea to show the young tribe the whole supply!

We grandchildren were also often sent to Grandmother's house on a weekday evening for half an hour or so to keep her company, and her children also visited her often, showing her their love and respect. But the old woman also went out on her own quite frequently, sat with us in the shop for a long time, and had an open ear and eye for everything. After that, she usually went over to the Birnbaums' house and always had a story to tell.

At appropriate times we often remember a conversation that the forgetful old lady had with her Catholic servant almost every day. "Marie, d'you want to go to church today?" asked Grandmother. When the girl answered: "Yes, Mrs. Heller," Grandmother remembered having asked the same question the day before and said quickly, "No, my dear. You went to church only yesterday, and one doesn't go every day."

In 1858 or 1859 Aunt Birnbaum died at a rather young age after suffering from an incurable disease for a long time. Aunt Leni had been Grandmother's favorite, and she was also proud that her daughter had become a very wealthy woman who owned a large, impressive home, her own horse-drawn carriage, and every other comfort. I will always remember the sorrowful words that she spoke as she wept, when she received the news of her daughter's death: "A person should die leaving such a house!"

My Maternal Grandfather, Jakob Herschmann Jeiteles
His Dream and His Experience with a "Clairvoyant"

My grandfather, Jakob Herschmann Jeiteles (born 1782), died in Vienna in the spring of 1842, one month before I was born. He is buried there in the Währing Cemetery. What I shall write about him here comes from stories that relatives told me!

My grandfather was said to have been a very handsome and impressive looking man. In those days, officers of high rank often went around in civilian clothes. Supposedly, the sentry at the main guard post in Prague once took my grandfather to be one of them, and presented arms to him! That is a story that Zepora told me. She came to my grandparents' house and business in Prague as a very young girl, lived to a ripe old age, and was part of the household up to the end of her life. Let's believe good old Zepora. The portrait of my dead grandfather does not exactly contradict the possibility, and several of his sons were also very handsome men. Nevertheless, in those days even middle and high ranking military officers were likely to make mistakes! In any case, Zepora's story demonstrates that the memory of my grandfather was treasured greatly by every person in the house!

Grandfather owned a wholesale business that dealt in fashion accessories in Prague. He visited and carried a large stock of goods to what were then the important markets at Pilsen, Königgrätz, and other towns in Bohemia, as well as the market in Linz. His contemporaries definitely considered him to be an enterprising and progressive man. He was the first person in Prague to think of going to Nuremberg on a buying trip. In those days, however, Jews who wanted to travel to other countries on business were confronted with all sorts of difficulties, and my grandfather had to petition for several years to obtain a passport. Prior to obtaining it, he was also obliged to pay all taxes and fees for a period of five years in advance! He also wrote his last will and testament before he left, and the farewell was as serious as if he were leaving for eternity!

My grandfather spent a large part of the year in Vienna, where he did all the purchasing for his firm in Prague. Running the latter was left to my grandmother, Rebekka Jeiteles. When my grandparents married, they had only a very modest fortune. A certain degree of affluence and flourishing progress with the business occurred only after a strange event, the occurrence of which, as incredible as it may seem, was confirmed by Grandmother Jeiteles and her children.

During the time of the Napoleonic Wars, there were large numbers of injured soldiers whose wounds were dressed with waxed canvas (oilcloth). The supply of that material was soon exhausted, the prices for it rose drastically, and still the required quantities were not available.

Grandfather was in Vienna, and Grandmother wrote to him every day, saying that he should find a supply of that waxed linen, at whatever price. Grandfather did try, but without any success. So it was no surprise that under those circumstances he thought about waxed linen day and night and even dreamed about it! The strange and curious thing, however, is how and what he dreamed and the result of his dream! He saw an old house on a street that he thought he recognized as a particular one in a certain suburb. In his dream he entered the house and saw mountains of waxed linen in one of the rooms!

When Grandfather woke up, the dream was so vivid that he could not go back to sleep. The next morning he made his way to that suburb and actually found the street and the same old house that had appeared in his nocturnal vision! Since the front door was locked, Grandfather rang the bell, and after a while a frail old man opened the door and asked him what he wanted. Grandfather had enough business sense not to reveal what had brought him there and sought instead to win the old man's trust. He involved him in conversation and after a long talk he asked him what was in the room next door. The old man replied that it was the remains of his former business, that he had retired many years ago, and that he had stopped trying to get rid of the goods. Then he took my grandfather into the room, which was indeed full of waxed canvas! You can imagine Grandfather's surprise. A deal was promptly made, the canvas was moved to Prague, and it brought my grandparents a huge profit!

Here I must tell another, similarly mysterious story that I also heard from my grandmother and other relatives. As I mentioned before, my grandfather visited the markets in Linz. There was a Jewish restaurant there, where he regularly went to dine. One day a Polish Jew approached him in the foyer, begging for alms. Grandfather gave him some money and asked him if he had had lunch. When he gave a negative answer, Grandfather asked the host to serve the poor man a meal, which the latter ate in a corner of the restaurant. In those days - and even today - a sense of intimacy existed between the owners of Jewish restaurants and their patrons. So the host asked my grandfather when he was planning to return home, and Grandfather replied that he intended to take a steamship back to Vienna the next day.

At that very instant the poor Polish Jew jumped to his feet. Excitedly he said, "Don't travel tomorrow, Sir! The steamer will not survive the trip to Vienna. It will perish in the rapids." In those days, many accidents did happen because of the submerged rocks in the Danube that have now been rendered harmless through the use of explosives. But back then it took a lot of care and skill to pass the dangerous spot without an accident.

My grandfather, who was quite shocked, asked the man how he came to know that, and received the brief reply from the man that that was his own business. But he implored my grandfather not to get on the boat if he valued his life! The event made quite an impression on my grandfather, who decided to travel by coach instead. Strangely enough, the ship really did sink at the rapids with all hands lost!

As I mentioned before, my grandfather spent a lot of his time away, partly in Vienna, partly at various other markets. He was very rarely actually in Prague, the headquarters of his business. The main reason for that might have been that between my grandparents there was not the kind of harmony that makes spending a lot of time together desirable! I am not very well informed about my grandfather's virtues and faults, but I know from all that I heard about him that he was a highly respected man. I am, however, in a position to form my own opinion about my grandmother, Rebekka Jeiteles, both on the basis of my own experiences and from the stories that her children tell.

My Maternal Grandmother, Rebekka Jeiteles

There can be no doubt that she was a competent businesswoman. She was also a prudent woman, who never hesitated to exploit circumstances to her own advantage, even when her children's interests should have been paramount. She was also proud, even vain, and expected everybody to treat her with exceptional politeness. In other words, she was not easy to get along with! At the same time, however, she was pious and charitable. Yet her quiet, reserved, and pensive disposition rarely allowed any glimpses of what was doubtlessly her good nature.

When I became acquainted with her, she was nearly sixty years old. I shall describe her appearance as well as I can. She was very impressive looking, of medium height, and of proud bearing. Her face was covered with scars from smallpox, but she was certainly not unpleasant or ugly. She had knowing eyes and her manner was very self-confident. Her speech was refined and precise. She dressed conservatively, but never without jewelry, which she seemed to value a great deal. That is how I vividly remember my grandmother, even today!

I cannot believe that she was ever a beautiful woman, and yet my grandfather was very jealous, especially of Uncle Goldschmidt, whose wife was my grandmother's sister. He was the founder of the jewelry business *Michael Goldschmidt and Sons*, which still exists today (1913). Grandfather's suspicion was certainly unfounded, but it was the cause of all of the calamities that were to follow. From all I have heard, both grandparents were fine, highly respectable people, but they were not a good match and did not get along well with each other.

Grandfather developed poor health. For years one of his adult sons had been at his side in Vienna. What a sad frame of mind he must have been in during the last days of his life and his suffering. His suffering is suggested by the repeated request that he made on his sick bed: "Please don't let Riwka come in here!" (Riwka is the Jewish short version of Rebekka.) In fact, she did not arrive in Vienna until after Grandfather's death!

In the year 1842, Dr. Mannheimer was the preacher for the Israelite congregation of Vienna. He was a man who will remain forever in the memory of the Jews there, because of his personality and his human qualities. This highly respected man had a strong influence on my grandfather, whom he befriended, and it was at his insistence that Grandfather wrote a last will and testament on his deathbed. In that will he expressed a very positive attitude toward his wife, naming her the sole heiress of his estate and beseeching her to take care of and provide for the children. The will is still in the possession of my brother-in-law, Max Jeiteles.

As far as my grandfather is concerned, the only other thing that I know is that he had a brother who had been baptized in his youth and was therefore "dead" for the rest of the family. He lived in Linz and was an umbrella maker there.

I will now return to Prague, to my grandmother's home.* She owned part of a house, i.e., the second floor of a building on *Zigeunergasse*.* The ground floor belonged to someone else, as did the third floor. There were very few houses in the Jewish quarter in Prague that belonged to only *one* person.

The owner of the rooms on the ground floor was far from being a model of cleanliness and order. That is why we had to pass through a wet, dark, and very filthy corridor and up an equally filthy and bad flight of stairs to get to my grandmother's apartment. The owner of the third floor apparently also abhorred a neat house.

But as soon as we pushed through the door to Grandmother's apartment, the scene changed completely. There was an immediate impression of entering a comfortable and elegant home. Good taste and prosperity were evident in everything, and tidiness and pleasantness were visible everywhere. One could recognize the sensitive mind and the careful touch of the mistress of the house.

Since Grandmother was a businesswoman and spent a large part of her day in the shop, Aunt Fanni Pick, her sister, supervised the household. Nevertheless, Grandmother did not allow ultimate control to slip out of her hands. As a child, Aunt Fanni Pick had suffered a serious accident that left her crippled for the rest of her life. She could only move around on two crutches. She remained unmarried and lived in Grandmother's home.

Uncle Pick, Grandmother's brother, was an old bachelor and still alive. He had a dreadful, squeaky voice that once caused an unfortunate encounter in Teplitz, where he was taking the cure. He wanted to buy a pair of gloves, and an unscrupulous joker purposely sent him to the shop of a brush maker instead, whom he knew to have a similar squeaky voice. Uncle Pick entered the shop and asked for a pair of gloves. The brush maker, furious that someone was clearly mocking him by imitating his voice, while at the same time ordering something that he obviously did not have for sale, replied very rudely, but in the same squeaky voice, of course. That got Uncle Pick all riled up, and if it had not been for the intervention of some passers-by, they would have ended up in a fistfight.

Now I want to tell you what things were like at Grandmother's house.

Nine children: five sons and four daughters, all of whom she brought up in the strictest manner. They all had tremendous respect for their mother, more reverence than love, more fear than devotion! The children were only permitted to address their mother as "Madam Mother," and the familiar German *du* form of address was supplanted by the more formal *Sie*. None of the children would ever have been bold enough to take more than the one slice of bread that was given to them, without first asking: "Madam Mother, do I have your permission to take another piece of bread?" In a word, the prevailing manners were like those at the royal court of Spain. They remained so even after the children had grown up, married, and had their own families. Upon arrival and departure there were kisses on the hand, and that was all the warmth that was allowed, for children and grandchildren alike.

I will have other memories of Grandmother to tell about later on, when I write more about my own youth. All I want to say at this point is that she died in the autumn of 1857 at the age of sixty-seven. She left a sizeable fortune, gave detailed instructions in her will about absolutely everything, and deposited the will with Dr. Porth, one of the most respected attorneys. He had always been her confidant and advisor, and she made him the executor of her will, along with her son Joseph Jeiteles, my future father-in-law.

However, that appointment worried Joseph Jeiteles a great deal. It gave him countless sleepless nights, because soon after my grandmother's death the most unsavory rumors about Dr. Porth began to circulate, and all possible means had to be employed to force him to release the fortune from his grip. Fortunately, that was achieved just prior to his complete collapse, when he lost his reputation as well as his own assets and those of many of his clients through acts of sheer negligence!

I was fifteen years old when my grandmother died, and I mourned her loss. She had always been quite nice and kind to me. However, I was also impressed with the fact that I had come into a small fortune at my age, even though, for the time being, it was kept in my name at the trustee's office. Even so, it allowed me to feel like a little Croesus!

Koppelmann Foges

Among those of my grandparents' generation, I want to refer to only one more person, my great-uncle, Mr. Koppelmann Foges, who was the father of my dear Aunt Rosa Jeiteles, my future mother-in-law.

He was the owner of one of the largest wholesale manufactured goods businesses in Prague. Most of the time his wife and sons were in charge of running the business, because he spent a lot of time away purchasing goods in Warnsdorf and other manufacturing towns in Bohemia. He was often away for months at a time and had to suffer many deprivations, because he lived on only coffee and eggs* when the supplies that he had taken along from Prague ran out.

Whenever he returned to Prague, he did not spend much time concerning himself with selling the goods, which his wife and sons were doing very well anyway. And they in turn were quite satisfied with that, because his passionate, energetic personality was not very well suited to dealing with customers.

I must take some time to describe that old gentleman, because I want to paint a picture of a person who would be very difficult to find today. He was a businessman, but at the same time an erudite scholar who studied the Talmud* and the Gemora, as well as contemporary classical and philosophical writings. His large library contained the rarest and most precious specimens of ancient and modern literature. He was very conscientious about fulfilling all religious obligations and even followed the rules regarding food preparation, despite the sacrifices that resulted from it. He did that mostly out of piety and habit but did not resent the fact that his sons were more inclined toward more liberated and more modern tendencies.

He was a great friend of music and the theater and never missed a good play, a good opera, or a good concert. He always took the cheapest seat, however, not to save money, but out of modesty. On the other hand, there was hardly a Saturday or a holiday when he did not have several poor people sharing the meal at his table. Moreover, he considered it a holy obligation to give one tenth of his annual income to the poor. When people without means got married, he not only put his large apartment at their disposal for the wedding, but he also provided for an appropriate banquet. Accordingly, this man was held in respect and high esteem by everybody.

MY FIRST BUSINESS TRIPS

First Experiences at the Markets (1853 to 1855)

After two or three years of working in the business, I had gained enough experience to be able to make a real contribution. That was made easier for me partly through my eagerness, partly because I had insight into all of the details of our activities that remained hidden from many other employees. But I also made a point of taking private lessons in a number of different subjects, languages among others, and used my evening hours to do it. I also had my father's permission to set up my own library and often stayed up reading into the wee hours.

One day Father surprised me by telling me that he was going to take me along with him to the next market in Brünn. That seemed to me to be a sign of how satisfied he was with my progress. As a boy of only thirteen years, I was not only glad about that, but also proud, and I looked forward to making such a major journey and to spending a length of time living in an unfamiliar city.

It was winter, and I was given new warm underwear for the trip. One evening toward the end of November, my father and I, along with ten or twelve other employees, climbed into the stagecoach that would take us to the train station at Aussig. The journey, however, was far from being as pleasant as I had hoped! It was bitterly cold, and there was a snowstorm when we boarded the train in Aussig at around midnight. Third-class compartments had no window glass in those days (1855). They had rather large window openings that could be covered by pieces of leather, each held in place by two buttons, but it did not matter whether a person was sitting close to the window or far away from it - there was no shelter from the incoming snow and frost.

In order to offer the public *something*, the railway management set up an iron stove in the middle of the car. When close to it, you almost roasted, but on the far side of it you could freeze to death. There was no hope of sleep in that crowded coach filled with tobacco smoke. My enthusiasm for travel faded quickly!

There was another bit of distraction for travelers in those days. Two hours out of Prague, a policeman, accompanied by two soldiers, boarded the train. He took away everybody's travel permits and in return handed out certificates that enabled the travelers to obtain approval for further travel from the office of the railway police in Prague. Without that paper a traveler would have gotten into the worst kind of trouble, because the police inspection was repeated every four or five hours.

Those were official provisions that might seem unbelievable today! The trip from Aussig to Brünn took more than twenty-four hours back then. There were no fast trains, but long stops at each station instead. We arrived in Brünn shortly before two o'clock in the morning and were very glad to get into a warm room and a comfortable bed!

Work at the markets in Brünn was truly exhausting, but it was also interesting. We had not only all the wholesale traders from Vienna as our clients, but even those from the entire Empire, including all the provinces. In those days even Lombardy was part of Austria. For three full weeks we constantly had large numbers of buyers in our storerooms. They were there all at the same time and bought large quantities of goods straight from the stock.

Whatever was sold during the day had to be invoiced and packed during the same evening - or better, the same night - since a further accumulation of work simply could not be permitted. So it was always one or two in the morning before we were finally able to rest. I could mention here a few things about the reputation of the markets at Brünn in those days, but I will come back to that at a later point. Until the end of the 1850s, for Austria they were roughly equivalent to what the Leipzig Trade Fair was, and to some extent still is, for the whole world - albeit on a smaller scale.

Until 1862 I returned to Brünn at least twice a year, but once a year, during the month of August, I also accompanied my father to the market in Linz. In Linz the work was as quiet and steady as it was exhausting in Brünn. Even the journey was a pleasant one, by train to Prague and from there to Budweis in comfortable horse-drawn carriages. Then the last part of the trip to Linz was accomplished by *Pferdebahn*,* a horse-drawn train - a sheer delight! It passed through a lovely countryside, for the most part along winding roads. A good two hours before arriving we could see Linz and the beautiful Danube from the top of the mountain.

The cozy and inviting impression that the city itself and its inhabitants made was also manifested in the business world. Every evening we were free from seven o'clock on, and Dad then took me to one of the numerous beautiful hostelry gardens along the Danube for dinner. On Sundays we undertook larger excursions on the Danube, and we were sorry when our time in Linz ended.

In 1858 I also took my first trip from Linz to Vienna. Between the end of the market at Linz and the beginning of the Brünn market in September there were only a few days. Instead of making the long trip from Linz to Teplitz and then from Teplitz to Brünn, I asked my father to let me travel to Vienna. I pointed out to him that the expenses that I would incur in Vienna would be cancelled out completely by the reduction in travel costs. My father agreed to my plan, but instead of letting the sixteen-year-old boy go to the big city on his own, he sent one of our oldest employees, a man by the name of Altschul, to accompany me.

The trip from Linz to Vienna on the Danube was delightful! The countryside is picturesque. I had also just finished reading the *Nibelungen*, and many places along the way brought the beautiful saga vividly to mind.

In Vienna we stayed at a rather cheap hotel, the *National*, on *Taborstraße*, but I was out from early morning until late at night. I spent my time in the city and its environs, and my Viennese relatives looked after me very well. I do not intend to describe Vienna and my stay there in any detail, but simply want to mention a few things. In 1858 all the city walls and gates were still standing. I was taken to the old bastions, where my Uncle Ignaz gave me all sorts of details about the Revolution of 1848 and the positions that the citizens' militia of Vienna occupied in those days.

I was not quite seventeen years old when my father entrusted me with the work of a traveling salesman. Prague was the first place I visited. It was easy for me to be successful, because my father's firm was well known and our goods were in demand. Everybody was always friendly towards me, and they gave me large orders. I was happy to be able to send such orders home every evening!

Vienna, approximately 1858, when the old bastions were demolished - Löwel Bastion

I took along two or three small suitcases filled with samples of our factory's products. I had them taken from one customer to the next and worked from morning until night. When the work was done, I either attended theater performances or visited Uncle Heinrich and Aunt Marie Wiener, who warmly welcomed me. I was joyful and light-hearted and told all sorts of hilarious stories. My adult cousins rewarded me with applause that I especially liked to receive from my cousin Klara. I also spent many entertaining evenings in the home of Uncle Joseph and Aunt Rosa Jeiteles, my future parents-in-law. On Sunday and holiday evenings, all the relatives met there for dinner, and everyone had a lot of fun.

As a result of my successful trips to Prague, one day my father surprised me with the news that I was to visit all the large cities in the Empire. I was overjoyed, for nothing can be more wonderful for a young man than travel! Of course, I had to carry out my business obligations most conscientiously, but beyond that I was a free and independent man, the master of my own free will! There had been no other traveling salesmen before me in our firm; I was the first and had to smooth the way for myself. There were a few difficulties in the beginning, but that soon changed.

I permitted myself to experience some pleasant hours, which were particularly enjoyable in Vienna, where I usually spent two weeks at a time. I went to the theater or to the opera, to open-air concerts in the evenings, and to the masquerade balls and the "Fool's Night" that were organized in the winter by the Vienna Men's Choir. In short, I attended everything that was entertaining and worth experiencing. In a word, I was on my feet all day - and a large part of the night - and enjoyed my existence! I was eighteen years old, had everything I needed, and was truly happy and contented!

With Vienna as my starting point, I traveled to all of the major cities in Upper Austria, Salzburg, Styria, Carinthia, Carniola, North and South Tyrol, and even went as far as Verona and Venice, which still belonged to Austria back in those days. In that fashion, I became acquainted with a fairly large portion of the world. Those journeys took place twice a year until I reached the age of twenty-two. One trip was made in the spring and one in the winter. I was thus able to admire the beauty of the countryside during the different seasons.

In the years from 1860 to 1864 there were still not as many railway lines as there are now, and I continued to cover many stretches and long distances in mail coaches, where a person can become much better acquainted with the country and its people. Furthermore, in that manner one gains far more pleasure from traveling than is possible behind a speeding, steam-powered iron horse! I became friends with my customers and was warmly welcomed into their homes.

Nearly every day I was able to send large orders home, and my success afforded me great contentment. I also learned a great deal from my travels. I was a young, eighteen-year-old man from the provinces, who had a few "rough edges" that caused me and others a bit of discomfort at first, but those problems were soon smoothed out along the way. I had the same kind of experiences as many of those who receive their education only through their contact with other people. For example, in almost every hotel where I stayed, I met either the managers of the firms themselves, or their sons, or sometimes their employees, and came to owe much to them. I was always the youngest and was treated in a fatherly manner by them. I was regularly invited to their tables at lunchtime and in the evenings. On those occasions I often received advice and sometimes reproach, to which I gave heed for the rest of my life.

An Arrest

There was one very embarrassing lesson that I learned during the very first year of my travels, and my memory of it is still vivid today.

While traveling from Linz to Salzburg, I took the mail coach to Lambach (there was no railway line then), went from there to Gmunden on the narrow-gauge train, and then traveled on by coach to Salzburg. Aside from me, there was only one other passenger in the carriage when it departed from Linz, and since the journey took about twelve hours, we had to get along with each other. By and by a lively conversation developed. It was late autumn, a cold, unpleasant, rainy day, and we sought to pass the time by talking. My neighbor, a gentleman of about twenty-eight or thirty years in age, introduced himself as Mr. Behrenz from Berlin. He said that he, too, was going to spend some time in Salzburg on business. We finally arrived there after nine in the evening, took adjoining rooms in the *Hotel Schiff*, and arranged to have breakfast together in Mr. Behrenz's room at eight the next morning.

I opened the door to my room at the appointed time. Breakfast was already served, and while we were happily digging in, there was a knock at the door. Without waiting for a response, a gentleman stepped into the room. A second man tried to follow him, but was pushed back by the first one. I noticed that the man who was pushed back wore a badge identifying him as one of the secret police, which caused me no small amount of concern and anxiety!

Nor was my apprehension dispelled when the first gentleman approached us, introduced himself as a police inspector, and asked my name, my status, and the purpose of my trip. After I had answered those questions, he wanted to know how it was that I had a close enough relationship with the man sitting next to me to be having breakfast with him in my robe. I was able to explain that, and when answering the next question, as to whether I was known in Salzburg, I mentioned the names of my business associates, G. Junger, I. B. Neumüller, and a few other companies.* I was satisfied to read in the eyes of the high-ranking policeman that I was not considered to be a serious criminal, for he ordered me to return to my room and told me not to leave it until further notice.

So I did that, and I wondered and brooded about it for a long time, until finally my door opened and the police inspector appeared and gave me back my freedom, but with a serious word of advice. He told me to be more careful in choosing my friends in the future, and not to be too accommodating to anyone on the sole basis of a decent outward appearance. Moreover, he told me sternly not to mention this incident to anyone in Salzburg.

That was a load off my mind! I went about my business with the intention of leaving Salzburg as soon as possible. Then, at around one o'clock that day I returned to the hotel, gave a wide berth to the few secret police agents who still stood in the doorway, and went through to the dining room. I had just sat down at my table when one of those "monsters" with a yellow badge came right up to me. Was the matter still not resolved?

The man, however, bowed politely and said, that Mr. Behrenz had urgently requested that I come and see him. "Well," I said, "I've really had enough of his kind. But just where is Mr. Behrenz? Where am I supposed to visit him?"

"He's in a small room right next door, with his hands tied, of course, and he's in custody. He will be transported across the border under guard by sled this afternoon."

"Ah, yes," I said, "and I'm supposed to subject myself to more inconvenience for him? Go and tell him that I've been through quite enough on his account, and that I decline the pleasure of seeing him again."

After a while, however, the "yellow badge" returned and announced that the police inspector had requested that I go and see Mr. Behrenz, and that it would cause me no further trouble at all. So I went and found the poor man in a very unenviable situation. He implored me to forgive him for causing me such problems and assured me that I could maintain my positive opinion of him, in spite of what had happened. Finally he asked me to visit the *Lobositz Company* in Prague on my way home, and to tell them everything that had occurred here during the last couple of hours. I promised to do that!

Even though he had been arrested and now had his hands tied, and was ready to be taken across the border, I could still not think of him as a criminal and bade him a friendly farewell. I did not shake hands with him, however, because first of all the inspector had warned me not to be too "friendly," and secondly because the poor man had his hands tied!

When I arrived in Prague several weeks later, I went to find the *Lobositz Company* on *Geistgasse* and told one of the directors the whole story. He pretended to be quite indifferent, thanked me, and eventually asked where and how long I was staying in Prague. That same evening, towards eleven o'clock, another one of the directors of that firm was waiting for me at my hotel. He asked me with great interest about every detail of the story. Unfortunately, I was unable to obtain an explanation from him, but I suspect that it was a matter of smuggling.

My travels brought me more than simply a lot of diversion. They also brought many happy, cozy, and sometimes even high-spirited and hilarious hours.

The Prestige of the Markets at Brünn and Their Gradual Decline after 1854

I have recalled the Salzburg episode many, many times. For that reason I now want to describe the circumstances that prevailed in those days and explain the events that brought about a fundamental change in direction during the 1850s.

As I mentioned earlier, the markets at Brünn* were extraordinarily important. The *Balduin Heller Company*, which enjoyed a good reputation, made its primary sales at those markets, which took place four times a year and lasted three weeks each. Not only companies from Prague and Reichenbach, but representatives of all the textile and calico print factories, Brünn manufacturers with their large variety of goods, and all the producers from Moravia were present and in great demand. But first and foremost, the entire respected and reputable Austrian business world and all branches of industry were concentrated there!

We leased three large business facilities there for the entire year, one that belonged to the Count of Sereny, next door to it a second one belonging to the Werner family, and a third on *Herrengasse* that belonged to the deputy mayor of Brünn, a Mr. Herlt. Those three storerooms were always packed full of goods at the beginning of the market, because our customers were the most important wholesalers from Vienna and Pest, from Galizia and Lombardy!

During one of those fairs a good 200 packing cases or more were sold, and business was quite easy, because we brought mostly goods from Germany and France to Brünn, goods that were otherwise not readily available to the large Austrian market. Most foreign goods were either totally prohibited from import into Austria or else taxed at excessive rates.*

I now want to explain how we business people from Teplitz managed to satisfy the Austrian demand for foreign articles. We had constant business relations with other countries because of our proximity to the border, and because we visited the fairs at Leipzig on a regular basis we also knew the best sources for foreign goods. We, the Teplitz wholesalers, took advantage of being so close to the border between Germany and Austria. Our proximity to it made vigorous and well-organized smuggling activities possible! It was not even necessary to be too secretive about it, because not only the local people, but "all of Austria" knew that Teplitz was *the* place from which most foreign goods were sent out into the Empire, and that there was not one firm there that did not participate! Many wealthy entrepreneurs had excellent contacts with the border police. Inside the customs department itself there were "confidants" who gave the person concerned a timely warning about any imminent official examination of any storage areas. So it was possible to hide the endangered goods for a while in the private houses of friends. The cellars of Count Clary and Duchess Colloredo very often contained valuable batches of goods, but even those of ordinary citizens were ready to accept such deposits at any time and without questions.

From time to time, certain quantities of goods were processed through the customs office so that receipts could be shown at the next review, but in the meantime much larger quantities moved across the border in a different manner!

Even though the government had taken measures to counter the practice, its own departments did not observe them strictly. Any smuggler who was caught red-handed was often punished severely, even incarcerated. But for merchants who were found to keep large quantities of goods for which no duty had been paid, a so-called "indulgence process" was in place. The duty had to be paid retroactively, even a fine, but there was no prison sentence or loss of reputation involved. The "protection mechanisms" were as effective as they could be.

This practice lasted until about 1860, and up to that time our business in Brünn was kept active - and had to be! As long as the railway system evolved only slowly and other means of transport were totally inefficient, the markets in Brünn still offered the most successful link between industry and commerce for all of the countries within the Austrian Empire.

But times soon changed! The modes of transportation improved markedly and brought with them an entirely new mode of operation: Factory owners and merchants engaged their own representatives, who traveled in their behalf throughout the monarchy and later even to foreign countries. Business volume increased enormously! The impact of this new era, however, resulted in enormous modifications, and the importance of the markets in Brünn decreased rapidly. My father quit going there and began to concentrate his activities on our metal goods factory in Teplitz. But there was yet another cause for the sudden expansion of Austrian industry. Our trade activities were forced into totally new guidelines. When the first trade agreement between Austria and Germany was signed in 1854,* ratifying the import of foreign goods into Austria, it initially seemed to be a severe blow for our factory owners! Until then they had operated freely and made immense profits, without fear of any competition and without having to improve their manufacturing equipment.

The new regulations, however, which were at first "cursed" as the ruination of Austrian industry, proved to be favorable because they "roused the industrialists rather roughly from their slumber," as German competitors literally flooded the Empire with their manufactured products! Beginning at that moment, Austrian industry picked itself up and reached quite respectable heights, and that occurred "out of necessity rather than voluntarily!"

The few statistical data in the following table give a picture of the Austrian trade figures during the last century, up to a time shortly after the signing of the first trade agreement between Austria and Germany in 1854:

Total Imports of All Foreign Manufactured Goods into Austria*

1835	CMfl.	2,957,360	crowns	6,210,296
1847	CMfl.	8,243,820	crowns	17,312,022
1854	CMfl.	24,373,282	crowns	51,183,892
1857	CMfl.	62,170,710	crowns	130,558,491

It continued to rise in the same staggering proportions. Thus, what was first considered a curse, turned out to be a blessing in the end!

Youthful Attempts at Independence and More Amusing Events

My frequent trips to Brünn and Linz, and later to Vienna, and all of the impressions that I gained during those travels caused quite a few of my opinions to change!

As I had been brought up in a religious household and was therefore burdened with all of the old traditional ceremonies, it was quite an effort for my father to get me to enter a Christian inn. He had to speak words of encouragement to me to get me to eat my first mouthful. But I became accustomed to it sooner than I thought I would and even found it pleasant. With that experience, the "first loop in the net" was loosened, and many others soon followed.

But when the Jewish holidays approached, my deeply-rooted religious sentiments stirred, and I felt drawn to the temple. I was able to pray fervently, fasted at Yom Kippur (Reconciliation Day) each year, and in so doing felt a deep inner satisfaction. That changed, of course, over the years, and I will talk about it later.

Working and traveling on Saturdays could not be avoided in the interest of business, so why shouldn't it also be permitted for the sake of amusement? Thus my cousin Friedrich Birnbaum and I started hiring a little horse-drawn carriage on Saturdays. We did not need a coachman and took entertaining little trips to Milleschauer Hill, another to Osseg or Billin, and little by little we became very well acquainted with the whole area around Teplitz! It was no longer done in secret, and our fathers were aware of our excursions. We were even allowed to smoke a cigar or a cigarette here and there and began to think of ourselves as halfway adult, as emancipated individuals!

After we turned sixteen, Friedrich and I developed a fondness for playing billiards. Not daring to ask our parents' permission, we secretly slipped away to a distant tavern and looked over our shoulders ten times before we dared enter. One day I was caught in there by one of our employees who liked to cause me grief with my father for the sake of revenge. My father listened to the accusation calmly and then simply said to me: "I would have preferred you to ask me first. I would have given you permission to play, just as I am giving it now, but I want you to do it in decent locations from now on. Friedrich should also ask his father's permission."

Addressing the accuser, my father said: "I think I know why you came to me to tattle on my son. From now on I will keep a very sharp eye on you, and you certainly did not gain anything by this accusation." At that, I felt a huge sense of relief.

EUROPEAN BUSINESS TRAVELS

First Journey to London and Paris (1862-63)

In the autumn of 1862, my father surprised me by announcing that I was to attend the exhibition in London, then visit Paris and some industrial cities in Germany. In the process, I was to strive to bring home a lot of things that would find innovative, practical, and useful application in our factory. As a twenty-year-old, the news that I would see London and Paris simply astounded me, and I was so happy and excited that I could hardly contain myself.

My nervousness reached its climax on the eve of my departure from Teplitz. I arrived at the station long before the train was to leave and spent the whole time walking up and down the platform. I began to worry about the fact that the journey was not for pleasure but for serious business, and that it therefore burdened me with great responsibility. It also dawned on me that I would be traveling to London without being able to speak a word of English. Back in 1862 traveling to England was still uncommon, and it should therefore not be held against me that as a young man my nervousness caused me to imagine that I would be subjected to all sorts of dangers and problems.

After my first night in the compartment I was able to calm down. I made the acquaintance of a Mr. Täubner, a factory owner from Brünn, who was also traveling to London and could speak English. He promised to look after me. I then felt safe and hoped to be able to enjoy my time in London. As we approached Calais, my buoyant mood suddenly disappeared. I saw the wild, turbulent sea and was reminded of my first journey by ship, which had not agreed with me at all!

Two years earlier I had traveled from Laibach (Ljubljana), where I had been on business, to Venice for the Pentecost weekend. The Venice of that time, which was still part of Austria, cannot be compared to the Venice of today. There were only a few houses along the Grand Canal that were not dilapidated. Few windows had glass, and even the wooden frames were missing. But the city still made an overwhelming, enchanting impression on me. The glorious weather of Pentecost added to that, and I boarded the steamer for Trieste delighted by the joyful experiences of the previous two days.

I was then still very young and naïve. I knew nothing about seasickness and simply did not believe that it existed. In my inexperience, I headed for the top of the ship to have just one last look at Venice. And because I, as an eighteen-year-old, wanted to be seen as a real man, I had a dark Italian cigar between my teeth and was smoking vigorously! When the ship started moving, the sky was sunny and blue, and I could see Venice spread out before me in its entire splendor. But as soon as we reached the open sea, with the lagoons still visible, things changed dramatically! A strong north wind was blowing. The ship rocked and my insides rebelled. The cigar had long since been thrown into the sea when I became acquainted with seasickness at its worst. I made one "contribution" after another, until there was nothing left.

Two gentlemen from Hamburg noticed and felt sorry for me, took me to a good place on the deck, and told me to lie down on the floor. In that position, I was not only able to watch the blue sky, but also to draw the conclusion that travel by sea is a very good way to clean out the stomach.

I remembered all of that when I looked at the choppy sea in Calais, and I shuddered at the thought. The trip to Dover confirmed my fears - I became very seasick. But as soon as I felt solid ground beneath my feet again, my zest for life returned. The awareness that I was in England filled me with a feeling of indescribable satisfaction. I gazed with admiration at the foreign countryside in its autumnal glory. It was so very different from our continent. The landscape, the glorious, lush green of the meadows, the magnificent architecture of the castles that I admittedly glimpsed only fleetingly, and the sophisticated culture that was visible everywhere had soon captured my complete attention. I was sorry that night approached so rapidly and put an end to my admiring the scenery.

When we arrived at London Bridge Station, it was already completely dark. Mr. Täubner, who had been my guardian angel until then, left me there and went to stay at a different hotel. I had booked a room in *De Kaysers Royal Hotel*, an establishment that was frequented by Germans. I was then on my own and had no knowledge of the language at all. I even had difficulty putting my luggage in a carriage and trying to explain to the driver where I wanted to go. We then proceeded to drive through both lively and quiet streets and did not make great progress because we were traveling behind a long line of carriages and moved no faster than at a walking pace. I thus had more than an hour in which to remember all the stories and novels about how foreigners in London were taken to some disreputable area, robbed, and thrown back on the street, penniless at best! Nervousness, youth, and inexperience can, of course, easily cause anxiety or unrest. But those torments came to an end when I arrived safely at *De Kaysers Royal Hotel*.

On the first night I soon made the acquaintance of a Mr. Fischer, the owner of a spinning mill in Neuenteich in Bohemia. He promised to look after me. The following morning he and I visited the exhibition. Just looking at everything made me very tired. I saw so many things that in the end I forgot what I had seen, but I was very upset that I did not find anything that would have been of use in the fabrication of metal buttons in Teplitz.

I am sure that I overlooked many outstanding exhibits during my extensive search, but one of them did remain in my memory forever. It was an enormous fountain that was exhibited by the well-known *Farina* firm of Cologne on the Rhine. Eau de Cologne sprayed forth from it continuously in a great arc, filling the entire room where it was displayed with a refreshing coolness and a pleasant smell. Hundreds of visitors rested on the chairs around the exhibit and moistened their handkerchiefs with the fragrant water. Although I, too, spent time in that delightful spot, I realized regretfully that the magnificent exhibit had nothing to offer that would make my trip worthwhile!

I remained in London for ten or twelve days, attending the exhibition every morning, but making no progress at all as far as my business interests were concerned. In the afternoons and evenings I toured London's sights and its historically interesting and magnificent environs. When it was time to depart, I promised myself that it would not be my last visit to London. I ended up keeping that promise!

Several of the German hotel guests, who were not aware that I had the same occupation as they, told me that they came to London twice a year with their button samples and made large sales.

That was enough to trigger my ambition to achieve the same success.

From London I went to Paris. I was looking forward to seeing that highly praised and beloved paradise and went to the boulevards the very first night, shortly after my arrival. I must admit that I was rather disappointed with my first impression of Paris.

I had come from London, where I had encountered milling crowds day and night, crowds that were probably inflated further by the exhibition. Paris, however, seemed empty and deserted, even on the main boulevards. *Tout Paris* had not arrived back from their vacations. The weather was cold and rainy, and that did not improve the gloomy impression. I seriously asked myself: Is this the famous Paris, the city that the whole world raves and dreams about? But over the years I have really learned to love and appreciate Paris.

I earnestly used my time there for business purposes, and Mr. W. Hirsch, who was our representative there and about whom I will later write more, was my guide. I learned a number of useful things and thought that I had reason to be pleased with my business successes. I did not see much of Paris itself, or its surroundings, but I promised myself that I would visit the city again, as I had done with London, to make up for lost time. I also discovered that German factory owners regularly came to Paris with their button samples and made good sales, so why shouldn't I have "two irons in the fire" as well?

On my way home I visited some German industrial cities, arrived home in a cheerful mood, and told my father everything that he needed to know. I also informed him of my plans regarding another trip to Paris and London to sell our goods. He consented immediately, and I was able to start making the necessary preparations.

At the beginning of November in 1863 I went there on my first sales trip, full of hope, and with my mind at ease in the knowledge that I was now able to speak English fairly well. (I had already been able to speak French.) In Paris I learned that the buying season would not begin until two weeks later. In a dejected mood I sailed on to London, where my business success was minimal, but I became acquainted with the taste and demands of the English market and consoled myself with the thought that things would improve in the future. Back in Paris, I then learned everything that I needed to know in order to get my feet on the ground in local business circles. Then I eventually returned home more than a little disappointed.

Father, however, was more satisfied with my success than I was, and he immediately decided that we had to take advantage of my experiences and that I should prepare for a new trip in May of 1864!

The next journey was really successful, with both fashion and demand working in my favor. In both Paris and London I gained a great number of new customers and received orders of a magnitude that was even extraordinary for our business at home, which was by no means small. We were pleased to see that the customers were satisfied with our merchandise, a fact that was confirmed by the repeated orders that arrived by mail. As a result, our father built a large factory in order to meet the increased demand.

All this continued until 1873, when a serious lengthy illness stopped me from traveling. My brothers were working very hard for the firm as it was, and they were forced to give up that part of the business, which could only be maintained through personal contact.

Our Subsidiary Factory in Dresden (1864-1866)

Just after my *first* trip, an unpleasant incident threatened our future success: In 1864, Germany and France concluded a trade agreement that contained special concessions facilitating the export of a number of German products to France. In those days Austria had no such agreement, and for that reason much higher customs duties had to be paid on Austrian goods than on similar products of German origin. That was also the case for buttons, and we found ourselves in the most unfortunate situation of missing out on large business transactions with France.

There was only one way out of that dilemma, and that was to manufacture our goods in Germany as well. I made that proposal to my father, and he agreed to it. A factory was supposed to be set up in Dresden - solely for the French market - and my brother Julius, in spite of the fact that he was only sixteen, seemed competent enough to be in charge. The Dresden factory would only exist until the customs regulations were changed in Austria's favor.

But then an enormous new difficulty presented itself. Incredible as it may sound today, fifty years later, in 1864 Jews were permitted to settle in Dresden only if they bought some real estate there.

We had a very capable attorney working for us in Dresden, who was also a member of the legislature. Through him, we managed to get an appointment with an important person of high rank, who expressed his delight at seeing a new industry established in Dresden, which had previously had only a few factories. He advised my father to buy an appropriate piece of real estate, which would promptly put an end to any difficulties. My father agreed and bought a property on *Rosenthaler Straße* in Dresden. The plant was set up in a great hurry, mostly using equipment from the Teplitz factory. My brother Julius was put in charge of it, and we did not have to miss out on a single season of business with France.

In 1866, after the end of the Austro-Prussian War, a trade agreement was established between France and Austria, putting Austria on the same footing as Germany. Julius returned to Teplitz, the manufacturing facilities were moved back there again, and after a while the Dresden building itself was sold at a reasonable profit.

Julius was back at work again in the factory at Teplitz. We had a chemist in charge of the laboratory. He was responsible for plating products with gold or silver or for oxidizing them. But whenever it was a question of producing something new, Julius could not be deterred from carrying out the experiments himself, and despite our repeated warnings he spent more time in the laboratory than was healthy for him.

In those days the fashion was to color brass objects chemically to achieve an intense blackness that would allow them to be polished to a dazzling shine without losing their intensity of color. Julius did not rest until he had found a way to accomplish that. But the vapors of the concentrated nitric acid and the corrosive ammonia had such a harmful impact on him that for several weeks he was down in bed with severe pneumonia.

Journey to London in November of 1865

In November of 1865 I traveled overnight from Paris to London. We arrived at Calais at around two o'clock in the morning during a severe storm. The weather was very cold and snow was falling. In those days, only small craft plied the English Channel in the winter. Even at the best of times, let alone in raging seas, they were unstable enough to make anyone seasick! But it did no good to hesitate. I had to board the ship come what may. And come it did! I felt absolutely miserable and suffered greatly.

After a journey of more than two hours, which seemed like an eternity to me, we arrived at Dover. Exhausted, weak, and almost frozen stiff, I left the boat, hurried to the inn, and asked for a glass of brandy with biscuits to revive my spirits. That did me some good. I ordered a second and a third glass, and if the bell had not started to ring to summon us to the train, I undoubtedly would have continued to try to restore my battered body in that fashion.

I had a substantial amount of hand luggage. I had it taken to the compartment, where I stretched out comfortably after having managed somehow to keep it all to myself. It was about five in the morning and still completely dark. Tired as I was, I soon fell into a deep sleep. I had no worries because the conductor had promised to wake me when we arrived in London.

Who could then describe my astonishment upon waking up to find myself undressed and in bed in a very dark room? Where was I? How had I gotten there? Who had undressed me and put me to bed? All of those questions rushed to my mind, and only gradually did I begin to remember having lived through a bad Channel crossing and having gotten into a train compartment in Dover. But I remembered all of that only vaguely, and whatever else had happened to me after that was a total mystery to me!

In vain I groped around for my watch, my wallet, and my briefcase. Eventually, ready for anything, I decided to press the button next to my bed. A young man with a serious expression appeared, looked at me scornfully, and asked quite disrespectfully: "What do you want?"

I was shocked at being addressed in that way. Gathering all my strength I asked curtly: "Where are my briefcase, my wallet, and my watch?"

He replied: "Mind your tone. They are safer with me than with you!"

"I want them back immediately!"

He responded: "Not for a while!"

At that point I really got angry and shouted: "For heaven's sake, what is going on here. Whose hands have I fallen into? Whose house is this? How did I get into this bed, and why have my valuables been taken from me?"

"I'll tell you," he replied. "A porter from the train station brought you here. You were staggering across the street. You were very lucky to have ended up no worse than in my hands!"

"Yes, but just where am I?"

The young man began to laugh out loud and said: "The porter brought you and your belongings here. As drunk and drowsy as you were, he had a lot of trouble getting you out of the compartment. At that point, fortunately, you stammered the words '*Royal Hotel.*' Since you were a well-known guest here, it wound up being my job to bring you up to your room and put you to bed." At that point he opened the curtains and said: "When you are awake and sober, you will realize that the person who took care of your briefcase and valuables was none other than your old school friend Karl Hartmann* from Teplitz, who is completing his training here!" Imagine that! That very embarrassing situation could not have come to a more cheerful conclusion.

Travels in 1866, Political Tensions Notwithstanding

Of my numerous journeys to London and Paris, I especially remember one that I undertook in May of 1866. There had been a lot of tension in the relationship between Prussia and Austria of late, but nobody wanted to believe that there could be a war, even though both countries had begun to mobilize troops. It was generally hoped that the differences could be ironed out. I myself had become exempt from military service by paying a special release fee,* so I had nothing to fear from the mobilization. I made the necessary preparations as usual and began my journey as planned.

First I went to Paris, and after concluding all my business there to my total satisfaction, I went on to London. When I arrived, my local representative reported that several of my clients were already expecting me. He also said that business would be particularly good this time, because almost all of our German competitors were prevented from coming to London by the mobilization. It turned out that business really was unbelievably successful. Clients who had bought from us before ordered twice the usual amount, and I received very substantial orders from several very large firms that I had previously not been able to win over as clients. As the orders increased, my satisfaction soared. Only someone who has been in such a position can imagine my joy. The only concern was whether it would be possible to deliver everything on time, but my youthful enthusiasm soon helped me to get over that worry!

One morning I was shocked to read some telegrams from Berlin and Vienna, which reported with certainty that diplomatic ties between the two countries would be broken off. Even though I would have preferred to spend a few more days in London doing business and also wanted to return to Paris, I decided to return home immediately.

The journey across England, Belgium, and France was quiet as usual, but as soon as I set foot on German soil I noticed great agitation. All the stations were packed with military personnel who could not all be moved in time, and there was an air of excitement everywhere. We arrived in Cologne in the evening, several hours late. The station was bursting with people, most of them soldiers, who were crammed into the departing train so tightly that they could hardly find room to stand. It was quite astonishing that I actually managed to regain my previously reserved seat.

In my compartment sat seven German officers, and just as many were standing. Those gentlemen expressed their joy at the impending war while soundly cursing Austria whose final hour would soon come! I had to listen to all of that, but did not participate in the conversation, of course, because it really is wiser not to run any unnecessary risks.

Nor was I bothered by anyone or anything during the whole journey across Prussia. Around two or three in the morning, the conductor announced, "Hanover, a thirty-minute stop." I wanted to use that time to get out of the smoke-filled compartment and get some fresh air. At that moment I saw a sight that I will never forget. A number of Prussian military engineers who had arrived on the same train began to tear up the tracks between Hanover and Cologne and to destroy the telegraph wires. Then I knew that war had already broken out and that Hanover was also considered to be one of Prussia's enemies.

I continued my journey with a heavy heart. When I arrived in Leipzig very late, I found there another nasty surprise awaiting me. The railway bridge across the Elbe at Risa had been blown up during the night by the Saxons, which made it impossible for me to get home via Dresden and Bodenbach. So I quickly went to Thüringer Station, got on the first train to Altenburg, continued my journey from there to Karlsbad by coach, and spent the night in Karlsbad. The next morning I took the express coach home.

Along the way I learned that the King of Saxony had arrived in Teplitz. A large part of the Saxon army had already entered Bohemia in order to join our army, and as we passed through Komotan (Chomotov), Brüx (Most), and the surrounding villages, we found them all occupied by Saxons. I was able to notify my father of my altered travel plans by telegraph, and when I arrived in Teplitz on Sunday evening, I had the pleasure of experiencing his joy in welcoming me home.

Even Teplitz itself had to house a large contingent of Saxon military personnel. We had received sixty men, who were fed and housed well and gave us no cause for complaint. We were able to keep the factory running undisturbed, and there was very little sign of any hardship associated with the war. After eight or ten days, however, the Saxon soldiers had marched on and Teplitz had no other protection aside from a few local policemen. Even the gendarmes had been called away, and there were some serious incidents.

There were many people out of work, who could not find any source of income. They got into serious trouble, and theft and crime became the order of the day. In order to deal with this situation as effectively as possible, the city council decided to set up a citizens' militia made up mostly of young people, to "defend and protect" our town. That became a "funny" institution.

At about eight o'clock at night we assembled in the large room of an inn to receive our orders for the night. There were more than a hundred of us young, high-spirited fellows meeting there, and groups of five were supposed make the rounds in their assigned areas for an hour at a time. Ten sections were set up, which meant fifty men. The others had to remain in the guard station until six o'clock in the morning, ready to deal with any incidents. That was in June. The nights were bright and clear, and our watchful eyes looked longingly for an excuse to demonstrate our bravery. Since we were not allowed to carry firearms, we had only iron rods with which to attack or to defend ourselves. But we rarely made use of them anyway.

Our main successes were in preventing burglaries, fistfights, offensive behavior on the part of drunks, and other such misdemeanors, but most of the time all we did was track lovers who were trying to hide. We often had a hilarious time doing that, and our knowledge of the "scandal chronicles" of our home town expanded enormously.

Our period of glory did not last long, however, and we were forced to surrender to the enemy. Prussian military forces arrived to assume the task of protecting the town. For more than two weeks we had been expecting the Prussians, and the people had all sorts of worries. The most ridiculous rumors about plundering and all kinds of cruel deeds were circulated and believed, and there was no doubt that our young men would be forced into military service in the Prussian ranks as soon as they arrived. In fact, many fearful citizens left Teplitz without any idea about where they would be safer than at home. They ran right into the enemy, whose positions were never known, but the latter refused to put them into service.

Day by day, even hour by hour, the excitement in Teplitz increased. Many people had experienced the arrival of the enemy at Zinnwald and Eichwald. Since those places were not even an hour away from Teplitz, the populace was extremely worried about coming events. For a long time those reports proved to be incorrect, until one day things became serious after all.

Our factory was situated in an elevated location at a crossroads, and from the attic we had a sweeping view of the surrounding countryside and the road from Eichwald. One afternoon, from that vantage point I watched a small group of soldiers approach

Teplitz. They were riding at a fast gallop, but they came to a sudden halt almost directly opposite our factory. There were five "Black Hussars," and one of them, who carried a ladder, dismounted and put the ladder up against the telegraph pole. The "clang, clang" of the hammer smashing the porcelain heads resounded in my ears for a long time after the event. The telegraph equipment itself had been safely taken away just after it had been used to report the arrival of the Prussian detachment.

The Prussians then galloped across the marketplace, down *Lange Gasse* to *Settenzerstraße*, past Prince Clary's palace, and then stopped abruptly. People "regretfully admired" the certainty with which they operated and their precise knowledge of the streets. We did not know the Prussians well enough in those days!

After about ten minutes, a group of twenty-four men came and occupied all access roads leading to the town. Then another squadron of hussars arrived and were followed an hour later by the bulk of the infantry under the command of General Vogel von Falkenstein. They assembled in formation in the large square opposite the town hall, and the commander "wished" to see the mayor.

In 1866, Carl Stöhr, a man who had rendered his home town great service, was the mayor of Teplitz. He was a highly cultured person with a sharp mind and was always aware of where leniency or strong action was required. His upright and affable character was held in very high esteem by all decent citizens. That was the man who now appeared at the head of the assembled city council, to face the Prussian general who was apparently intent on impressing the mayor with his rough and provocative behavior. He replied to the mayor's greeting by shouting the following question: "Tell me, Mr. Mayor, are there soldiers in this town?" Then, not trusting the negative answer, he repeated the question in an even more petulant tone. When the mayor responded that he had already given his word that there were no defense forces of any kind in the town, not even in hiding, the general drew his saber from its sheath, put its point to the mayor's chest, and shouted excitedly: "You must give me your word of honor!"

At that, the mayor very calmly pushed the blade aside with the back of his hand and declared in a firm voice: "My simple word is no different from my word of honor."

Stöhr's behavior apparently impressed the general greatly, and he immediately began to talk with the mayor in a quiet, more businesslike manner about the accommodation of his soldiers. It was certainly a difficult task to house and feed around 2,000 men. Supplies were already running short because of the earlier prolonged presence of the Saxon soldiers, and it was impossible to obtain fresh ones. Any justified requests, however, were taken into consideration as much as possible.

We had to house and feed eighty men in the factory, and because the troops that occupied Teplitz included some rather rough and aggressive elements, quite a few unpleasant events took place. There were even small excesses, but they were severely punished. The soldiers' superiors took the strictest action against them.

It seemed strange to us that the soldiers who were stationed with us required that each meal and each drink be tasted by the host or his deputy before they touched it. That was an order, however, that was based on the fear of being poisoned. After a few meals that unnecessary requirement was abolished.

A large number of young girls were employed at our factory. They became "points of attraction" to five or six soldiers, who entered the factory buildings, behaved inappropriately, and were disruptive. They ignored my demands that they leave, and I was therefore forced to report it to their commanding officer. He immediately had the recalcitrant gentlemen arrested. When they had completed their detention, they were given far less comfortable quarters than they had had with us. That had the desired effect, and we had no further problems with unsuitable behavior.

We all worked in the factory with increased diligence to fill the orders from England and France. Unlike elsewhere, we were not short of workers, because the other factories in Teplitz had either closed altogether or were operating at a reduced capacity. We produced goods in large quantities, but we were worried about their delivery. The question was how to move the goods to Dresden, which was occupied by the enemy, i.e. the Prussians. And even if we succeeded in that respect, the question remained as to how Austrian goods could be moved unhindered to England and France. The Prussian administration in Teplitz was unable to give us any information with regard to the latter question. The exchange of mail between Austria and Germany had come to a complete standstill, and thus there was only one last possibility: to risk making the journey to Dresden by coach.

A Problematic Journey to Dresden in 1866

I spoke with the banker Bernhard Mayer, a very good friend of the family, about my intentions. He immediately decided to accompany me, because he had some urgent, long-postponed business in Dresden and Leipzig! He also promised to arrange for our transportation to Dresden, and early in the morning of the day appointed for the journey, a carriage stopped at my door. I was more than a little surprised, however, to see a starving horse in front of a very shabby open carriage. I commented that even a good carriage drawn by two horses would take eight or nine hours to reach Dresden. My friend Mayer replied that the horse was a good runner despite its appearance, and that two horses would have cost twice as much. I finally had to accept the situation, but then I was confronted with another surprise! My friend Mayer informed me that we would be accompanied by a third traveling companion in the person of the poultry dealer Dasch, who weighed at least a hundred kilos!

"For God's sake," I yelled, "how is that poor horse going to lug four people (including the driver), with an absolute giant among them, all the way to Dresden in one day?! And why did you allow him to come with us?"

My friend Mayer responded very cleverly: "You know, my dear Heller, Dasch is a very strong fellow, and these days you never know what might happen along the way. Dasch is a form of security for us, and that's why I asked him to come with us!"

Mayer undoubtedly had other reasons for taking Dasch along, but since I could do nothing about it, we eventually all got into the carriage. I had to plug my nose immediately, because Dasch, who was sitting opposite me, smelled almost unbearably of chicken, geese, and duck coops. But that was not all. The man had such long legs that they completely filled the interior of the coach, and I did not know where to put mine. Eventually, Dasch had to sit with his legs hanging out the side of the carriage, which had the rather pleasant result that I was less irritated by the odor.

After a long and painful journey, we finally arrived in Dresden late at night, without any problems. We felt as if we had been on the rack, but were glad to have completed that tortuous trip. The next morning I attended to my business and learned to my great satisfaction that our goods would be forwarded promptly once they arrived in Dresden. That fulfilled the purpose of my trip, and I could have gone home immediately, but I was obliged to wait for Mayer, whose business in Leipzig would take another day. A rumor was spreading in Dresden that sometime that afternoon several trains full of Austrian prisoners would pass through the city, and everybody flocked to the station. I joined them with a heavy heart and very soon saw something that I would not forget for the rest of my life.

Long trains, consisting only of freight cars, rolled into the station with their doors wide open. Inside them were many Austrian riflemen of the *Jäger* military corps, and most of them were wounded. The poor wretches were sitting in the open doors with their legs hanging out and covered with blood, and many had bandages around their heads. It was a pitiful sight! The wretched men were given refreshments and many gifts by the people of Dresden, since their sympathies lay with the Austrians.

When I returned to the hotel, I found Mayer there. He had returned from Leipzig and was anxious to leave for home immediately, because he had urgent business there the next day. At first I did not want to leave the same evening, but then I decided to give in after all. Rumors from several sources were floating around that a Prussian army unit was going to move toward Teplitz the next morning, and that could have hindered our journey home.

We left Dresden at around eight o'clock that night. It was raining and stormy, and we felt quite uncomfortable in our open carriage. The two days of rest seemed to have done the horse some good, because it trotted at a lively pace, but Dasch still reeked of the chicken coop and his legs were still as long as before. I had to change the position of my legs from moment to moment, and it was all most uncomfortable, but after traveling for several hours and after the driver had extinguished the lamp to save fuel, everyone fell into a light slumber. But suddenly we were awakened by a loud "Stop! Who goes there?" And we found ourselves surrounded by a Prussian patrol.

We showed the sergeant our permit to travel back to Teplitz, which had been issued by the Prussian commander in Dresden. He found it very suspicious that in wartime we were traveling through the night and fog in an unlit carriage, and he sent off two men with a report to his commanding officer. At the end of a very long hour, another officer appeared and put us through another sharp cross-examination. He finally believed our assurances that we represented no threat to the Prussian state. He pointed out, however, how unwise we were to travel at night and advised us to turn back to Dresden, because we could certainly expect to have many more unpleasant encounters like this one during the night.

He would not, or could not give us a definite answer to the question of whether a similar encounter could not also happen on our way back to Dresden. We therefore decided to continue on toward home. The officer ordered us to keep the light on the whole time. He also advised us to make our presence known in some way or other in order to demonstrate clearly that we were not involved in any secret and sinister plot, for we would undoubtedly encounter several more Prussian patrols on the way.

We thanked the officer, lighted the lanterns, and left, but then asked ourselves what we could do to make our presence known in order not to be taken for spies. We thought of singing, but Dasch said: "I can't sing, but I can shout 'cock-a-doodle-do,' and I can imitate geese and ducks very well. That's at least something!" So he shouted cock-a-doodle-do and quacked and crowed out into the night! Mayer and I were shaking with laughter, but eventually Dasch got tired of it and said: "That's all, no more!"

But it still did not seem advisable to travel on quietly, and so we decided to try singing. Mayer said that he was tone deaf and did not know any songs other than temple songs. "That's good enough," I said, and we began. First we sang *Lechau Daudi*, then *Hallelujah* and *Matowu*, etc. Then, to our surprise, Dasch was no longer tired. The Jewish songs electrified him, and his full baritone drowned out both our voices. After each temple song, Dasch shouted cock-a-doodle-do so loudly that it could be heard far and wide. We laughed heartily and began another temple song.

As it turned out, we could have saved ourselves all of our singing and Dasch's imitations of his stock in trade, for we encountered no further delay and arrived at daybreak in the town of Dippoldiswald, where we stopped at the inn.

Although we had not seen any other Prussians on our journey, the inn was full of Prussian officers who had arrived there by other routes and were on their way to various destinations. Our arrival created a stir, and we had to relate the story of our nightly adventure before receiving a warm welcome. Mayer, the banker, handed out his business cards and did not miss the opportunity to recommend himself as trustworthy for any currency exchanges. After an hour's rest, we continued our journey home, arrived in Teplitz tired, weak, and hoarse, and had completed a trip that has probably remained in the memories of all of the participants!

Then the goods were swiftly packed into boxes, and after a few days we had a full load ready to be sent off. A large freight coach, supplied by the *Zehra Transport Company*, was loaded, and our accountant, Mr. Josef Sittig, was ready to accompany it to complete the customs formalities at the Saxon border. He made certain that he had the correct permits for himself and the freight and arrived unhindered in Dresden. Once there, he transferred the boxes to the *Fischer Transport Company*, and they were moved to the railway unencumbered. Mr. Sittig made that journey many times in the course of a few weeks.

These days Mr. Sittig is a factory owner and owns a house in Vienna. Many years ago, I negotiated his purchase of my father-in-law's horn button factory, which he then proceeded to enlarge. Today he is a wealthy and well-respected man.

Journey to Vienna in 1866

The considerable decline in the value of our currency helped business, of course, but people began to fear all sorts of things that they had seen happen before and preferred to own "things of real value" rather than worthless paper money, even if the former obviously increased horrendously in price. That was the reason for another uncomfortable journey to Vienna. At that time, several hundred people, both men and women, were employed by our factory, and we had sufficient work for them. Thanks to my father's foresight, we also had enough liquid capital available to carry on all operations without interference. My father had deposited a portion of the capital with Mayer, the banker, with the explicit proviso that it had to remain at our disposal at all times.

One day, this otherwise reliable friend explained that he had over-extended himself and that he intended to travel to Vienna to withdraw a large amount of money from his account there, which would allow him to cover his debts to us in a short time. It so happened that we also had a large amount of money deposited with our subsidiary in Vienna, which could not be moved during this time of war. So I decided to accompany Mayer on his journey to Vienna.

Even though peace negotiations were well under way, it still was not easy to travel long distances, for railway and postal traffic had come to a total standstill and the country was occupied by enemy troops. On top of that, unemployed people roamed the country roads, making travel uncertain.

Nevertheless, we were not deterred, and with the necessary permits in our pockets, which had been issued by the Prussian commander in Teplitz, we departed by carriage on our way to Prague. We stayed there for two days, and after receiving permission from the Prussian headquarters in Prague to travel on to Vienna via Budweis and Linz, we hired a reliable looking carriage to take us as far as Budweis (Budejovice).

When we got into the carriage, however, it turned out that the driver either *could not* or more probably *did not want to* speak German. Since neither Mayer nor I spoke any Czech, the situation became quite unpleasant. All our requests were greeted by the driver with: "Can't understand."

We left Prague around three o'clock that afternoon. The driver took a break every two or three hours to feed the horses and eat. Out of principle, and probably to save money, he never stopped in a reasonably large town or at a decent inn, but rather always just before or just beyond a larger village. We therefore never had a chance to eat anything hot and could not even get out of the carriage, because in the places that our driver favored there were never any rooms where we could have stayed.

Fortunately, we had taken some "ammunition" with us from Prague, and things were tolerable until nightfall. But we were forced to remain in the carriage at night as well. To stretch out, even at the stops where we often stayed for two hours, was unthinkable. We were so glad to see the sun rise after all those hours of torture! At around four o'clock in the morning, the coachman stopped once more in front of one of those lonely houses along the road, knocked to awaken the owners from their sleep, and signaled to us after a while with hand gestures to get out of the carriage. It was a frosty morning. In fact, the whole summer of 1866 was quite cold, and we were freezing. And even after we were shown to a so-called "room," we did not get any warmer. After a while an old peasant woman arrived, dressed in rags. Using sign language we conveyed to her the idea that we wanted coffee or some other hot drink. Our wish was even fulfilled, but in what an unpleasant manner!

In a rather large, flat, wooden bowl we were "served" a gray liquid with bits of bread floating in it. The bowl also contained two wooden spoons. Mayer and I looked at each other in surprise. "We are supposed to eat *that*?" We forced ourselves to taste one spoonful, but did not take another! We were sustained by the hope that we would have to reach Budweis sometime, and that we could recover there.

We arrived at around noon and spent the night there, since the horse-drawn railway departed for Linz only once a day, early in the morning. Along the entire route from Prague to Budweis, and from Budweis to Linz as well, there was no sign of any military presence, and we arrived in Linz without any problem.

The journey on the - long since abandoned - horse-drawn railway from Budweis to Linz, was very pleasant. We had comfortable compartments with good suspension and - because of the railroad tracks - no shocks or bumps of any kind. Compared with our journey from Prague to Budweis, it felt like paradise. Even the countryside there was very pretty, and excellent food was provided along the way, making the journey truly pleasant.

After arriving safely in Linz in the evening, the next day we traveled on to Vienna by train. That route was kept open without interruption throughout the war period. Thus along the entire route from Prague to Vienna we did not get the impression that we were and paid for it in cash in the amount of 40,000 florins in convention currency.

A Lost War with Positive Consequences, 1866

During the last months of the war, the populace of Vienna had been very nervous. The defeats that our armies had suffered and the various military proclamations that were issued by the highest authorities all produced resentment, and that had led to turbulent excesses on more than one occasion. Very sharp measures were taken against the people involved, which understandably only added to the provocation.

In those days Vienna had a very capable, energetic, and liberal mayor, Dr. Zelinka. A modest statue of him can be found in the Vienna Municipal Gardens. That man gathered the courage to declare openly and freely to the Emperor that if the strict police measures were not soon abolished, he could not guarantee that the city would remain calm, nor that "extensive popular unrest" could be avoided. Those circumstances forced the "highest authorities" to give in. Out of necessity, the mayor's frankness was "graciously" tolerated, and the police became "modest."

Our impression of Vienna, however, was once again that of a welcoming and friendly city. Everyone knew that in Nikolsburg peace negotiations were being conducted, negotiations that were not unfavorable for us as a nation. Kaiser Wilhelm of Prussia wanted some Austrian territory as a prize for winning the war, but Bismarck was against it and was satisfied with compensation in the amount of, I believe, thirty million gilders. He did that with clever foresight, hoping to transform us into allies in the long run.

It is doubtful that Bismarck would have been successful in convincing Kaiser Wilhelm to accept his moderate plans, if he had not been supported by Napoleon III. Napoleon's power was so great in those days that nobody was able to oppose him, and *he* did not want to see Prussia's influence increased through the acquisition of Austrian territory. However, we were forced to give up the province of Venetia* in spite of all our previous victories in Italy. Yet that was not perceived as terribly painful, because we knew not been supported by Napoleon III. Napoleon's power was so great in those days that nobody was able to oppose him, and *he* did not want to see Prussia's influence increased through the acquisition of Austrian territory. However, we were forced to give up the province of Venetia* in spite of all our previous victories in Italy. Yet that was not perceived as terribly painful, because we knew that it would happen someday and that the Italian provinces were a heavy burden for us.

We found Vienna in its usual serene mood, even though the enemy was a mere three hours away and trenches and fortifications continued to be built outside the city. Everyone knew that the war was over, even though it had been lost, but in all honesty people were happy about the defeat, which was correctly recognized as resulting from the old, rotten system of absolute monarchy, and they were looking forward to more liberal times.

Even though it turned out later that those times did not become what everyone had expected and hoped for, and that another reactionary period intervened, the war of 1866 did revive Austria and provide it with new energy. Unfortunately, because of our circumstances, because of the character, the natural peculiarities, and the manifold aspirations of our nations, all progress was soon suppressed again.

Business activity, which had really lost momentum at the beginning of the war and was brought to a complete standstill after our severe losses, suddenly began to flourish again. The favorable peace agreements brought optimism to the population, and Vienna was throbbing! It was the beginning of a period of enormous growth.

Stock Market Fever

The prospect of the immanent formation of a new parliament, that is, of the establishment of a liberal government, revived all of Austria, and that mood of expectation was soon reflected in hitherto unknown activity. Trade and industry flourished, and even the upcoming settlement with Hungary - the work of the great Beust* - contributed enormously to the self-confidence of the citizens.

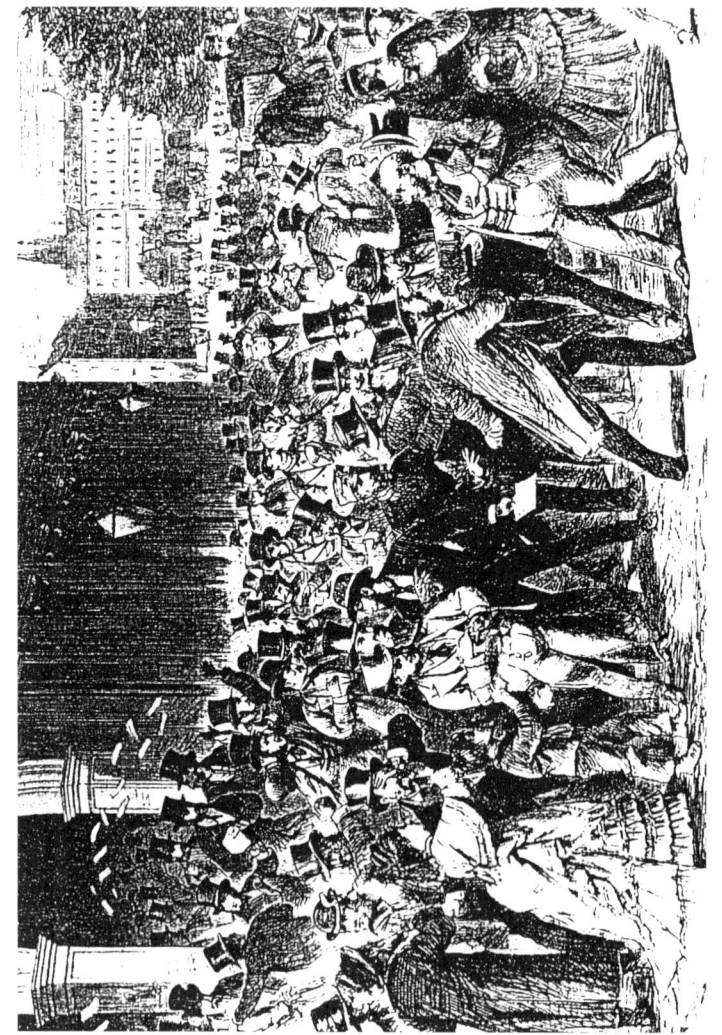

A scene in front of the old stock exchange at the time of the great crash of 1873

Easy, previously unimaginable profits resulted in "wild dances" at the stock exchanges in Vienna, the provinces, and elsewhere. Year after year there was nothing but profit, which fostered limitless gambling and encouraged the wildest speculations. New banks sprang up like mushrooms in fertile soil and were never short of customers.

The mad frenzy did not seem to come to an end, up until the moment when "the big crash" put a sudden stop to speculation on "Black Friday" in the exhibition year of 1873. The whole "rotten structure" was swept away with a single blow, and an untold number of people were suddenly plunged into misery, or their lives were totally destroyed. My brother Leopold and several of my close relatives also participated in wild speculation in the stock market and fell victim to it. They suffered great losses. Some of them lost almost their entire fortunes, plunging their families into poverty. Some of them, however, succeeded in rebuilding their lives.

My Uncle Josef Foges (my mother-in-law's brother) had surrendered to the temptation of insane speculation, which caused him huge financial losses. After the "crash," he and his family were unable to survive financially. His brother-in-law, Joseph Jeiteles (my uncle and father-in-law), came to his rescue. Back in 1867, he had purchased a horn button factory in Vienna to provide at the time a secure, permanent income for his brother Michael. The business ran very successfully for years. Demand was so high that some orders could not be filled for an entire year. My Uncle Josef Foges was made a partner in that business.

The horn button factory was located near the west railway station, in a building on a side street that was not yet fully developed and was therefore not very busy. That changed after a few years, much to the disadvantage of the factory owner Foges and his son. The material to make horn buttons comes from oxen hooves. They must be soaked in large barrels for a period of time so that they become pliable and can be shaped. This produces a pervasive, very strong, unpleasant smell. The smell bothered the whole neighborhood and led to legal intervention that ended with the closure of the factory. But that only happened after the death of Uncle Josef Foges, who did not live to old age.

There is something, however, that Vienna owes to that period: its embellishment. The most magnificent streets, the most splendid palaces, and both public and private buildings were erected during that time and have become a permanent adornment for the city of Vienna.*

WORK AND LEISURE

The Trade Fairs in Leipzig

I will never forget the wonderful times that I enjoyed during the trade fairs in Leipzig. Emboldened as I was by my successful journeys to London and Paris, I felt brave enough to attend those famous fairs as well, as a salesman with samples, and had the satisfaction of enjoying not only business success, but also stimulating entertainment! The hotel *De Baviere*, where I stayed, was one of those establishments that rented some of its rooms to salesmen for their sample collections and was thus also frequented regularly by buyers who visited the fair.

The owner of the place was a certain Mrs. Eicke, a former actress who was very popular with her former colleagues because of her kindness and generosity. For that reason all the reputable artists who visited Leipzig stayed with her. During the fairs, which brought the theater extremely large audiences, there were always several famous figures from the art world in Leipzig, and without exception they were regulars at the *De Baviere*.

I cannot remember what it was that earned us Mrs. Eicke's particular favor - by us, I mean my brothers-in-law George and Max and myself. But we were included among those few guests at the fair who were invited to dine with her and all of those actors and actresses in the "Glass Salon," which was used as the dining room.

It was not so much the exquisite *table d'hôte* that we really enjoyed, but rather the fascinating hours that we spent in the company of all those intellectually stimulating, freethinking actors and artists. I have the most vivid memories of them. In the evenings, we often sat together until one or two in the morning, listening to their experiences or following their brilliant, witty exchanges. We even had the satisfaction of holding our own in that kind of company. That filled us with joy and pride, and even when we sacrificed quite a few hours of sleep, it did not weary us. On the contrary, we fulfilled our business obligations very thoroughly and loved and enjoyed doing it. But in those days, doing business was easy and pleasant. Sometimes it seemed to me as if the whole world were only just now coming into existence and still very young.

Our customers were always pleasantly surprised by whatever we could offer them, and they gladly accepted it. We did not have to go and see them; they came to us. Most of them were companies from South America, Westphalia, and Hamburg, which had their outlets overseas. They gave us orders of a magnitude that we had not previously experienced. Not only did they come to see us at every trade fair, year after year, but we also received written orders from them in the interim. That demonstrated their satisfaction, and those ties lasted for many years.

Freemason Lodge, 1869

In 1869 I was admitted to the brotherhood of Freemasons, the "Black Eagle" lodge in Frankfurt am Main. It was the fulfillment of a wish, something that I had wanted for a long time. One of my friends had signed for me as an applicant to his lodge, and after several months of exhaustive research on their part, I received the news that nothing stood in the way of my admittance.

In May of that year I stopped in Frankfurt on my way back from Paris. On that occasion I was inducted into the brotherhood in a very solemn manner. The ceremony of affiliation is intended to make the applicant reflect on his motivations. He is required to state his reasons for seeking admission to the assembly. The rites are supposed to instill within the novice's mind and thoughts an everlasting impression of the celebration of his own admission. They remind him of the establishment of the first association of Freemasons and their death-defying obligation to keep "the secret" in those days. The awareness of belonging to an organization that spreads across the world, and the feeling of being entitled to count on the care and friendship of every single member at any time, do fill you with awe.

Unfortunately, I could not take full advantage of my membership during the early years, because there were no lodges in Austria before 1871. I went to Frankfurt only on rare occasions, but when I did go, I never missed the opportunity to visit the lodge, and they always made me feel very welcome. After I moved to Vienna in

1877 or 1878, I became affiliated with the local "Humanitas" lodge, and on April 14, 1909, on the occasion of my 40th anniversary as a Freemason, I was made an honorary member there.

In recent years, due to age and illness, I have unfortunately not been able to attend the lodge as often as I would have liked. But I remain a loyal member in my heart and mind, even if I can no longer participate in its leadership as I formerly did.

Freemasonry is a peculiar thing. It unites people of all different classes of society, of very different professions, and of different approaches to life. Neither religion nor politics form an obstacle to acceptance into the group. All of those contrasts disappear once a person has crossed the threshold of the temple, where total equality and fraternity reign. The informal mode of address *du* that is used among the members is not an empty matter of form. It contributes greatly toward binding us closer and more sincerely to each other. The evenings that we spend together are often elevating for each of us, but they always bring recovery.

The Freemasons are often reproached for putting too much emphasis on formality and ceremony, but that is not justified. A protective covering is required to keep the contents intact, and if the covering and the formalities were dropped, the contents would suffer as well.

Many people also ask if it is necessary to keep the contents of Freemasonry secret. The answer could quite easily be *no*, because there really is no secret. But the whole thing can only be understood and appreciated by people who have the required inclination and understanding. To all others it will remain a total mystery that they will never be able to unravel. It is therefore just as well not to divulge the so-called "secret."

The meaning of Freemasonry and its aims can be given in a few words: propagation of enlightenment, cultivation of friendship, fraternity, and humanity in the broadest sense, and readiness to alleviate human suffering. The "Humanitas" lodge has rendered a great service to the general public since it founded a children's sanctuary in the village of Kahlenberg almost fifty years ago. Hundreds of children have been placed under care there from infancy, and they owe their very existence and everything else in their lives to that home.

My Teplitz Circle of Friends

Now I want to tell you about my circle of friends.

In a small town, everyone notices everything. Thus everybody knew that I went on many business trips. It was assumed that they were successful, and I therefore had a good reputation and even a certain image! That is probably why, at a very young age, much earlier than my contemporaries, I was not only invited to all social events in the Jewish community, but was also one of only a few who were invited to very exclusive Christian parties.

There were balls, concerts, theater performances, and pantomimes called "living pictures" that were performed by amateurs, as well as other such pastimes. It was all very entertaining. I interacted with families, frequently talked with pretty young ladies, and had just about everything that could make a young man happy and content. There was no lack of flirtations, which contribute, of course, to youth's appeal, and I believed in real and imaginary conquests and paid extensive homage to the "sweet and lovely foolishness of youth."

Despite all of that, I also continued striving to educate myself, and many a burned-out candle and many a burned floor near my bed provided evidence that I read until I was exhausted.

I had a small but close circle of friends, and although I was the youngest, I was extremely proud to be a part of it. I was particularly attached to my cousin Ludwig Glogau, and he had great influence on my character, my beliefs, and my development.

Glogau, who was nine years older than I, was witty, steadfast, and well-educated. He was an excellent speaker, funny, ironic, and even sarcastic, and I was often the target of his sarcasm. All in all, he was a splendid person, and everyone enjoyed his company. He was one of those people who do not much care about the opinions of the world, who speak the truth frankly and openly to everyone, and who are self-confident without being immodest.

In spite of the difference in our ages, Glogau really was a true friend, and we remained in contact until 1875, when I moved to Vienna. He remained unmarried for a long time, and I spent many happy hours in the comfortable home that he shared with his mother and his cheerful young sister Fanni. On free winter afternoons several young men and women met there regularly for simple but good coffee and cake, which were served in the big kitchen. There was not much fuss but always a pleasant atmosphere. There was often piano playing, singing, and dancing in the room, and sometimes we were able to enjoy the performances of good visiting artists there.

This is how it came about: Ludwig Glogau was a close friend of Ascher's, the lessee of Prince Clary's *Herrenhaus*, a rooming house for patients who were taking the cure at the spa. Glogau visited there daily, presumably because of Ascher's niece Sophie, who later became his wife. Guests from the upper social circles who needed the cure stayed at the *Herrenhaus* during both the summer and the winter, and Ascher's winning manner enabled him to make friends with many of the guests. On winter evenings they regularly gathered in Ascher's apartment, where many stimulating conversations took place. Among the guests there were also writers, composers, and performing artists with whom Glogau was on friendly terms, and we often had the opportunity to listen to them at *his* home.

During the winter of 1864-1865, the *Herrenhaus* was particularly lively. Many Austrian and German officers who had been wounded in the Schleswig-Holstein war were recuperating in Teplitz, and there were parties at Ascher's every night, which I, too, often attended.

Ascher was at least fifty years old by then. He fully enjoyed life and had the spirit of a young man, and I cannot resist telling a little bit about his life in the pages that follow.

Richard John Ascher was born in the small town of Tachau in Bohemia. He usually liked to talk a lot about his later life, but remained completely silent about his parental home and youth. It was probably just as well, because everything we heard about it was not particularly good. His parents were said to have been from a very low social class, poor Jews who did not care about their son's education and development. Some people claim to have seen him as a thirteen or fourteen-year-old peddler who moved from town to town. It is also said that in later years he engaged in a sideline of financing officers. He came to Teplitz at the age of twenty-one or twenty-two and was noticed because of his good looks and good manners. People were amazed at what he had become. He also hinted that he had some money, but did not establish a business in

Teplitz, although he settled there. He traveled often and returned home from time to time. Ascher was really a strikingly handsome man with an expressive face. He was tall and conveyed the impression of being an officer in civilian clothes. He had good manners, as mentioned earlier, and even spoke French. It was no surprise that the girls in Teplitz found him attractive.

He even got engaged, although people were surprised at his choice, because his intended was an exceptionally ugly woman and stone deaf besides. But she had a sizeable fortune, and that was what Ascher was after. The "lovely" lady was so in love with Ascher that all the warnings of her parents, brothers, and sisters fell on "deaf ears," and all doubts that arose were extinguished by her fiancé's ardent love. The wedding took place, but soon afterward, when Ascher had gained possession of his wife's fortune, he divorced her and left Teplitz. It was often said that people saw him at aristocratic parties, that he was living a fast life, and that he must have had plenty of money.

Years passed, and Ascher did not return to Teplitz. Then he suddenly reappeared as a wealthy man with a horse-drawn carriage and servants. He bought the beautiful house *Zu den drei Kosaken* (The Three Cossacks) on the castle square, where he held extravagant parties that were attended by even those who knew about his past but were not able to avoid associating with him because his charming and fashionable manner did not permit them to offend him.

In addition, Ascher was an excellent storyteller, a brilliant, witty, and vivacious conversationalist, and since his parties were only for gentlemen, the stories that he told about his adventures and conquests had such a powerful impact that the listener was reminded of Boccacio! In a word, Ascher was soon completely integrated into Teplitz society, and even the ladies gladly endured his tender attention.

But why did Ascher settle in Teplitz again, where the divorced wife whom he had made so unhappy still resided? A new love, a new conquest brought him here. But once again, that flame was neither beautiful nor young. She was, however, suitable for Ascher's purposes because she was rich, very influential, and completely independent. She went by the name of Miss Kathrin and had been the chambermaid of Prince Edmund Clary's wife for many years. She was not only the maid, but also the confidante and private secretary to the very cheerful princess, who preferred to spend her time traveling and staying at her palace in Venice, rather than living in Teplitz, Prince Clary's place of residence. Miss Kathrin was the woman whom Ascher needed, and he knew how to win her over so that she would give him money and everything else that he wanted. He owed his fortune primarily to that relationship, and to show his appreciation, he was baptized, became a Protestant, and promised to marry the very wealthy Kathrin. Nevertheless, he cunningly postponed the wedding again and again and continued to live in grand style.

He built a match factory* on the *Königshöhe* [royal heights] in Teplitz. A short time later it burned down, and he was not able to claim any damages because no insurance company would insure such factories. Soon after that, Ascher's glory seemed to wane. Furthermore, in the meantime he had assumed a new liability by taking in two nieces who were sisters as housekeepers. Sophie, the older of the two, married my friend Ludwig Glogau a few years later.

Nevertheless, Ascher worried neither about himself nor about his nieces, because Miss Kathrin, the "almighty" private secretary of her high-ranking mistress, loved him! Very soon Ascher became the lessee of the *Herrenhaus* under very favorable conditions, had a nice position in society again, and earned a lot of money. His two nieces were able to help him run the large hotel, and once again Ascher was on top of the world!

To ensure that things would stay that way, Ascher continued to postpone the wedding to Miss Kathrin. She, on the other hand, after hearing about her "Don Juan's" many affairs, often threatened to end the relationship. But Ascher always knew how to calm her down, and each reconciliation added strength to the bond.

As I mentioned earlier, I often spent the evening at Ascher's house. One evening I pricked up my ears when he said, "Tomorrow I'm going to Dux for my Franzl's seventh birthday. I'll give him a nice birthday present, and his mother won't come away empty-handed either." Soon after that, it was a Roserl from Türnitz, then a Hansl in Bilin. On and on it went, until one evening, when a large number of particularly jovial people had gather at his house, Ascher introduced them to his large family. He had sixteen children in and around Teplitz and kept a book with the names and ages of all the children. He never missed a birthday and was a good father to all of them. Ascher had the kindheartedness that is common among unscrupulous people.

When he was over fifty years old, however, he pulled off a coup that exceeded all the previous ones and became his crowning achievement, a coup that was probably unique and one that he planned out carefully. He began to make the arrangements for a new ten-year lease of the *Herrenhaus* through Miss Kathrin. As soon as he had it in his possession, however, he broke off the relationship with her completely. She was getting too old for him, too ugly, and too troublesome. But the main thing was that he wanted to win over a beautiful young girl.

Her name was Minna F., and she was the daughter of a poor and somewhat half-witted, but otherwise kind and decent father. Her mother had already been dead for a long time. Ascher tried very hard to persuade the pretty Minna to submit to his desires. He gave her plenty of jewelry and was very attentive to her, but she was clever enough not to be caught. Having no better offer at the time, however, she indicated that she would become his "only with a ring on her finger!" The expensive presents appealed to her, and she really did not want to do without Ascher altogether.

Ascher was so infatuated with Minna that he proposed. But then the following situation arose: Ascher, who was Jewish by birth, had become a Protestant, but Minna was Jewish. Her father was a strictly observant Jew and refused to give permission for his daughter to be baptized. He thus also refused to consent to the wedding, if Ascher did not want to return to the Jewish faith.

That, of course, was simply too much for Ascher and he did not want to agree to it at all. He therefore requested some time to think about it and then used the time well! After a few days, he asked to speak to Minna's father and told him that he was willing to revert to Judaism. Nevertheless, he refused to take that step in Teplitz because it would create too much of a stir and could be harmful to him. Instead, he wanted to celebrate his return to Judaism and the wedding in Hamburg, and Minna and her father were to go there with him. At the same time, Ascher gave the penniless man a large sum of money, with which he was to buy new clothes for both Minna and himself, so that they could arrive in Hamburg in a manner befitting their social status.

The old man was overjoyed with the idea of gaining such a generous son-in-law and agreed to everything. Minna continued to receive valuable gifts, and everyone in Teplitz talked about the upcoming wedding.

Minna's father had received the Jewish given name of "Joile," but Ascher always called him "Uncle Julius," because he intended from the beginning to keep his father-in-law as far away from him as possible. Then came the day when "Uncle Julius" and Minna departed with Ascher, and the latter showered both of them with attention. But despite Ascher's generosity, and despite the sumptuous life that was being offered to him, "Uncle Julius" kept a very close eye on Minna. Upon their arrival in Hamburg, they were welcomed by Richard B., an old friend of Ascher's who was a well-known Hamburg merchant. He took them to a hotel on the *Jungfernstieg*, where rooms had already been booked.

The baptism and wedding in accordance with the Jewish rites were to take place the following Sunday, and preparations for the wedding ceremony were made in one room of the hotel. Sunday came, and with it an old, very respectable-looking rabbi, who was accompanied by two gray-bearded Jewish gentlemen. In the presence of "Uncle Julius," Ascher's friend Mr. B., and two witnesses, the rabbi married the beautiful Minna in her wedding dress to Ascher, who was beaming with joy.

A wedding certificate was issued and signed by the witnesses. Later on, Ascher very often showed it to his friends as something that he had kept as a valuable rarity.

The wedding ceremony had started immediately after the arrival of the officials. Minna's father, having been entertained by Ascher's friends who acted as his drinking companions, had completely forgotten about Ascher's conversion to the Jewish faith. He had been completely satisfied by the presence of the three honorable officials from the Jewish congregation. After the ceremony, the guests happily sat around the wedding table, and Minna's father had such a good time that he was soon dead drunk and had to be taken to bed.

The following day, the newlyweds met the young lady's father for lunch. The atmosphere during the meal was very cheerful, and after several glasses of wine had been consumed, Ascher said, "My dear friends, I have to tell you that yesterday, because of all the excitement, my conversion back to the Jewish faith was completely overlooked. Since the wedding itself was Jewish, it has no official validity whatsoever, particularly since I am a Protestant. Now, now, don't get so upset! If Minna wants to become a Protestant, I am very willing to marry her legally in Teplitz!"

Minna was crying her eyes out, while "Uncle Julius" was cursing and swearing never to agree to the baptism. But Ascher remained calm and said that he had no intention of forcing anyone, and if Minna did not want to become Protestant, she would have only herself to blame. He also then thought it wise to give father and daughter some privacy, so that they could discuss the situation and make their decisions. Then he said that he had a few things to do in Hamburg, but that he would be back in time for dinner.

When he returned, Minna greeted him happily and explained that she was compelled to make a virtue out of necessity, and "Uncle Julius" also agreed to his daughter's conversion. He really had no other option!

The last day of their stay in Hamburg ended with a lavish dinner that Ascher's friends also attended. After that, the newlyweds returned home in a cheerful mood. Minna soon converted to the Protestant faith, and the baptism and wedding were kept secret. It was not until sometime later that Ascher told his friends his latest story, which he called "Uncle Julius or The Trip to Hamburg."

Their happiness did not last, however. Ascher's health began to fail and he fell seriously ill. Nor could he bear the fact that his wife was unfaithful to him several times. They had many arguments, and finally Ascher ended his very turbulent life. Minna was left penniless. Since she believed that Teplitz could not offer her sufficient means for a good life, she moved to Vienna with her father. Fortune did not smile on her there either. She finally accepted a position as a sales assistant in a shoemaker's shop, but was laid off soon afterward. She died in poverty and misery a few years later. Her father was supported until his death by some people from Teplitz who lived in Vienna.

THE IMMEDIATE FAMILY

My Brother Heinrich

This chapter is in memory of my eldest brother Heinrich, whose short life was filled with hard work, and who was unfortunately not allowed to reap the benefits of well-earned success. To begin with, however, I must describe the general situation of the merchants in those days, in a time that suddenly experienced very decisive technical and political changes (1850-1860) and therefore demanded incredible adaptability. I have already mentioned the profound upheavals that businessmen had to master in the middle of the century. All previous business standards and methods were no longer valid! Previously unknown difficulties were caused on the one hand by the exacting demands of the customers, and on the other by the industrial mass production of goods and the many social problems. As a result, new approaches had to be discovered.

As a ten-year-old boy, my brother Heinrich moved to Grandmother Rebekka's house in Prague to attend school and then the technical college. But after a serious illness he followed the doctor's advice, interrupted his studies for a year, and returned home to recuperate. Soon, however, Heinrich was helping in Father's business, where he proved to be very useful. Then, when our dear mother died a few months later, he had to give up his studies completely in order to partially "replace" her.

I shall now skip over a few years that were spent in hard work and therefore went by quickly. In all that time, Heinrich was entrusted with responsibilities at home and ran the Teplitz business during my father's frequent absences. He also soon had a circle of friends of his age, and thanks to his tact and good manners he was accepted among the best families.

Heinrich had made good use of his student years in Prague, and despite his business activities, he continued to educate himself. He was very interested in all new literary works and was considered to be an educated young man - for good reason!

He was especially popular with the young ladies, whom he courted vigorously, and who liked him for his gentlemanly style!

Nevertheless, Heinrich did not remain in Teplitz long. My father had taken over the relatively important Moravian subsidiary of an affiliated Vienna wholesale company that sold Viennese and Austrian goods at the markets in Brünn and Olmütz. It was necessary to supply eight markets a year, and the time between the markets had to be spent in stocking the warehouses and purchasing new products. For that purpose, Heinrich then moved to Vienna, where he had a room for purchasing and storage next to his apartment at *Mariahilferstraße* 67.

I believe that the years of his brief stay in Vienna were the best and happiest of his life. He made many friends, associated with good families, was introduced into artistic circles, and became acquainted with all aspects of bachelor life in the big city. Without being reckless, my brother liked to present the image of a gentleman. He loved a comfortable life and good company.

Nevertheless, two years later he decided to move to Brünn. From a business perspective, he could no longer justify remaining in Vienna. Although our storage facilities in Brünn were rented year round, until that time they had been used only during the markets. Now he was able to turn the market there into a permanent business enterprise.

In Brünn, Heinrich was introduced to Miss Minna Gompertz, the daughter of I. M. Gompertz, a well known industrialist. The young people fell in love, and their happiness was sealed by the announcement of their engagement. Unfortunately, it did not last very long. Some weeks later, my brother became seriously ill, and some members of Minna's family, who were not well disposed toward him, insisted that the engagement be dissolved. A year later Minna was forced to marry a wealthy wine merchant in Eisenstadt.

I do not wish to dwell more than necessary on this incident, which was painful for everyone involved, but I do want to mention that Minna's brother Heinrich Gompertz and I were good friends even before their engagement, and that in spite of this sad situation our friendly relationship remained unchanged.

Heinrich Gompertz was a very well-known personality in Brünn. He left his substantial collection of paintings and books to a museum there.

Then my brother also made plans to establish his own home. In his cousin Pauline, the daughter of our Uncle Wiener and Aunt

Marie (my mother's sister), he found a dear, kind, and devoted wife. Pauline was a likeable, well-mannered, and pretty girl, but one who was not spoiled by her parents. Her father was a rather prosperous man who had to provide for a large family of twelve children, of whom Pauline was the oldest. The youngest, Rudolf, was only three months old.

Heinrich's home was furnished solidly and comfortably, if not luxuriously. After more than fifty years, many of his furnishings and paintings still adorn the apartment of his son, my nephew (and son-in-law), Dr. Robert Heller.

But even in Brünn Heinrich's business success was rather disappointing. He therefore moved back to Teplitz with his family in 1868, in order to assist our father. Then, by coincidence, upon the death of the owner, my father was offered the old, well-established knitwear factory that had belonged to Carl Asconas. He purchased it in order to give Heinrich an independent life again. At the same time, Uncle Josef Heller joined the new company as a partner.

This factory produced cheap, common consumer goods, such as men's and ladies' jackets and blouses, as well as fine woolen luxury items. Above all, their production required good taste and appreciation for suitable new items. Aunt Regie, Uncle Josef's wife, and my sister-in-law Pauline were a great help in that regard. In the early years the business made a satisfactory profit.

It soon turned out, however, that home workers in the small Bohemian villages produced the goods so cheaply that it was not possible to compete with them. It was therefore necessary to focus primary attention on exclusive fashion articles, and that was possible only in Vienna, the center of fashion and good taste. Accordingly, Uncle Josef moved to Vienna with his family in 1876 and settled there. Heinrich followed one year later.

Unfortunately, in spite of all their efforts, and despite the eager and understanding assistance of their wives and children, the two men were not destined to achieve satisfactory success. It was only many years after their deaths, and after a hard struggle, that a brighter future opened for their children.

Uncle Josef Heller died in November of 1879 and left his wife and children penniless. But Aunt Regie was able to continue her business with the help of her experienced adult son Karl, although it required some small loans.

After a brief illness, my poor brother Heinrich died on December 29, 1882 at the age of forty-eight, and his poor widow and five destitute children looked anxiously toward the future. I shall write about my dear sister-in-law and her children in more detail later.

My Brother Julius

I have gotten ahead of myself in my story and now want to return again to the earlier years. I particularly want to describe my relationship with my brother Julius when he was a child. When our dear mother died, he was only four and a half years old. Father was often away on business, as was Heinrich, and although I was only eleven years old, I instinctively felt a responsibility to look after Julius. The little fellow also felt drawn to me because he knew that I liked him very much. I played and spent time with him whenever I could. We went for walks, and I was particularly happy about his intellectual development and his progress. I think that my feelings for him were even warmer and deeper than they usually are between close brothers. I never missed an opportunity to have fun with him, and during his later school years in Dresden his letters were usually addressed to me, because my questions always gave him a reason to answer.

He entered the public elementary school in Teplitz when he was six, also received very good private lessons, and soon turned out to be a talented and able child. He was especially good at drawing. As a six-year-old he drew pictures of horses, dogs, and birds in a manner that was rather outstanding for a child his age. While drawing, however, he often became lost in thought and daydreams. That is why our father often called him "Napoleon III," who was also said to have been a dreamer.

Even as a child, Julius often developed views that seemed too liberal to my father, who then hurled insults at him, such as: "You're a forty-eighter" (a revolutionary), or: "You're a democrat." When Father became quite irked at Julius's comments, he called him "*Schlomele Drehkopf*" or a "deranged lawyer."

Julius really was very different from all of his brothers, and in my opinion he was the most talented among us. At a very young age he already demonstrated a certain degree of independence. He insisted upon his own views and had a strong character and the ability to get his way.

When he was eleven or twelve, he was sent to Dresden to continue his schooling. For several years he remained at the *Jacobson Institute*, which was considered to be one of the best schools in Dresden, and he took full advantage of his stay there.

He returned home when he was fifteen and received employment in our metal wares and button factory. It soon became apparent that partly due to talent and partly thanks to diligence in his studies he had acquired skills and knowledge in mechanics. These, combined with his good drawing ability, paved the way for him to become a manufacturer.

At an early age I acquired the reputation of being the anxious one in our family. Thus, when Julius suffered from severe pneumonia, I was extremely concerned. Fortunately, he recovered completely, and afterward I was very happy to be able to make a rather long journey with him, primarily for recuperation and pleasure, but also for business purposes.

That was in 1867, a year after the Austro-Prussian war. First we traveled to Berlin and stayed there for several days. We took in many sights, including museums and the Babelsberg and Sanssouci castles in Potsdam, and noticed many flags and trophies that had been taken from us in the previous year's war. I remembered then, just as I do today, various details concerning them, and it pained me to see our defeat displayed on a Prussian parade ground.

I think that every Austrian who experienced the year 1866 as I did feels the inner conflict between heart and mind. For the defeat that we suffered was beneficial for Austria. The close relations that now connect us with Germany must completely satisfy every sensible Austrian, and I think that many people of my age would agree. I only wish that my clever mother-in-law's words may never come true: "An old enemy is not a new friend."

From Berlin we traveled to Elberfeld, Barmen, and Lüdenscheid, towns that have not only been centers of button manufacturing almost forever, but are also where the latest and best machines and tools for that purpose are produced. Our father and both of my brothers were convinced that because of the growing demands and the expansion of our business we could not continue with our current manufacturing method, and that changes had to be made by introducing more practical machines and facilities. By letter, we had made careful preparations for this trip, and we had connections and friends in all of those towns. They helped us with recommendations and addresses. At home we had been given "full authorization" to buy any machines that we found suitable, because father trusted Julius's technical understanding and my business skills. So we went to work.

My brother was in his element, and even though I did not agree to everything that he suggested, we still bought a number of very practical machines, the purchase of which absolutely guaranteed a favorable change of direction in the manufacturing of our products. The acquisitions represented a rather large sum of money, and the thing that worried me about them was the fact that several expensive, complicated machines that we saw in operation had to be packed in disassembled form. I feared that we would have to get specialized mechanics to come to Teplitz to assemble them again. Julius, however, allayed my fears about that, and later on at home, when they were all assembled perfectly under his supervision, our own factory mechanics started them up without the least trouble.

The business part of our trip was then over, and the remainder was devoted to pleasure. First we went to Cologne, explored the environs, and spent two pleasant days there. I had obtained my father's permission to take Julius to the 1867 Paris exhibition, but that was to be a surprise for him until the last moment. When he asked me in Cologne where we would be going next, I replied that we would be returning home after a trip along the Rhine, and he was quite happy with that.

On the morning of our departure from Cologne, I made sure that he was busy with our luggage, so that he could not follow me to the ticket office. I then bought two tickets to Paris, returned to him, and handed him one of them, saying, "Now have a look and see where we are going." Julius took the ticket from me and read slowly, "P a r i s, P a r i s. I've never heard of a place on the Rhine called Paris. Where is it?" He had not expected that we would go to PARIS, and when I told him, he was so happy that he could hardly contain himself. The surprise was a complete success, and we arrived in Paris in the happiest of moods. We stayed for about two weeks, visited the exhibition regularly, saw the sights of that unique city, and also spent many hours at the Bois de Boulogne, Versailles, and in the magnificent environs.

During the years 1868-1869, many improvements and expansions were made in our factory. A motor was also set up, and mechanical operations were introduced step by step under Julius's supervision. Business was going well, and the main problem was (and always remained) to produce sufficient goods.

I married in 1870 and became a partner in the company. Julius was only twenty-two then, but based on his diligence and his performance, I saw to it that my father also made him a partner, as well as my youngest brother Leopold, who also worked in the business. Both of them were enormously surprised and very happy when I told them the news.

I was away traveling for at least three or four months a year, and the rest of the time I enjoyed living with my family in my beloved Teplitz. My work was not as exhausting as it had previously been, and I was able to enjoy many free hours. That continued until the year 1873, when, as I said before, I was unable to continue with my business trips because of a severe illness.

The Jeiteles Family: Cousin George's Childhood

In order to be able to talk about my cousins and future brothers-in-law George and Max Jeiteles, I should first give some details about their parents, my dear Uncle Joseph Jeiteles (my mother's brother) and his wife Rosa, née Foges, who later became my revered parents-in-law. Later on I shall dedicate a more detailed chapter to them. Here, however, I simply want to tell about their eldest son George and his childhood.

I knew George from a very early age, when I stayed with his parents in Prague during my travels, and I was able to observe his very peculiar development. He was born on January 18, 1852, was a very talented and clever boy, but caused his parents and teachers a lot of trouble. Because of his stubborn and obstinate character and his overbearing and opinionated nature, kind words, urgent pleas, affectionate admonitions, and even punishment left him cold and unwavering. I shall present here an episode involving the ten or eleven-year-old George:

George could not stand his private tutor, Dr. Kahn, and played tricks on him whenever he could. One Sunday evening, when George's parents were at a party, Dr. Kahn did not return home until about ten o'clock. He found his room locked from the inside, because George, who lived in the adjoining room, had thought it a good idea to lock the door from the inside. Dr. Kahn knocked, and George, who lay awake in his bed, did not answer at first. After the man had knocked for a long time, however, he finally said in a sleepy voice, "Yes, just a minute." But then he did not move and kept the poor tutor waiting in the hallway for more than half an hour on a bitterly cold December night. When all admonishments and threats availed nothing, an extremely angry Dr. Kahn was about to call for a locksmith. So George finally opened the door, slipped outside, half naked, wearing only a nightshirt...and was gone! Then the tutor's anger turned to worry that George would become ill because of the cold weather. He shouted and searched everywhere, but could not find him. After an hour of anxious waiting, George's parents came home, and the whole house was searched with lanterns from attic to cellar. Finally the boy was found in a corner of the cellar almost frozen stiff. It then took a long time and many kind words and assurances that he would not be punished, before George decided to leave his hiding place.

Similar incidents happened quite frequently, but otherwise George was the most diligent and conscientious pupil in the school. He was often held up before his schoolmates as a model. My parents-in-law dealt with George's peculiar character with great patience and did their best to prevent any further excesses.

Meanwhile, George had turned sixteen and had completed his lower secondary education. His parents would have liked to let him continue his studies, but on second thought they decided to introduce him to their extensive business, where so many outsider assistants were employed. George was sent to Gablonz and put under the supervision of the manager there. He had to work his way up from the bottom. It was a difficult time for him. The manager there, a Mr. Teveles, whom I knew very well, was competent and efficient, but also a coarse, uneducated, and recklessly firm person who knew how to command George's respect and did not permit George's stubbornness to get the upper hand.

It thus became apparent - as it so often does - that people who do not belong to the family exert a more powerful influence than parents or relatives. The tough school at Gablonz was very beneficial for George. After two years of hard work, he had acquired sufficient skill regarding products and business that his father could send him on a provisional sales trip with samples. He did so well that he gradually became good enough to travel across most of Europe. Thanks to his diligence, in time he became a pillar of the business.

George never quit educating himself. He was particularly eager to learn languages, which aided him very much during his trips to Italy, France, England, Spain, Russia, and Scandinavia. Traveling also had a very positive influence on the young man, who was well liked for his good manners, his elegant and pleasant behavior, and - last but not least - his handsome appearance.

Purchased Release from Military Service

The business activities of George and his brother Max were not interrupted by military service, something that they owed to their mother's foresight. At the end of the 1850s and after the mid-1860s, laws were introduced that permitted young people to buy themselves free of military service. Until then every young man who was deemed suitable had to serve. Initially, the sum of 600 gilders of convention currency was required to purchase release, and anyone who could afford it took advantage of that fact, especially because military service lasted for seven years back then, and that fact often threatened the existence of young people in many respects. A family's "mourning" when a member was conscripted into military service was hardly less than when a death had occurred in the family.

The 600 gilders, however, did not have to be paid until the young man had reached the age at which he was liable for military service. Then suddenly a law was introduced stating that the amount of 600 gilders had been increased - I believe - to 1200 gilders, with the provision that not only men who were already of age, but boys of any age could be bought free, as long as application was made within an unusually short period of time. The regulation stated that general compulsory military service would be introduced shortly, but in reality the short period of time for the application was a result of the financial straits that were being experienced by the public treasury.

Then everyone who was financially able hurried to pay the exemption tax, which brought in a huge amount of revenue for the state, because even baby boys who were only a few months old had their release purchased by their parents. Aunt Rosa had spoken with her husband several times about buying the release of their sons, but he did not want to make the decision until they had reached the specified age. He also thought that after the introduction of general compulsory military service in Austria his sons should not be an exception and should serve their country.

The law and the regulation regarding the exemption tax happened to be introduced at a time when my father-in-law was at a spa on Helgoland. All things considered, Mama felt it wise not to contact him regarding the matter, first because she did not want to perturb him while he was taking the cure, then because that way he could not disagree with her. She therefore decided to act independently and buy the release of both her sons by all means. She did not take the money from the business account, but sold all her jewels to buy her sons' release from service.

My father-in-law happily accepted the *fait accompli*, and in this case as in many others, my dear Aunt Rosa demonstrated her kindness and generosity.

Uncle Joseph and Aunt Rosa Jeiteles

I was already related to my wife's parents before we got married. My father-in-law, Mr. Joseph Jeiteles, was my mother's brother and therefore my uncle. I was still very young when I first met him. He came to take the cure in Teplitz, and in my spare time he often took me along on his walks and coach drives, which certainly increased the conventional love of a nephew for his uncle!

My father-in-law had a very fine appearance and a calm and prudent nature. He was definitely the most likeable, straight-thinking, and capable of his father's sons. His open and upright character prevented him from pursuing ideas or actions that would be more damaging to others than advantageous to him. Not all of his brothers thought and acted that way.

Uncle Joseph Jeiteles and his brothers Michael and Hermann were employed for many years by their mother Rebekka. She ran a tight ship and did not pay them very much. Joseph was her favorite son, however, and she held him in very high regard. She also trusted him completely, and he was the only one of her sons who - although he worked in Vienna - was often asked to manage the primary business in Prague. When Rebekka Jeiteles retired from the business at a very old age and turned it over to her three sons, they still retained equal shares in the Prague and Vienna enterprises.

Hermann Jeiteles,* however, forced a complete separation, such that Joseph Jeiteles would become the sole owner of the parent business in Prague, while Michael and Hermann Jeiteles would share ownership of the Vienna subsidiary. Uncle Joseph and his wife Rosa often told us about the difficult situation that confronted them because of the demand that the business be divided, about their sleepless nights before they agreed to it. For the business in Prague, although well reputed, had been managed by the elderly owner in an excessively old-fashioned manner and showed only a moderate profit, while the Vienna subsidiary was much more profitable. The final determining factor was the recognition that harmonious and successful cooperation, especially with Hermann Jeiteles, could not be expected. It was therefore preferable to turn the Prague business in a new direction and remain independent.

Uncle Joseph Jeiteles then had a large task ahead of him. He mastered it completely thanks to his energy and diligence, but mostly because of his excellent business skills. He made a fortune, and the firms that he built up are still flourishing today (1913).*

He was fortunate to have a dear, outstandingly clever, and competent wife at his side, who enabled him to carry out his far-reaching plans, and who devoted herself to the business eagerly and efficiently. Aunt Rosa, together with her mother, had worked in the *Koppelmann Foges* manufacturing business until her marriage. She therefore had experience, but the *Jeiteles Company's* line of trade was completely unfamiliar to her.

From left to right: Auguste, Jakob Ludwig, Rosa, Joseph, Max, George, and Antonie

She now labored diligently and attentively to acquire specialized knowledge about the products and finally achieved a dominant position supervising the large group of employees. Nothing was made easy for her, however, and in her old age she often talked about how much it upset her, when good old Mrs. Zepora, who had been employed in the business for forty years and had gained and enjoyed complete trust, said to her yet again: "Young lady, they are all mocking you."

But that did not last long, because her diligence, cleverness, and eagerness helped her to overcome all of the difficulties. Uncle Joseph, who was often away from Prague, was able to leave knowing full well that the management of the Prague business was in good hands.

The first reforms that he made in the Prague business included enlarging the warehouse and adding more saleable products, where previously only expensive luxury items had been the primary stock. Then he stopped going to the markets in Königgrätz and elsewhere because it cost more time and effort than the benefits warranted. Instead, he hired several traveling salesmen, who visited all of Austria and acquired new sales territories and new customers. Uncle Joseph himself repeatedly traveled throughout Italy in order to become familiar with the country and its people, as well as to learn which products could be introduced successfully. During those trips he came to the conclusion that the specific articles that were manufactured in Gablonz would be of significance not only for Italy, but for the entire world market.

Gablonz

Today (1913), Gablonz is one of the most important cities in Bohemia. Next to Prague, it has the second busiest postal service. A large number of international companies are based there. It has large factories, elegant houses and villas, theaters, hotels, and all the amenities of a city. It boasts of colossal world-wide trade and is very wealthy. Back then, however, it was a small town of three or four thousand inhabitants and had the most primitive facilities imaginable.

Admittedly, a few small glass factories already existed near the town, but everything else was cottage industry, specifically not so much in Gablonz itself, but within a radius of several miles. The workers lived in remote huts on high mountains, where it was very difficult to get to them, especially in the winter. But in order to be successful, it was necessary to reach them and become acquainted with the people, their products, and their productive capacity.

In those days, the workers, who are now highly regarded, had to carry their products to Gablonz themselves, where some of the local business people bought and sold the items as a sideline. Uncle Joseph was already dealing with some of those Gablonz middlemen, but he decided to open his own purchasing business. He rented the necessary premises, took some able employees from the Prague business to Gablonz, and remained there until he could entrust the running of the business to the most capable of them. He returned there at frequent intervals to check on everything and make necessary arrangements.

Uncle Joseph was one of the first to recognize the value of Gablonz for world trade and set up a business there. He was soon followed by others. He then began to implement his far-reaching program by employing several very efficient traveling salesmen with language skills, whom he sent not only to Italy, but also to France, England, Spain, Scandinavia, Russia, and Switzerland. He also had them attend the Leipzig Fair. By these means he came into contact with a number of important North and South American companies, and his business expanded substantially in a relatively short period of time.

After a few years, Uncle Joseph was able to introduce his sons George and Max to the business. Both of them proved to be capable, were placed under the supervision of the Gablonz manager, and became useful employees. George was soon able to undertake extensive business trips. Max followed him and also achieved satisfactory results.

Among my uncle's employees was a young man named Adolph Schwenk, who had first worked in the Prague business and then in Gablonz. He turned out to be not only unusually efficient and useful, but also highly principled and loyal. He expressed to his employer a desire to settle permanently in Paris in the interests of business, citing as an argument his successes during his travels to

France and Paris in particular. He also pointed to the continuing active relations with the involved Paris companies.

Uncle Joseph agreed to the plan, and Mr. Schwenk went to Paris to represent the company there. From that moment on, the already successful business experienced an even greater boom because Mr. Schwenk knew not only how to make himself popular, but also how to command high prices. He was fully supported by the excellent management of the Gablonz business, which was then already in the hands of George Jeiteles.

Max, the younger son, felt that his role in the business was not challenging and independent enough, and that his current work could also be carried out by an employee. He therefore suggested to his father that he build a hollow-glass factory for him in Hayda and let him manage that factory by himself. My uncle agreed to it, and Max managed the business to his complete satisfaction. Moreover, he took upon himself the tiring task of traveling to England, Spain, etc. with twelve or fifteen large cases full of vases and similar products, and of taking a number of samples from Gablonz with him as well.

It finally turned out, however, that because of the steady growth of the Gablonz business, Max's help was needed there, and that there would be sufficient independent work for him. The house and business in Hayda were sold to Mr. Reich, the owner of the large glassworks, which resulted in a nice profit.

The Difficulties and Worries of a Successful Businessman, Uncle Joseph Jeiteles

In 1867, Uncle Joseph Jeiteles decided to buy a factory in Vienna, in order to provide a permanent and secure livelihood for his brother, my Uncle Michael. That business was quite successful, and the horn button factory that I mentioned earlier was sold many years later at a good profit.

From what I have said thus far, one might too easily get the impression that my uncle had good fortune in everything that he did. I must therefore also mention the numerous difficulties and worries that are inevitable when a person runs a major business.

First and foremost, the company's office staff and the traveling salesmen often caused sleepless nights. Despite the fact that their salaries were high and their conditions were good in every respect, they began to make excessive demands when they realized that the business was prospering. The traveling salesmen in particular often made demands that were almost impossible to meet. They justified their demands by mentioning that they had received much better offers from rival companies. But in order to emphasize their demands further, they also encouraged the good office staff to ask for a pay raise at the same time, or to give notice. Usually, those tactics were used by two traveling salesmen simultaneously, so that in one day the English and the Italian traveling salesmen and two or three of the senior staff gave notice. Such incidents occurred frequently, and even when they were resolved by making rather large sacrifices, the constant fear that they would be repeated still remained.

Another time, the traveling salesman in Spain became ill. His samples and traveling funds disappeared, and his illness, which lasted for several months, cost the company several thousands, not to mention the loss of business. After he was discharged from the Spanish hospital, he returned home to Bohemia to recuperate fully. During that time he continued to receive his full salary, and after he had recovered completely, he showed his "gratitude" by immediately going to work for a competitor and by trying to harm his former employer as much as possible.

Even my uncle's calmness and confidence suffered greatly from these and many similar incidents, but they had a much greater effect on my aunt, who had a pessimistic disposition. My uncle benefited from his optimism, but my aunt was consumed with grief and worry, especially when such unpleasant events took place during her husband's absence. It was in her nature to be forever scared and worried, and the state of her husband's health undoubtedly gave her reason for that.

Uncle Joseph was not a healthy man. He suffered from nervousness, which manifested itself in different ways. He was an insomniac, had various ailments, and largely owed the fact that he reached the age of seventy to his wife's careful, loving, and self-sacrificing care.

Gegründet 1810. Telegramm-Adresse: JEITELES GABLONZ.

Jacob H. Jeiteles Sohn

Gablonz a. N.
Paris, 57 & 59 Rue Réaumur

Export von Glas- und Bijouteriewaren
aller Art nach allen Ländern der Welt
**Perlen, Knöpfe, Hutschmuck, Kleider-
schmuck, unechte Bijouterien.**

Die Firma Jacob H. Jeiteles Sohn ist im Jahre 1810 gegründet worden. Der derzeitige Besitzer ist Herr Victor Schwenk, gleichzeitig Inhaber der bekannten Firma Ad. Schwenk Fils in Paris. Das Unternehmen befindet sich heute im Besitze der vierten Generation.

Die Firma Jacob H. Jeiteles Sohn hat sich im Laufe der Jahrzehnte zu einem der bedeutendsten Exportgeschäfte am Platze emporgearbeitet. Es ist nicht ohne Interesse, daß die Firma ihren Sitz Mozartgasse 19 seit dem Jahre 1882 inne hat und daß das imposante Gebäude mit dem anschließenden großen Hofgebäude eines der ersten Exporthäuser war, das in einem solchen Ausmaße gebaut wurde. Im Jahre 1892 wurde die Fabriksanlage in Wiesenthal errichtet.

Das Unternehmen gilt durch die stete Verbindung mit der ihm alliierten Firma Ad. Schwenk Fils, Paris, als eine der bestorientierten Firmen über alles, was die Pariser Mode jeweils bringt.

Facsimile from a Gablonz yearbook, 1932

Founded 1810   Telegraph Address:
JEITELES GABLONZ

Jacob H. Jeiteles, Son
Gablonz a. N.
Paris, 57 & 59 Rue Réaûmur

Export of glassware and costume jewelry
of all kinds to all countries of the world

Pearls, Buttons, Hat Ornaments, Dress
Accessories, Costume Jewelry

The firm of *Jacob H. Jeiteles, Son* was founded in 1810. The current owner is Mr. Victor Schwenk, who also owns the well-known company of *Ad. Schwenk Fils* in Paris. The business is now in the hands of the fourth generation.

Over the decades the firm of *Jacob H. Jeiteles, Son* has assumed the status of one of the most important export business in town. It is an interesting fact that the company's headquarters have been at *Mozartgasse* 19 since 1882, and that the impressive edifice with the large adjacent courtyard building was one of the first export houses to be built on such a scale. The factory in Wiesenthal was built in 1892.

The company is considered to be one of the most well oriented firms with respect to Parisian fashion trends, because of its constant cooperation with the company of *Ad. Schwenk Fils* in Paris.

During the time that my uncle was at home, my aunt treated him like a guest. The dishes for him were more carefully selected and prepared than were the ones for her children and herself, and she insisted that he get the necessary rest after meals.

In the summer, when the whole family stayed in Bubentsch,* my aunt had her lunch brought to work, while my uncle ate in peace and comfort at home and went for his walk afterward. It was evident that the "lord" of the house and the family provider always had to be held in the highest regard. The children noticed that as well, and although Aunt Rosa was an excellent mother who watched over her children devotedly and gave them a good education, they knew that their father enjoyed the greatest care. As a result, the children rightly learned to value not only their father, but both of their parents.

What a difference from the way things are today!*

It is no longer the father who rules the house, nor the mother. It is the children! And how could it be otherwise? These days the mothers no longer help earn a living and no longer assist their husbands in their work. In the best cases, they do not have to worry about the struggle for existence at all, for the husbands now cope with it on their own. In the worst case the women have to deal with it only when it is too late, i.e. when the ship has already sunk or when their husbands have physically or materially gone under during the struggle. Consequently, wives do not know the value of their husbands' individual responsibilities, nor do they properly appreciate their endless toil. Therefore they do not give them the care and attention that they deserve, which more considerate women formerly gave their husbands!

The children now realize that it is not the father but they themselves who are the important ones in the house, and that their parents, both father and mother, devote all of their care to them. They see that their parents do whatever they can to make everything as easy and pleasant as possible for them, both at home and in school, and that they remove any obstacles. When they are systematically brought up that way, it is no surprise that the children become arrogant and demanding. We only have to look at the young ladies and gentlemen between the ages of eight and fifteen. They are so carefully dressed. They know the difference between the latest and yesterday's fashion, and everything must be of high quality and extremely elegant, so that *their parents'* vanity is satisfied. Children should, of course, be dressed nicely, but in a plain, simple, and modest manner, and not in bright, striking colors. For the parents who introduce their children to expressions like "chic" and "latest style" at an early age will learn all too soon that they have turned them into vain dandies and demanding people. They will see that the pampered upbringing at home has decreased their children's robustness, and that the struggle for existence will be twice as hard for them because they have been spoiled from an early age.

Now I shall leave this troublesome issue and return to my story about Aunt Rosa.

Aunt Rosa hardly ever treated herself to a holiday at a health resort. She contented herself with her summer apartment in Bubentsch, although it brought her more trouble than pleasure. She had to leave the house early every morning and walk to Prague, because there was no cheap and convenient mode of transportation available then. She also had to walk home again at night, weary from the day's work. Her only opportunity to get some rest was on Saturdays, when the business remained closed, and on Sunday afternoons, for she had to work in Prague even on Sunday mornings. In December, however, Aunt Rosa was already considering which health resort would be beneficial for my uncle the following year, and she discussed it with her family doctor, the renowned Dr. Duzensy.

Various places, such as Teplitz, Johannesbad, Marienbad, and several other cold-water spas, had not achieved the desired results, and therefore the doctor found it difficult to recommend a specific resort, because my uncle was very nervous, but did not have a definite illness. Then one day my aunt asked for the doctor's opinion about a seaside resort and gave Helgoland as a suggestion. To that the doctor replied, "Well, if you want to spend that much money, very well. I did not dare suggest it to you because it would cost a lot of money. But it would definitely be the best option for your husband."

That was in the mid-1850s, when only aristocrats and very wealthy people enjoyed the luxury of a stay at such a health resort. Uncle Joseph did go to Helgoland, which was very beneficial for him, and he returned there in many subsequent years. Not only was the stay beneficial for his health, but the resort was also very entertaining and he found pleasant company there. Auguste, his eldest daughter and my future wife, accompanied him on those trips, saw Berlin and Hamburg for the first time, and became acquainted with the world in general. She had pleasant, unforgettable memories of her visits there, with the weekly dances, the casino, and all the new experiences.

It is difficult to describe the troubles that my dear aunt had to endure while my uncle took the cure in Helgoland or Ostend. She even worried when a letter from him was delayed, and it was only her strong constitution that enabled her to endure it relatively well.

Year after year went by. The Gablonz business grew steadily, and Uncle Joseph built the new business and residential building where the company is still headquartered today (1913).

The Prague business, on the other hand, did not remain as successful as it had been in the past. The manufacturers who had formerly supplied the Prague wholesalers now sent their traveling salesmen everywhere, which meant that the Prague wholesale trade almost ceased to exist. Moreover, life in Prague became very unpleasant because of nationalistic disputes, the provocative actions of Czech mobs, and the frequent and prolonged street riots. My uncle therefore decided to give up his business in Prague and move to Vienna, so that he and my aunt could rest and reap the benefits of their many years of hard work.

Uncle Joseph had always had a special predilection for Vienna, where he had spent many happy years. It had always been his wish to move to Vienna some day. Aunt Rosa was not as eager to leave Prague and abandon the work that she was accustomed to, but after a while she got used to the idea because several of her brothers and many of their friends had already moved to Vienna. In addition, her elderly father had recently died. Thus the move took place in 1871.

The home of my parents-in-law was very comfortable. They had a small but pleasant apartment in the first district of Vienna at *Elisabethstraße* 24, where my aunt and uncle, and especially my unmarried cousin Tony, soon felt at home. On Friday evenings, the close relatives who lived in Vienna regularly gathered there and spent many happy and memorable hours.

On December 31, 1874, we celebrated the silver wedding anniversary of my parents-in-law, and everyone met in Vienna. George and Max came from Gablonz, my wife and I came from Teplitz, and a great number of friends and relatives took part in the celebration as well.

My father-in-law suffered greatly during his final years. All of his organs were more or less affected by his weak nerves, and he had to undergo a serious eye operation. He died on June 30, 1889 in Bad Ischl, a few weeks after his 70th birthday. Aunt Rosa devoted all of her care and attention to him up to his last minutes, and she mourned him until her dying day.

Aunt Rosa Jeiteles

I am driven to write some more about my dear mother-in-law.

She had been given a religious upbringing in the ghetto of Prague. Thanks to excellent teachers, she also received what was for that time a very good education.

Earlier, when I wrote about her father, Mr. Koppelmann Foges, I mentioned that he had studied not only Jewish works but also modern classics and philosophers. For him it was therefore very important that his children grow up to become educated people.

My mother-in-law was intellectually very gifted, and later, when she was an efficient and earnest businesswoman, she spent her free time reading good books. She was very interested in history, French history in particular. There is a legend in the Foges family, who used to spell their name "Voges," that they originally came from the Vosges, a mountainous region in eastern France. The actual story is that the "Voges" were originally French Huguenots who had emigrated and converted to Judaism rather than to Catholicism! That fact may account for her fascination with France. She held Napoleon in particularly high esteem because he granted full and equal rights to the Jews.

Aunt Rosa remained deeply religious until the end of her days, but was not overly devout. In memory of her dead mother, she celebrated Friday evenings according to ritual and looked forward to Saturdays, when she could rest completely.

She was also a very charitable woman, especially when she could avoid manifestations of gratitude. She was thrifty with regard to herself, but unusually generous with others. When she managed to make someone happy, a warm, sweet smile crossed her face, revealing her heartfelt satisfaction. That kind of smile also appeared when she was given good news by others.

Her keen intellect and her quick and accurate judgment were impressive. She knew quite well that she tended toward pessimism and distrust, but took that into account when making decisions and therefore usually made the correct ones.

On the whole, Mama was very modest, reserved, and even shy, but when there was a need for it, she could be very firm and self-confident and knew how to voice her opinion. She was vivacious and hot-tempered by nature, but also exceptionally kind-hearted. Whenever she scolded someone or thought that she had wronged somebody, she tried to make amends as soon as possible.

Here are some of her favorite sayings:

"An old enemy (*Szoinje*) is not a new friend."
"Think of everybody as a *Maloch* (angel) and trust him like a *Galloch* (clergyman)."
"Love me less, but love me for a long time."
"If you don't do your own calculations, things will be calculated for you."

One saying that she often used was characteristic of this unusually capable woman's modesty: "A woman's efficiency is like a bench with three legs."

She died on July 11, 1904 in Baden and was buried two days later in Vienna, deeply and sincerely mourned by her children, grandchildren, relatives, and everyone who knew her.

Of the four children of Uncle Joseph and Aunt Rosa, I have already mentioned George. Later I will talk more about his subsequent fate and that of his brother Max, since they are both part of my immediate family. Regarding their sisters Auguste and Tony, the latter has been married to Adolph Schwenk since 1877 and has started a family with him in Paris.

Cousin Auguste Becomes My Wife

My cousin Auguste, who was born on January 6, 1851, experienced a careful upbringing, received a good education and excellent schooling, and developed mentally and physically in a most satisfactory manner. She was a very ambitious and assiduous pupil who developed a fine intellect and became what could rightfully be called an educated young lady. With her simple, modest character, her pretty face, and her graceful manner, she made very favorable impressions on everybody.

We became engaged on April 10, 1870 and were married on July 10, 1870. She was nineteen and I was twenty-eight years old. We entered into marriage in the happiest, most blissful spirit and began our honeymoon that same evening. We were supposed to go to Paris by way of Switzerland, but that plan could not be carried out. The Franco-Prussian War broke out a few days after our wedding, so we were able to travel only to Munich, and from there to Zurich and then to Ragatz.

Unfortunately, from there we had to return home. We had to overcome many obstacles and lost an enormous amount of time, because nearly all trains were used only for military purposes. If we had hesitated only one more day, our return journey would not have been possible for several weeks. Nevertheless, we spent some happy days in Munich, where we visited galleries and art collections, and we enjoyed the beauty of Zurich. That was followed by six or eight very happy days in Ragatz, until we were jolted out of our joyful mood by the dramatic rumors of war. We did not listen, however, to the advice of many German visitors to Ragatz, who had been ordered to return home because they were being called up for military service. We did not leave until the declaration of war became a reality.

After traveling in the same compartment without interruption for three days and nights, during which we often spent five or six hours in one spot, we finally arrived in Prague, much to the delight of my worried parents-in-law.

Two days later we returned to our new home in Teplitz, where my father, my brothers, and our relatives welcomed us warmly. All of our employees were standing in the courtyard waiting to greet us. The house, courtyard, and apartment were decorated festively with green boughs, flowers, and emblems; people cheered, gave speeches, and congratulated us when we entered.

We had a very beautiful and large apartment that I had equipped in the current fashion with elegant furniture that was made by good Prague cabinetmakers. Many of those pieces are now in my own apartment here in Vienna and are still in perfect condition after almost fifty years.

The apartment had been completely furnished before I left to get married, and my young wife was delighted with everything. At her parents' home everything was nice, but our furnishings were more modern and suited the tastes and wishes of my young wife. In her parents' home she had had only a very small room at her disposal, and her mother had been very strict with her. Now she owned a spacious, elegant apartment and had absolute freedom to do what she liked, and that made her happy and contented.

Auguste was accustomed to acting in strict accordance with her parents' wishes at home, and she was similarly submissive, I would almost say obedient, toward me. I did not want that, and I therefore asked her repeatedly to tell me frankly whenever she did not agree with my views and wishes. I would then be very willing to agree with her opinion, if I thought she was right, but I did not want her to be a submissive wife. After some time, I succeeded in those endeavors, and she gained independence and self-confidence!

I had relatives and many friends in Teplitz, with whom we were very close and to whom I introduced Auguste. There was also a performing arts circle in Teplitz, albeit a modest one, which often delighted the local inhabitants, especially in the winter. Very good concerts were held, featuring out-of-town artists from the capital city. We attended events and balls, and in the summer the health resort and its beautiful surroundings provided much entertainment. Our life was therefore pleasant and comfortable. Auguste looked after her home meticulously, and I had regular work at the factory, but I always found time, both summer and winter, to spend a few hours with my wife outdoors.

Thus the first year of our marriage passed, and on July 18, 1871 our daughter Alice was born. My mother-in-law had been our guest for several weeks. She and I breathed sighs of relief when the danger to Auguste from the Caesarean section was over, and we were delighted to hear the child's first sounds. Auguste found it difficult to recover following the birth. She had previously believed that nervousness in women was imaginary and had made fun of it, but now *she* was afflicted with the same thing. She suffered from moodiness and uneasiness, and after that had gone on for several months, we went to Berlin, because our doctor advised a change of air. We stayed there for two weeks, visited theaters and all the other sights, and thus fulfilled the trip's purpose. Auguste became cheerful again and finally also admitted to me that she found life in Teplitz slightly monotonous as compared with that of her home town of Prague. Back then, Teplitz was a rather small town, where people minded each other's business more than was necessary.

On September 9, 1872 my dear daughter Grete was born. We then had in our home two dear creatures who brought us much happiness. But that rather carefree mood was not to last for long.

My Severe Illness

On the sixth of January 1873, my wife's birthday, we had invited several friends to come for the evening. After dinner everyone was in high spirits. There was dancing, and our guests did not leave until the wee hours of the morning after assuring us that they had spent a pleasant time.

When I went to bed, I suddenly felt a pain in my right leg. I tried at first to ignore it, but then it became so intense that later on I had to ask my doctor for advice. But the agony only grew worse, and a second doctor had to be consulted. The pain and my general condition were becoming so bad that my doctors in Teplitz advised me to consult two professors from Prague.

I was suffering from severe inflammation of the hip joint, and there were some extremely unpleasant complications. My condition improved only very slowly. I was bedridden until the end of April, and I was not in condition to be sent to the Franzensbad health resort until the end of June. By then I was still unable to move, and it was only after consultations with doctors from Vienna and another long stay in Franzensbad that I could at last tell my wife that I felt a slight degree of mobility, which gave us both some hope! However, a whole year went by before I could even think of returning to work, and even then, at first I was unable to work full time.

While all of that was going on, I did not receive the kind of sympathy from my brother Julius that I would have expected. I tried to excuse that by arguing to myself that he possibly felt more deeply than he wanted to show, and by remembering that because of my illness he had to work harder in the business than before. But I was very surprised and upset about the extensive and expensive purchases and changes that he had made and the equipment that he had bought while I was away from the business due to my illness.

During my absence Julius had gone ahead with almost all of the plans that he had developed earlier, but which I thought should only be carried out gradually. He had done that despite the costs and without informing me. In part, Julius ignored the serious objections of our father, who still owned a large share in the business, and in part he knew how to make him give in by constantly pressing him. As a result, my father was as unhappy about it as I was. Julius had been aware of the fact that I would disagree with such rash actions and had used my absence to carry out his plans quickly.

I frankly admit that my father and I were less upset about *what* he had done than about *how* he had done it, particularly at a time when I was gravely ill and my life was in danger. Such a time was not suitable for making such costly changes without my knowledge or consent, when many of them were at my expense. Julius, however, was very pleased with himself and thought that his actions had been appropriate. Moreover, because business was going well during that entire time, he exhibited a sense of superiority and self-confidence that had a very negative effect on our previously affectionate relationship.

We began to argue. His ambition and a desire to prevail played an important role for him, but my feelings were hurt, and my vanity was offended. I felt that successful cooperation could no longer be expected.

And what is more, my youngest brother Leopold, who had no outstanding abilities, permitted himself to be guided by Julius in all matters, including his attitude toward me. Therefore, at the end of June in 1875 I decided to leave the company, which seemed to coincide with the wishes of my brothers. At the same time, my father also decided to retire completely from business, and my brothers Julius and Leopold were now joint proprietors of the company.

In December of 1875, my wife, my two little daughters, my son Konrad,* who was born on July 10, 1875, and I moved to Vienna. At the beginning of 1876 I opened a costume jewelry factory there. I ran it with varying success until 1887 and eventually sold it to my brothers, who joined it to their Teplitz factory. For a year I then worked in the interests of the company, but then dissolved the partnership by mutual agreement.

Brother Julius: The Horse-Coach Accident

In September of 1881, the warm brotherly feeling that I had once had for Julius returned completely, when I learned that he had had a serious accident and was in critical condition. I felt very anxious about him.

On the morning of September 16, 1881 I received a telegram from my dear father with the words: "Julius had an accident with his horses yesterday. He was not hurt and is not in danger. Details to follow in a letter."

In the evening of the same day I received another telegram, from my brother Leopold, with the following content: "Julius suffered no injuries, but has pains in his stomach, possibly peritonitis. The horses bolted. Julius was hurled against a tree. Father is composed, calm, and healthy. No danger. No need to come home. I will write again tomorrow."

The letters that I received the following day stated that on the morning of September fifteenth Julius had gone for a drive with his two frisky young horses and had driven the coach himself. The singletree to which the off-side horse was harnessed broke. The broken parts of the singletree and the traces slammed backward between the legs of the off-side horse, frightening it. Both horses bolted and galloped away out of control. The coachman, who was sitting next to Julius, jumped off the coach and tried to grab the horses to stop them, but was unable to reach them. The whistle of an approaching train frightened the horses even more, and they fled in the direction of the railway embankment, giving rise to the fear that the coach, Julius, and the horses would be thrown onto the tracks. Julius, who still held the reins, mustered his remaining strength and purposely steered the horses and carriage into a ditch, causing them to fall over. But unfortunately, he was hurled against a tree in the process. The people who brought back the horses reported the accident to my father and my brother Leopold. Accompanied by several doctors, they immediately drove to Weisskirchlitz, which was near where the accident had occurred. They found Julius lying completely exhausted in the little cemetery building, which lay about three hundred paces from the scene of the accident. Julius had lost consciousness when he was thrown from the coach, but recovered shortly afterward and with the help of the coachman was able to reach the cemetery building.

During a superficial examination, the doctors could not find any external injuries, and Julius was taken home on a stretcher at about four o'clock in the afternoon. Later letters from my brother Leopold stated that Julius no longer felt the pressure in his chest from having been thrown against the tree. Although he had severe stomach pains, after receiving some injections he was able to sleep for several hours during the night. The doctors established that he had peritonitis, which could mean a mild and brief illness. But he also had a fever, a lack of appetite, and impairment of his abdominal functions, and for that reason the doctors were unable to make any reassuring statements and felt that they would have to await further developments in the illness.

My brother Leopold also wrote that our dear father had not been informed of the seriousness of the situation, and that he remained strangely calm but often wept in secret.

My poor father also wrote a long letter of his own, informing me about the incident. At the end of it he wrote: "You can imagine how much this incident has upset me, but my faith in God gives me the strength to cope with adversity, and thus I hope that He will keep me healthy and strong and permit me to enjoy happy times with my children and grandchildren in the future. Do not worry about me. The doctors have given me hope that my Julius will soon recover!"

Two weeks later I stopped in Teplitz on the way back from the Leipzig Fair. Julius was still bedridden and very weak, but well on the way to recovery. The danger was over and we all breathed sighs of relief.

December 8, 1881, Fire at the Ringtheater in Vienna

In 1881 Julius came to Vienna for a short time, where he had an experience that fortunately ended with his escape from great danger. He came to Vienna to meet a family that did not live there either, a family that wanted him to marry one of its members. I have forgotten the exact details and remember only that Julius visited us one afternoon, told us about the purpose of his trip, and mentioned that he would meet the family at the theater that night. We did not ask which theater he planned to attend, because it did not seem important to us.

That was on the fateful 8th of December 1881, the evening of the fire at the *Ringtheater*.*

My parents-in-law had invited me over for dinner that night, and I had left the house at just after seven o'clock. As soon as I stepped out into the street, I saw the sky lit up, as far as the eye could see, with an extremely bright fiery glow, and an excited crowd was rushing toward the city. People said that there was a fire in the Leopoldstadt district. I returned home, informed my wife, who was not able to go out, and later learned on the street that the *Ringtheater* was on fire!

People who have lived in small towns all their lives find structural fires far more frightening than do people in big cities. There one can rely on the fire brigade and the rescue service, and as a rule people are more curious than excited or scared. But a person who has repeatedly experienced the horror of a fire in a small town is unable to shake off the feelings of fear and terror in later years and in other circumstances. That was how it affected me. I reached the apartment of my parents-in-law pale with fright. They already knew about the fire. We watched the sky from the window. One column of fire after another rose into the air with ever-increasing force, and the news that the servants brought back from the street grew more dreadful and more dramatic. It sounded so horrible that we thought they were exaggerating.

In all the excitement, I had forgotten about my brother Julius, and that he might be at the *Ringtheater*. Otherwise I would have been even more terrified. At around half past nine a messenger* came from my wife and informed me that my brother Julius had arrived safely at our apartment, and that a remarkable coincidence had protected him from great danger.

I hurried home, and Julius told me what had happened. He had remained at his hotel too long, had not gotten dressed in time, and had thus been forced to take a horse-drawn cab to get to the theater on time. In spite of that, it was already after seven o'clock when he arrived in front of the theater.

Everything was still calm and quite in order there. Julius wanted to pay the cab driver, but dropped a silver coin that he had intended to give him as a tip. "Don't worry, Sir," said the cab driver. "I'll pick it up all right! Don't worry!" Julius, however, tried to find the coin, and when he handed it to him, the man exclaimed, "Don't go in there, Sir! The place is on fire!" At that moment, Julius saw the flames flickering from several places, and people rushing out of the theater. But then he immediately thought of the family that he was supposed to meet in a theater box and ordered the cab driver to remain at his disposal.

The family was able to get to safety, as Julius learned the next day, but Julius took other families home in his carriage, people who had been driven from the theater by indescribable fear and horror and were halfway unconscious. He put himself at their disposal for two hours, before he returned to my home exhausted from the excitement.

The catastrophe had made such a terrible impression on both Julius and the family that he was supposed to meet at the theater, that they saw it as a bad omen and avoided all future contact.

After Julius's engagement was prevented by that tragedy, he married Miss Helene Fischl from Prague on March 25, 1883. Their marriage has been a very happy one. Of their children, the older daughter Minni lives in Berlin and is married to a physician, Dr. Harry Markuse. Their younger daughter, Ilse, is still single. The older son, Hans, is a physician, and Paul is a qualified engineer and currently works in his father's factory.

My brother Julius owns a very large factory in Teplitz and has made a considerable fortune thanks to his efficiency, energy, and diligence. These days, in spite of his sixty-six years, he still works very hard. The one thing that can be held against him is that he is too egotistical, too self-satisfied, and has too low an opinion of everyone else's efficiency, a trait that is rather common among very successful people.

As he himself says, my brother Julius has been striving for almost ten years to become more dispensable and to simplify the running of his large factory, but so far without success. Nor does he want his son Paul to take over, because he thinks that managing the firm is far too difficult and that the business is much too complicated. He does not seem to know what should happen to the factory when he himself is no longer able to manage it!

My Brother Leopold

I now want to write about my poor brother Leopold, whom I have scarcely mentioned so far, and who did not have much happiness in his life. He was born in 1851 and was a weak and sickly child. Two years later our dear mother died, and Leopold was spoiled and pampered badly by Miss Minna. It may have been the result of his disposition or his upbringing, but Leopold was never really cheerful, never satisfied, neither as a child nor as a young man, and not even later with his wife and children around him. He did not lack intelligence, but he did not have the aptitude to use it effectively. He had no sense of humor at all and therefore obviously had no friends and few acquaintances.

In order to tear him away from his constant ill humor, Father sent him to Vienna for a year, where he was supposed to work for a few hours every day as a trainee in a major company that belonged to a friend of the family. In his spare time he was supposed to profit from living in the big city. At the time, Leopold was twenty years old. After two months, however, he returned home. He said that he could not stand it in Vienna any longer, argued about the way of life there, and bombarded us with reproaches for sending him there.

In Teplitz he kept a riding horse and took several major trips. As the "joint owner" of a thriving factory, he could afford a lot of things, but as a result he became all the more pretentious and dissatisfied. Then he wanted to get married, and because his financial status made him a "good match," he was soon able to fulfill that wish. In 1879 he married Miss Erna Frank from Prague, who was a sweet, pretty nineteen or twenty-year-old girl and the eldest daughter of a Bohemian parliament member, the tobacco merchant Heinrich Frank. But even after he got married, Leopold remained the same, and even the vivacious, lively, cheerful young woman could not change him. She, on the other hand, often had ample reason to become disgruntled!

In addition, Leopold and Julius began to have disagreements. That was not surprising, of course, given their personalities. Leopold, who was always dissatisfied with everything, resented the fact that Julius had the upper hand in running the factory. He felt confined to his area of activity and was discontented with his performance. Julius, on the other hand, often displayed his superiority more than Leopold would have liked. Thus Leopold became irritable and irrational in business and at home.

Eventually, my brothers dissolved their partnership, and Leopold retired to private life with a sizable fortune. At that point he was his own master. He did not have to get annoyed or grieved, but he did not like idleness and retirement either. He had grown used to working early on, and he therefore looked for a new field of activity. After not having found anything suitable for a long time, he bought a large brickyard. It turned out to be unprofitable, however, and he soon sold it at a considerable loss.

After that, in order to be doing something, Leopold was led to try his luck in the stock market, where he lost the largest part of his fortune after only a few years. He then grew immensely weary of life. He recognized the emptiness and the unsuccessfulness of his existence and therefore decided to commit suicide. We carried him to his grave on July 20, 1903. He left his wife and children a modest fortune that was large enough to ensure a simple livelihood for them.

In the casual letter that he wrote shortly before his death, which was found on his person, he said: "In order not to lose the rest of my fortune speculating on the stock market and thereby leave you with nothing, I choose to leave this life voluntarily."

In the autumn of 1913, I traveled to my home town of Teplitz and had the opportunity to visit my sister-in-law Erna during my twelve-day stay. She is very well respected in Teplitz as the president of the German School Association. As a leading member of several charities she regularly associates with the town's upper class and its dignitaries. Thanks to her tact and her organizational abilities - in particular with respect to planning parties - she is of great value to the institutions that she manages. By virtue of her distinguished, yet modest manner, she is well liked by everybody, as I have repeatedly observed.

Her financial situation is also favorable. All of the securities and shares of stock that her husband left her have increased significantly in value, yielding her a good profit. Moreover, her sons no longer depend on her funds as much as they once did.

Max, the oldest son, is an agent for several companies in Berlin. Franz, the second son, has a doctorate in law, is a smart, attractive, and kind person, has been married to his childhood sweetheart Lilli Porges for several years, lives in Innsbruck, and is a partner in a successful legal practice. The third son, Walter, has a position here in Vienna, but is not very popular within the family. The fourth son, Ossi, is studying in Charlottenburg, and it appears that he will turn out to be a capable person.

My Sister-in-law Pauline

With great respect and deep emotion, I now write about Pauline, the wife of my brother Heinrich, who died in 1882 at the age of forty-eight.

After Heinrich's death she was obliged to give up the business because she did not have a trustworthy man at her side. Her only son, Robert, who was sixteen years old at the time, attended secondary school, achieved the best grades, and intended to become an attorney, and there was no reason to change that plan.

A son and four daughters, of whom some were of marriageable age, had to be supported. The available means were the least imaginable, but nevertheless Pauline knew how to keep up an appearance of prosperity and coziness in the apartment that was her home. I never heard her complain or feel sorry for herself. Instead, she and her daughters constantly worked until late at night to earn money with their needlework. Robert also helped his mother to manage by giving private tutoring.

Pauline was very fortunate to have good, well-behaved, and serious-minded children, and foremost among them was Robert. At a very young age he already exhibited a clear mind, firm and purposeful aspirations, and a strong character. He was always an unusually devoted son to his mother and brother to his sisters. It pained his sensitive nature to see his loved ones in financial difficulty, and he always remembered the various distressing circumstances of his youth. As a result, he still has a warm heart and always lends a helping hand to the poor and distressed.

I was appointed guardian to my brother's children, managed their small fortune, and was therefore in constant contact with my sister-in-law Pauline.

A few years before Heinrich and his family moved from Teplitz to Vienna, my dear father wanted to give him a sizeable present for New Year. He asked me for my opinion on whether to give him money in cash or in some other way. I recommended that my father buy several one-fifth lottery tickets for 1860, which Heinrich deposited with my father. When I was appointed guardian, I had those tickets sent to me in Vienna so that I could deposit them at the *Giro- und Kassenverein* bank with the rest of the securities that belonged to the inheritance.

My sister-in-law Pauline endured her unfortunate situation in a way that was admired by everyone, and people liked her even more than they had before. The whole family now endeavored to find a suitable husband for the eldest daughter Sophie, and they were successful in doing so. The choice that was made was a good one in every respect. Sophie married Arnold Weishut, an earnest, industrious, and kind-hearted man from a good family. His sole purposes in life are his family and his business, and he is now very well-to-do. These days he is the owner of a large house and a large, splendidly equipped printing business that his eldest son Heinrich already helps to manage.

Thanks to that happy marriage, my sister-in-law Pauline had one less worry, but she and her other children had to continue struggling in order to afford the bare essentials. Unfortunately, Pauline's strength was waning. She was often bedridden because of ill health and weakness, and her children had twice as much to worry about.

The First Prize

At lunchtime on the second of May 1887, a messenger from the *Giro- und Kassenverein* in Vienna delivered a letter to me. It was from the director, Mr. Kanitz, and contained the following statement: "This time Dame Fortune was not blind. The one-fifth ticket for 1860, with the number..., from the deposit of your sister-in-law Pauline Heller, has been drawn as the first prize, and I congratulate you and your sister-in-law most heartily."

I cannot describe the joyful excitement that I felt upon receiving the news, and I could hardly wait to visit Pauline and tell her about the lucky and unexpected windfall. Pauline was not feeling well and was in bed. I was shown into the room, however, and inquired first about her health, but did not receive a comforting answer. After a while I said to her, "Pauline, I have some good news for you today. You are aware that some lottery tickets are deposited for you at the *Giro- und Kassenverein*. Well, one of them won you a small amount of money."

Pauline was indifferent to the news and said, "Really?" as though it had nothing to do with her. Nor did she ask how much money she had won.

I then wanted to arouse her interest and said, "Pauline, you have won 10,000 crowns." I thought that by mentioning that sum, which was then considered a large amount of money, I would get her attention and excite her curiosity, but Pauline remained completely indifferent. She seemed to me as if she had finished her dealings with the world and no longer expected anything from it.

After a while I said, "Pauline, you have not won 10,000 but 20,000 crowns," but the effect was the same, and even when I gradually increased the sum to the actual amount of the win, not a muscle in her face twitched. Her face took on no happy expression. After a few seconds, however, she said, "Now I will have an iron fence erected around Heinrich's grave, which I would have liked to have done earlier, if I had had the money."

I left, and thus ended one of the most interesting episodes of my life, one that I will always remember. It became obvious to me that a desperate human heart that has been tortured for a long time and has given up all hope of finding joy cannot suddenly be healed, not even by a powerful stroke of good fortune. It requires time and patience to become accustomed to good luck and happiness again.

That time also returned for Pauline. The great worries had left her, and she could rest and take care of herself. She had the pleasure of seeing her second daughter, Helene, happily married to an honest and kind-hearted man, Bernhard Schlesinger, and her third daughter, Olga, also married, although without her full consent. She married a Mr. Adolf Schmeichler, whom she probably loved more than he deserved. Then several precious grandchildren were born, who brought a great deal of joy to their grandmother.

But Pauline had special reason to be particularly proud of her son Robert. Under truly difficult conditions that required many sacrifices, with resolute diligence and tough perseverance, he completed his studies in excellent fashion and obtained his doctorate. Yet he never ceased to be a good son, a loyal brother, and an understanding advisor to his family.

Through a presiding court councilor, under whom he received his court practicum, and whose esteem and affection he gained, he was recommended to Dr. Lichtenstein in one of the top legal practices in Vienna, where he became highly respected in every regard. My sister-in-law Pauline had every right to be extremely proud of her son.

But all those years of worry and privation had left their mark on her. She was ill for years, and all of the medical help and care proved to be in vain. She died on November 11, 1895, at the age of fifty-five. After that, Robert needed only to provide for his unmarried sister Else.

For years a certain secret understanding had seemed to exist between Robert and my daughter Grete. We were thus overjoyed to celebrate their engagement on November 18, 1897, and their wedding on April 3, 1898.

At almost the same time, my niece Else entered into a happy marriage with Mr. Viktor Langstein.

Uncle Josef Heller and Aunt Regie

I must now come back to the story of Uncle Josef and Aunt Regie.

In 1854, at the age of forty-two years, Uncle Josef became engaged to a charming, delightful, and intelligent seventeen-year-old girl named Regine Ehrlich. She was a poor orphan, and in all honesty she was forced into the marriage by her wealthy relatives. I know for a fact that during the weeks before the wedding Uncle Josef told both his brother (my father) and his old mother (Rachel) that his fiancée had no affection for him. He said that Regie left him in no doubt with regard to her feelings and openly admitted that she was marrying him only because she was forced to do so.

As a result, Uncle Josef informed Regie's relatives that he wished to cancel the wedding. That obviously had serious repercussions for Regie. Nevertheless, the outcome of all of those difficult deliberations was their eventual wedding on March 25, 1855.

In spite of everything that has been mentioned here, and despite the great differences in age and character, the marriage was a happy one. Uncle Josef dearly loved his wife and did everything to please her. Aunt Regie recognized that, and she was very happy to have her own comfortable home. She was also relieved not to have to live in surroundings any longer that had made her earlier life so bitter. As time went on they became the parents of lovely, sweet children. Today, at the age of seventy-five, as a grandmother and great-grandmother many times over, Aunt Regie would be thoroughly content if she were not in ill health.

I visit Aunt Regie often and enjoy those occasions. It always gives me pleasure to be able to talk with her for an hour or so. She has been through a lot. Her parents had once been wealthy, but, as she herself told me, her father had been reckless. This had had a bad effect on her mother, their fortune was soon lost, and her parents died shortly afterward. She had to go to live with her grandparents. Her grandfather was the wealthy Teplitz leather merchant David Kohn. Those people treated her like Cinderella and were only too pleased that somebody turned up who would marry the poor, penniless girl. At a time when their parents were still well off, Regie's older sister had married a physician, a certain Dr. Stein of Kühlen, but she died shortly after Regie's wedding.

Her other siblings were scattered all over the world. One brother was living in America. She had not heard from him for a long time. Another brother served for years in the military as a non-commissioned officer. A third brother was a "musical genius" who gave music lessons, but *only when it suited him*. All three brothers were thoughtless, and even those who lived in Austria did not keep in touch. Thus Regie was happy to have found a "safe haven."

Up until now, Grandfather has told the story of close family members from the point of view of a child or a young man. However, he wrote much more about his numerous relatives. After all, he did have a total of twenty-one uncles and aunts on both sides, and there were sixty-eight cousins in his own generation alone.

He is a goldmine of information about all of them, or at least mentions them by name, beginning with the generation of his grandparents and ending with that of his own grandchildren. Five generations are covered in all.

We have learned about "adventurers," lazy people, and even dishonest ones. Some are well educated and some are conceited, but all in all they are decent, diligent, and competent people. By their intelligence and their untiring efforts they rose from relatively poor backgrounds to respected positions and true prosperity.

The family members were always willing to help each other.

On the intellectual side of things, many made their marks in liberal professions. Doctors, lawyers, authors, scientists, and artists can all be found in the family.

The following chapter will bring to life some of the characters who deserve special mention.

CHARACTER STUDIES

The Heller Family

Uncle Joachim Heller

My father's eldest brother, Uncle Joachim, was a little odd. He was carefree, light-hearted, not too fond of work, and did not have too much faith in order. He was, however, good company and rather gifted. He was a little hard of hearing, which in later years intensified toward deafness. His right hand was slightly withered, but he was nevertheless known as one of the best billiard players in all of Bohemia. He was often in Prague for business purposes, and much of his time there was "well spent" on the game. With the help of his wife, who was the backbone of his business, he earned a name as a respected businessman and industrialist and managed to amass quite a fortune.

His marriage to Betti (née Freudenberg) was very strange. The couple lived harmoniously beside one another, but not with one another. For example, Betti loved her elderly parents dearly and visited them every evening. She did not return home until late at night. For his part, Joachim spent his evenings just as regularly in the taverns. He never stayed long in one place and left each tavern after a single glass of beer. After he had finished the rounds at about 11:00 p.m. he went home. His day's work was done!

Uncle Schmule Heller

Now I want to tell you the story of my father's youngest brother, Uncle Schmule (Samuel) Heller.

I never knew him, but I know from stories that he was a tailor. He was also a windbag who never wanted to work and relied completely on his siblings to support him. My father told me that he once received a letter from Schmule asking him for ten gilders. Schmule threatened to throw himself into the castle gardens pond. My father responded as follows: "Dear Brother, I would impart to you the following advice. If you really want to throw yourself into the castle gardens pond, you should tie a heavy stone around your neck before doing so. Without that, you are so flighty that you surely would not sink. I am not sending you ten gilders."

Uncle Schmule's family sent him to America in 1840. He apparently learned the meaning of work while he was there. After a couple of years he reported that he had married a girl from Bavaria. In 1850 he sent his mother a picture of his wife and himself. It was a Daguerreotype, the first of its kind to be seen in Teplitz. Everyone was amazed.

During the war between the North and the South, Schmule developed a type of "stocking underpants"* that were apparently incredibly practical for soldiers. That made him quite prosperous, but his affluence did not last for long.

In 1871 or 1872, my father received a letter from Schmule's wife. She wrote that my uncle had died and that he had left no fortune behind. She asked only that the relatives bear the cost of making a gravestone for him, which we did. Uncle Schmule and his wife had no children, and we heard nothing more from his widow.

Cousin Heinrich Heller

Heinrich is my youngest cousin and the son of Uncle Josef and Aunt Regie. His thirst for knowledge and his desire to learn are illustrated in the following true episode from his school years:

When he was ten or eleven, his father asked him, "How many children are there in your class?"

Heinrich promptly responded, "Fifty-nine."

"And where do you stand?"

"Dad, I'm the fifty-ninth."

"Aren't you ashamed, you rascal?"

"Yes, Dad," Heinrich answered without embarrassment, "but someone has to be last."

Heinrich never turned out to be a genius. Instead he became a bon vivant and was quite extravagant. He lived in Bucharest for a while and successfully represented the business of his brother-in-law, Isidor Hirschl. But the latter found Heinrich's lifestyle a little bit too expensive and he was recalled.

Back in Vienna he worked successfully as an agent for a large Bohemian spinning mill. He lived well, kept a horse and carriage, but became a much more serious person. Some years ago he married a poor Christian girl to whom he had been attached for many years. They did away with all superfluous luxury and now live in a childless but happy marriage. His wife's relatives fervently wish that her younger sisters would also marry Jews, because "they don't have as good a life with us Christians as they would with the Jews."

Cousin Karl Heller and His Family

My cousin Karl Heller, a son of Uncle Josef and Aunt Regie, was a handsome, but very wild boy who did not especially enjoy studying. For that reason, at the age of ten or eleven he was sent to the *Freemason Institute* in Dresden, a school where the boys were reared in a very strict and military manner. The years that he spent there certainly did him a lot of good. After that, he attended a knitting and weaving school in Chemnitz, Saxony. There he obtained theoretical knowledge that was very beneficial to him in his later work.

As I previously indicated, his parents and my late brother Heinrich had owned a wool and knitwear factory in Teplitz for many years. In 1877 they moved to Vienna, and there they established the same type of factory. After Uncle Josef's death in 1879, Aunt Regie and Karl continued to run the business, but it was not overly successful.

In the meantime, Karl had grown into a good-looking, well-mannered young man. One day, while in Venice on a business trip, he was introduced to Mrs. S. Heit and her daughter, who were also from Vienna. He already knew Mr. Heit, having done business with him for a number of years.

Now he had to devote all his leisure time in Venice to the Heit family. He apparently made quite an impression on young Miss Charlotte. Mr. Heit was a very wealthy man, and he knew that the Heller family's material situation was only modest. Nevertheless, Karl was often invited to their home, and the parents let him know that they would like to have him as a son-in-law. Miss Charlotte also gave signs of her favor.

Miss Charlotte was a very pretty and pleasant girl and made a very favorable impression on everyone. She won everybody's favor by the kind-heartedness and charm that were written all over her face. Karl was no exception, yet he thought that it would be best to withdraw because he learned from a reliable source that Charlotte's nerves often gave her parents cause for serious concern. That was a painful thing for him for two reasons. First, he had really grown fond of her and found it difficult to refrain from seeing her. Second, such a union would also have put an end to any material worries.

For a couple of months no approaches were attempted from either side. Then one day Karl was invited to an exclusive ball at the Heits' home. He could not decline, but went to the ball quite determined to remain very reserved. It became obvious, however, that Charlotte was intentionally ignoring him, and he became both jealous and annoyed. But by acting in that manner she achieved her goal, and before the dance had come to an end Charlotte and Karl were engaged!

They married, but as was to be expected, the happy atmosphere was seriously marred by Charlotte's health. The young woman went through the most diverse phases. For example, for months she remained in bed all day, but then her spirits would revive and she would be more cheerful than ever in the evenings. Karl had to take her to the theater, to concerts, and to parties, but on the following day Charlotte would lie in bed, ill in both body and soul. She was critical of her own behavior, asked Karl to forgive her, and pitied him for having such a wife. There was really no reason to be envious of Karl. But he had a happy temperament, a phlegmatic character, and did not take life too seriously. That helped him to survive some of the more trying hours, and he was able to maintain his joyful approach to life.

Shortly after his marriage, Karl opened a knitwear factory in Wöllersdorf, near Vienna. Several years later, however, he was obliged to shut it down, and he entered his father-in-law's well-known business. He was then financially secure, and as time progressed he became a well-to-do and well-known man. Moreover, as time passed, his wife's condition became somewhat more normal.

Karl's oldest daughter was a beautiful girl and many men vied for her attention. But she rejected the best and the nicest of them.

As it turned out, the recipient of her affection was a young man by the name of Schütz, and like her mother, she knew how to get her way, even in the face of serious difficulties.

The chosen man was from Russia. From what I have heard about him, he has no special qualities whatsoever. Before their wedding could take place, Schütz had to bring himself to change his faith for the second time. He had been a Jew, was then baptized, and now returned to his original faith. The bride was worth it, and old Grandfather Heit, who was a religious Jew, got the satisfaction of having "saved a soul"!

Although the two "got each other," the joy did not last long. Mr. Schütz found that the Sundays before his marriage, which he had spent on the Rax and the Schneeberg, were much too much fun to be given up. As his wife did not want to go climbing with him, he went alone. He was, however, a caring husband and asked a good friend to keep his wife company while he was away.

One Sunday it was the good friend who climbed the Rax, and Schütz stayed home. The friend had an accident and was found dead. Since they had often been seen together, Schütz was informed of the occurrence by telegram. Extremely saddened, he rushed to the scene, took care of the burial arrangements, and also took his friend's rucksack with him. To his astonishment, while looking through the rucksack, Schütz found a bundle of letters that had been written by his wife. They clearly indicated that his friend and his wife had gotten along a little *too* well. Touché!

Divorce quickly followed. During the process Schütz apparently behaved most decently. He immediately deposited his proceeds from the marriage into an account for their child. The young woman and her child returned to her parents' home.

That is the end of that part of the "novel," but the second part of it is just about to begin!

Many years ago, a young man by the name of Epstein married a Miss Kohn in Vienna. She was a niece of the wealthy Salomon Kohn. It was common knowledge that it was a marriage of love. Mr. Epstein and his young wife left Europe and went, if I am right, to Brazil, where he had a very good job with tenure for life. They lived there happily for many years, but the climate did not suit his wife, and she had to endure great suffering. For that reason, Epstein gave up his position and decided to return to Europe with his wife and settle in Brussels. But the decision was carried out too late. The poor woman died during the crossing and was buried in a watery grave.

Epstein was inconsolable. He was a broken man and tired of life. A few months after the sad event, the deeply grieving young widower went to Vienna to visit his relatives. As fate would have it, he met the divorced Mrs. Schütz at a social gathering. They both had pleasant memories of earlier encounters...and they have now been married for a long time and live in Brussels.

I hope that the young woman's "novel" has come to an end. She cannot be more than thirty, but her story would be weighty enough for a woman of fifty.

The Jeiteles Family

Uncle Israel (Ignaz) Jeiteles, 1811-1886

I now want to write about the relatives of my Jeiteles grandparents, and I shall begin with their oldest son, my Uncle Israel Jeiteles, who is commonly called Ignaz.

He was a very intelligent man who had received a solid education and good training because great importance was attached to them in his parents' home. As a young man he moved to Vienna, where he joined his father in business. After a few years he married a Miss Mayer, whose parents owned the large Kettenhof calico printing factory. Her family not only possessed a large fortune, but they also had good connections and were extremely influential in Viennese society.

This union did open brilliant material opportunities for Uncle Ignaz, but it was regrettable that they satisfied more ambition and vanity than heart and reason. Aunt Zilli was by no means a good match for my uncle. She was neither pretty nor intelligent. She had no charm and could not have pleased any man, let alone Uncle Ignaz. I must admit, however, that she was kind-hearted and patient. However, the decision to marry Aunt Zilli was, I believe, the initial great mistake that caused all of the subsequent misfortune that befell the family.

Through the connections of his parents-in-law and his wealthy and influential brother-in-law Boschau, Uncle Ignaz succeeded in obtaining permission to open his own firm under his own name in Vienna. At the time, that privilege was only rarely granted to Jews.

I must mention here a few characteristic circumstances of the time.

Before 1848, only a very small number of Jews were permitted to run businesses in Vienna, just as only very few Jews were given leave to reside in Vienna permanently. Jews from outside the city who wanted to remain in Vienna for a prolonged period of time had to apply for extensions of their residency permits when the initial time limit expired.

The following example may serve to illustrate the prevalent selfishness of the Viennese Jews back then:

Permanent residency had been granted to forty or fifty Jewish families that had given proof of sufficiently large fortunes. Those families knew very well how to capitalize on the privilege. Because of their small number they were able to go into many different types of business and did not have to compete with each other. They were able to expand their wealth freely, and their relationships with each other were very amiable.

They formed a small community and chose a leader to represent them in dealing with the authorities. Then, whenever the authorities received an application for residence from a Jew who lived outside the city, not only provided evidence of sufficient wealth, but also had very good references in every respect, the representative of the Jewish community in Vienna was asked to provide his own comments. The recommendation would usually be something like this: "Dear Sir, we could not possibly have any objections to the man, but there are already fifty of us here, and we think that there are enough of us in Vienna!"

That said, I shall now describe how the rules and regulations were bent and circumvented with the full knowledge of the authorities:

Jews from outside the city sought for and found respected Christians who, for a quite significant yearly sum, permitted the Jews to run businesses using the Christian firms' names. After her husband's death, my grandmother, Mrs. Rebekka Jeiteles, obtained such an authorization from a Mr. Johann B. Zorn. Three of her sons, Michael, Josef, and Hermann, ran the business in Vienna. The firm's name was *J. B. Zorn*. All business dealings were conducted under that name, and the true owners were registered with the authorities as employees of Mr. J. B. Zorn.

Private agreements were signed in which Zorn identified the Jeiteles family as the real owners of the business, but he made good use of his sovereign rights, and his yearly monetary demands increased exorbitantly! But the existence of the business depended on the borrowed name, and it was necessary to comply.

Now back to Uncle Ignaz. He started a business in Vienna dealing in wholesale haberdashery and fashion items. It went reasonably well and had a large turnover, but by expanding it too much he exhausted himself. He was a vain man and wished to be viewed as a first-class businessman. He thought that a careful and considered approach was "small-minded." That attitude repeatedly resulted in financial problems. Relatives helped him out of his troubles on several occasions, but even that did not make him any more prudent.

His family also lived in high style. They kept a summer residence in the Hinterbrühl* area, a luxury that only very wealthy people would have had the means to afford. But Uncle Ignaz wanted to keep up with his rich in-laws, who had properties of their own in that area. He only went out there on Saturday evenings. No railway line existed yet, and the journey was fairly lengthy and costly. On Monday morning he had to be back at the business in Vienna.

My uncle placed too much confidence in the family's willingness to help him out and in the weight of the reputation that he believed he had. Striking proof of his carefree nature and his nonchalant manner lies in the fact that he spent one Sunday in the countryside without being perturbed in the slightest at the prospect that on Monday morning he would have to pay an account of 10,000 gilders, although he did not have a single gilder at his disposal.

What I write here is not an assumption by any means, but a simple fact. On that day my uncle had said to a friend: "My friends are willing to lend me any amount, and tomorrow morning I will have the money to the last penny."

That approach worked for a while, until it did not work anymore. People's confidence in him faded. Being of a quarrelsome and opinionated nature, he finally broke off his relationship with his in-laws and had to get along without help from that side of his family.

One day, Uncle Ignaz disappeared completely. Nobody knew what had happened to him, and his wife and children were worried to death. Accounts that were due and payable were presented at the business, and the employees could not pay them and did not know what to do. After five or six days, Uncle Ignaz reappeared healthy and fine. He had spent the time in various small towns along the Danube, and now he set about making arrangements with his creditors. That process repeated itself several times, until at last the final collapse occurred.

It was no wonder then that his wife did not take her duties very seriously either, given the example provided by her husband.

When she saw that the whole enterprise was crumbling, a housekeeper who had been with them for many years presented a bill for several thousand gilders. In part it was for house-keeping expenses that she had borne, in part for back wages that she had not been paid regularly. As the accounts had not been kept properly for years, nor any control established, nobody was in a position to challenge the amount in question, and relatives paid the bill.

After this "shipwreck," the family lived in very lean circumstances while receiving some support from relatives. Aunt Zilli and her two daughters Lori and Gusti produced fine handicraft items for a shop. In order to make some money, my uncle wrote a number of quite successful articles about the national economy. At the same time, however, he concerned himself with obtaining a steady income and was eventually employed by the Vienna Jewish congregation as a secretary. He served that congregation very well for many years because of his great knowledge, diligence, accuracy, and righteous manner. That fact was generally acknowledged. On the occasion of his seventieth birthday, he received not only a great number of valuable gifts from the congregation and some of its members, but also many tokens of respect and high esteem.

I got to know Uncle Ignaz only after he had lost his fortune. For that reason I find it difficult to conclude my report about him at this point, especially because most of what I have said so far does not speak in his favor. Nevertheless, my Uncle Ignaz was a personality to whom we could offer respect and kindness. Although there was a large age difference between us, I cherished him as a dear old friend.

He was able to adapt to the times and was thus always a modern man with a true sense of beauty. It was specifically in the second half of his life, when he lived in very modest circumstances, that he demonstrated that a person can remain upright, even after suffering serious setbacks. He also showed us that consciousness of doing one's duty makes it possible to erase an unhappy past to some degree.

Uncle Ignaz died in the year 1886 at the age of seventy-five.

Aunt Zilli reached the same age of seventy-five. She adapted to the changing circumstances with decency and made every effort to make herself useful in the house of her daughter, about whom I now want to report.

Lori Jeiteles

A few days ago I had the great pleasure of having my dear cousin Lori as my guest. I now intend to report about her life, a life that she has mastered admirably despite great adversity.

Lori is the eldest daughter of Uncle Ignaz, my mother's eldest brother. She was born in 1841 and was given an excellent education. She combines the natural gifts of a sharp intellect and clear vision with those of kind-heartedness, altruism, modesty, and great energy.

The collapse of her father's business, which was described earlier, affected her deeply, but she did not remain inactive for long. She undertook tutoring responsibilities in the homes of friends and acquaintances, and her work was satisfactory enough that she was recommended to others. During the day she walked from one suburb to another to carry out her occupation. At that time there were no public transportation facilities as we know them now. Then she, her mother, and her younger sister Gusti used their remaining free hours, until late into the night, to produce fine handicraft work, for which Gusti was and still is especially gifted.

Nevertheless, Lori did not feel that all that was sufficient to provide her parents with acceptable living conditions, and that something more had to be done. That feeling led her to make plans to establish a college for young women, but as she pursued her plan, she encountered great obstacles. Despite her wide knowledge and skill, she lacked the specific qualifications that were required to run such a school and to obtain the necessary license from the authorities. Lori, however, did not let herself be deterred and pursued her plan with admirable tenacity. Despite the constant increase in the number of hours that she had to spend tutoring outside her home, she did not waste a single moment as she pursued her goal. Eventually she passed all of the examinations and was granted the desired license. But that was in the disastrous year of 1873.*

Starting a new enterprise at such a time, when everything was in a state of total economic collapse and one had to depend on the prosperity and willingness of wealthy parents to make sacrifices, was a risky undertaking. But Lori took the risk and eventually succeeded.

People trusted her. In the beginning the school had only a few students, but the reputation of the school grew, and she was able to justify that reputation completely. It was important to Lori to establish and maintain an exemplary college. She managed to attract the best and brightest teachers in Vienna, including university professors and specialists in each field. She accepted the necessary costs; the school grew from year to year and its good reputation became well known.

Moreover, in her own apartment she provided a pleasant home for a number of young ladies from outside Vienna and offered them room and board.

The success of her undertaking gave Lori a great deal of satisfaction. Her parents and sister now lived in less precarious circumstances, and the school enjoyed a reputation that she could be proud of.

She really accomplished an amazing feat. The college* occupied two large floors and had about twenty-five rooms. A large number of servants were required to maintain it. The kitchen had to serve forty people, because many of the Viennese girls stayed for the entire day and were offered lunch on the premises. There were some 130 or 140 students attending seminars and lectures. Lori supervised all of it by herself. Her work included the regulation of the teaching activities, interaction with the faculty and the parents of the students, and all of the other tasks that such a large undertaking creates. She even did some of the teaching herself. Her efforts were truly admirable!

In spite of all the work and effort, however, the economic returns were rather limited. Lori did not focus as much on material success as on offering her students the best in every respect. She felt fully compensated by the love and admiration of her students, by the trust of their parents, and by the general high esteem in which she was held.

Lori remained in charge of the institute, which was commonly known as the *Jeiteleum*, from 1873 to 1901. Thousands of young women from every social class received an education there during those twenty-eight years. Even today she is loved and highly regarded by all of them.

In the year 1901, as a sixty-year-old unmarried lady, she turned the institute over to Dr. Eugenie Schwarzwald.* Worn out by the many years of demanding work, she no longer felt up to the task of remaining in charge. Yet she continues to give lectures there and to teach evening adult classes. She also does volunteer work for different charities.

All who know Lori, her life's work, and her love and sacrifice for her parents will heartily wish her enjoyable twilight years.

Notice from the New School Principal

As previously announced, at the beginning of the next school year I shall take over the girls' college that has been directed until now by Miss Eleonore Jeiteles. I do not need to stress my firm intention to employ everything in my power to maintain and further the reputation of this well-established school as a solid and reliable educational and cultural institution. I ask the public to take special note of a few innovations that will, I believe, meet the aspirations of modern education to provide broader and more far-reaching instruction for girls and thus fulfill a real need. In these endeavors I shall expect to accomplish much through the active cooperation of the parents of my students. Only through the constant cooperation of school and home can I hope to remain in touch with and fulfill the expectations of women.

In the following material I offer an overview of the curricula for the various courses and the enrollment regulations for the coming school year of 1901/1902.

Vienna, July 1901

Eugenie Schwarzwald, Ph.D.

Uncle Hermann Jeiteles

I formerly had more contact with Uncle Hermann, my mother's youngest brother, whom I have mentioned previously and who is now eighty-seven years old. He is a jovial man and is able to adapt to people easily, but he is not entirely honest and exhibits a great deal of cynicism and a few other characteristics that do not make him very likeable.

Uncle Hermann had settled in Vienna, where he owned a rather large business. He was unmarried and was considered a "good catch." He became engaged to a Miss Spitzer, who had a good family background. She was a sister of the then well-known author Daniel Spitzer, who wrote very witty and intelligent newspaper features under the pen name "The Viennese Wanderer." Uncle Hermann, however, soon managed to destroy the confidence of his fiancée's family, who could not tolerate his extravagant and ridiculous ideas. A pertinent example of his behavior can be found in the fact that he presented himself at her home one winter morning at eight o'clock and refused to leave, just to see if she would be ready to receive him and what she looked like at that hour of the day! Uncle Hermann actually boasted about that little prank to his friends.

Later he married someone else, a lady whom I never got to know. She is said to have been very kind, although not pretty. In any case, the marriage was not a very happy one. The household was run in a lavish manner with a pretty young children's governess in charge of everything. The wife died at a young age, and several days after her death something took place that has never been cleared up. The wife's valuable jewelry had disappeared. There were all sorts of conjectures. The police were notified and the governess came under suspicion. Even my uncle was interrogated repeatedly by the police, but the jewelry never turned up and the mystery remains unsolved to this day.

Shortly after his wife died, my uncle got into serious financial difficulties. He had to give up his business and lost his fortune, which was especially sad because he had to provide for young children and could not rely on his relatives because they had suffered serious losses in the wake of his financial collapse.

Through special patronage, a wealthy Viennese Jew, who owned large estates in Hungary, hired my uncle to run one of his estates as a commercial manager. He remained there for many years, and in time he saved up a modest fortune that he used to move to Kapozvar* where he established or shared in a book printing business.

During his stay there, his oldest daughter Leontine fell in love with a man whom she then married. But soon after the wedding the only place that she could see him was in jail. The man was a crook. The second daughter married a goldsmith, and she did not fare any better. Uncle Hermann did not have much luck with his sons-in-law.

The book printing business did not work out either, and my uncle had to leave Kapozvar.

In the meantime, a different family event took its course. For many years a woman had been living in my uncle's house. She had looked after the children and my uncle himself while the family lived on the estate. The lady was Catholic, but my uncle was willing to marry her if she converted to Judaism. And that is what she did.

She came to Vienna to complete the necessary rituals. She learned Hebrew and was immersed three times in the ritual bath, which allowed her to take her place under the wedding canopy as an orthodox Jewess. It was quite interesting to hear in her own words what she had been required to do, what her impressions had been, and with what earnestness she experienced all of it. I was invited to the wedding, which took place in the *Seitenstättengasse* synagogue. It was a ceremony that did not leave a pleasant feeling behind.

The young woman was not able to enjoy her Jewish identity for long, because she died in Budapest, where my uncle had settled. Afterward he spent some time in Graz in order to avoid contact with his daughters and sons-in-law, who all lived in Budapest. Recently, however, he moved back there. He is not well off, but with the support of his relatives he is able to live in a modest but adequate manner.

It is interesting that as a youth Uncle Hermann suffered from a chest ailment and a number of renowned professors predicted that he would not live long. Now, however, at the age of eighty-seven, he exhibits a high level of vigor and zest for life. He survived three life-threatening operations last year, for which he was unable to be anesthetized. Even today he still takes a lively interest in everything. His writing style and handwriting are so clear and consistent that one cannot help but be astonished.

May God continue to give him an enjoyable old age!

The Foges Family

Uncle Jacques Foges ("The Peasant Foges")

Uncle Jacques Foges, who was later commonly known as "The Peasant Foges" in reference to his appearance and style of dress, was one of my mother-in-law's brothers, a son of Koppelmann Foges.

In his youth he showed little ambition and talent for school, and therefore his parents decided that he should learn the tanning trade. His mother worked in her husband's business, as was the custom in those days, particularly in Prague. It was typical for the children in such families, beginning at a tender age, to be sent to stay with respectable families out in the country, and for them to remain there until they started school. Similar arrangements are still common in Paris today (1913).

Thus it was that Jacques Foges, like his brothers and sisters, was sent to stay with the very same family in the country, and every

Sunday their parents came to see how they were doing. The children grew up with those of their foster parents, and among them there was one who had a bad stutter that Jacques picked up. He stuttered until his dying day, although with some effort it would have been possible for him to speak normally. That slight impediment, however, suited my uncle quite well. He was an extremely kind and handsome man with a good-natured appearance. His minor stammer gave his speech a very friendly tone, and it was by no means irritating.

Uncle Jacques learned the tanning trade in Prague. After his apprenticeship, at the age of sixteen he became a traveling journeyman. That was probably in about 1849-1850, and in those days the traveling craftsman was still a common and welcome sight. Back then, each trade or guild had its own hostel in almost every town, and the ambiance that prevailed in them was very cheerful. In the first larger hostel that a newcomer visited, he received a nickname that was entered into his journeyman's record and he kept it permanently. Uncle Jacques was given the nickname "the jolly Praguer," and he certainly never brought discredit to that name. He was always in the mood for jokes and pranks. He traveled through all of Germany, Belgium, and France, became very proficient in his trade, and finally worked in Paris, where he acquired skills that later became very useful.

In dealing with the master craftsmen, he pretended that he was just a poor journeyman and therefore would not become a competitor to them. He was then also able to gain their trust and thus learned about many innovations, techniques, and other production secrets that remained unknown to many others.

When Jacques Foges returned to his home town after a few pleasant and profitable years, he wanted to establish himself independently, and his parents offered him the means to do it. Then he also married. His wife, Lotti, was the daughter of the very well-to-do Cologne leather merchant Polatschek. She was a pretty, extremely intelligent, and well-educated woman who had extraordinary common sense. That characteristic was much more apparent than the emotional side of her nature.

"Peasant" Foges

Jacques then pursued his tannery business and was able to produce beautiful, high quality work. It turned out, however, that he did not have the business sense that is needed to run any enterprise successfully. He therefore took on a partner to be the manager. But the man in question worked so efficiently in his *own* interest, that within a few years he had dishonestly acquired Jacques's fortune, leaving him penniless! After that, his wife and daughter were adequately supported by relatives on both sides of the family, while Jacques himself obtained a very profitable position as the manager of manufacturing in one of the major Russian leather factories.

The factory was located in the far reaches of Russia, a two-day journey from Moscow and far away from civilization. The "jolly Praguer," who had only himself and some of his employees to rely on in that isolation, had to adapt to those conditions as best he could. The situation and the necessity to provide for his wife and child forced him to do so, but he did it with a heavy heart.

His life at the factory was very monotonous, but his work occupied all of his time. In his leisure moments he read and socialized with some of the senior personnel, who soon became his friends because of his likeable nature.

The factory lay in the middle of a huge estate that contained a large farming area. The farms and stables were full of horses, cattle, and all kinds of other domestic animals. By Russian standards it was an extremely efficient operation, and Jacques Foges, who had always been a lover of nature and animals, had the opportunity to acquire new skills. In later years he frequently enjoyed talking about his stay in Russia and his experiences there.

He told incredible stories about the stupidity, bigotry, and superstition that existed in Russia. According to him there were even more public holidays than in Austria, and on those days, as well as on Sundays, of course, absolutely no work was permitted. And that was true even to the point that they were not allowed to feed the livestock, and thus on holidays the poor, hungry animals made a dreadful noise.

Jacques enjoyed it when Russian Jews visited the factory to do business, some to purchase finished leather, others to sell raw skins and other materials. Since it was always a matter of major business deals that were beyond the means of any one of them, they came in groups of three or four. But they did not trust each other and tried to outsmart one another. Accordingly, during their discussions they always spoke Yiddish and did not suspect that Uncle Jacques, with whom they were dealing, was also a Jew and could understand every word. Uncle Jacques, of course, was always able to derive benefit from that, and he always enjoyed hearing them praise him for his efficiency after a deal had been struck, when they themselves had provided the means for him to obtain favorable results.

My uncle also mentioned the various major and minor attempts at bribery. One day he had a group of those "noblemen" thrown out of the factory and told them categorically that they were never to set foot in the factory again. After that he became known everywhere as "that peculiar saint."

Then several years passed, during which Uncle Jacques felt quite comfortable in his position. With his high income he was not only able to provide for his wife and child, but could also save a substantial amount each year. His relationship with his subordinates was rather pleasant, and he therefore decided to have his wife and child join him, remain there for a few more years, and then return later to his home town with sufficient means to start a new existence.

My aunt had grown up in the country, and she also enjoyed their stay. She managed the household, helped out on the farm, and had a pleasant life. But it did not last very long.

One evening the director of the estate came to see Uncle Jacques in a very agitated frame of mind and informed him that the workers had learned that he and his family were Jews. He said that the workers intended to cause trouble and therefore advised him to leave the estate that very night. Otherwise he could not guarantee their safety!

Thus Uncle Jacques and Aunt Lotti returned to Austria and settled in Vienna. That must have been around 1872. Uncle Jacques continued for some time to correspond with one of his former employees at the factory. From him he learned that after their departure the tables, cupboards, and all the furniture that they had used had been burned. The walls were scraped down, and clergymen arrived with incense and holy water and spoke long prayers before the apartment could be used again!

Uncle Jacques set up an imitation leather factory in Vienna and was rather successful with it. He dealt only with the manufacturing process and supervised the workers, while Aunt Lotti expertly took care of the commercial side of the business. It was not long before he could afford to acquire the house in Gaudenzdorf,* which he had only rented until then. From year to year his fortune grew larger, and Aunt Lotti ensured that they lived very economically at home. It could not be claimed that she was interested in comfort and tidiness. On the contrary, visitors usually left with rather unpleasant impressions.

I remember the first time that my fiancée and I visited Aunt Lotti in Prague. It was in the year 1870, and Uncle Jacques was still in Russia. We arrived at her apartment at about noon. We were announced and immediately shown in and welcomed by my aunt. But what a state she was in! She wore only an underskirt and a vest. A table stood in the middle of the room. Still on it were the breakfast dishes, a loaf of bread, a bowl of butter, a wash basin with dirty water, and a soap dish. In addition there were various more or less discrete items of underwear of questionable cleanliness.

The room itself was untidy and reminded me of the paintings of William Hogarth. But the strange thing was that Aunt Lotti thought that the situation was completely natural. She did not hesitate to admit us, asked us to sit down, and made no mention at all of the fact that the apartment was not in suitable condition for welcoming visitors.

She also lacked appreciation for a comfortable home when they later moved to Vienna. As a result of the personality differences and mental inequality between husband and wife, my uncle spent most evenings in the *Café Schwender*, where the respectable suburbanites and local officials were always very pleased to see him. As to my aunt, she spent her time eagerly reading books and saw to her only daughter's education.

Nevertheless, peace and harmony prevailed at home. Intellectually, my aunt was very superior to my uncle. She was an exceptionally intelligent woman who knew how to judge and guide her husband. He, on the other hand, was good natured and compliant, and thus there was no friction and they went their own ways.

Uncle Jacques began to suffer from asthma, and neither doctors nor medications were able to relieve him. By mere chance, one day someone whom he knew from the *Café Schwender* invited him along on a trip to the country over two successive holidays.

The tourist industry and mountain climbing were still in their early stages at the beginning of the 1880s. The first trip that my uncle made to the Rax* had an extraordinary effect on him. During the climb he soon felt very comfortable. His asthma vanished, and the stay on the Rax itself was so beneficial that he decided to repeat the experiment. And it was again a success! From then on he used every free day to go to the country. He regularly hiked on the Rax, the Schneeberg, or the Semmering. There was one spot that he particularly liked. On a plateau above the village of Klamm he found an old dilapidated hut with a magnificent view, which he acquired along with the meadows and forests that belonged to it. My uncle allowed the elderly former owner and his wife to continue living in the hut and occupied only one room on his visits. The former owner's only income, apart from poaching and gathering wood, came from providing board for the few tourists who climbed mountains in those days. Now my uncle himself became their most frequent visitor.

He often came and stayed there for rather long periods of time. He roamed through the fields and forests, climbed the Semmering Pass, which was only about an hour away from his property, and felt exceptionally well, in spite of his very primitive accommodations and life.

As a result of his friendly and good-natured manner, he also became known in the wider vicinity and was well liked. The *"Fogesbauer* [peasant Foges]," as he was commonly known, was very popular in the entire area. One reason for that was his manner of dress. My uncle could readily be mistaken for a down-and-out farmer, and people thus easily regarded him as one of their own. Besides that, he often helped them with word and deed, and the man whom everybody knew to be Jewish restored not only the "holy" pictures of the saints* on his property, but also all those that were entrusted to his care. Even the many poachers trusted him completely because they knew that he would never betray them.

Uncle Jacques often went for walks in the woods late at night and early in the morning. On one such occasion he met some rather suspicious looking characters. They, however, immediately recognized "Peasant Foges" and let him pass. Yet after that experience he never went out by day or night without a loaded gun.

After several years he built a rather large house as a permanent summer residence for himself, his family, and any occasional visitors. He also sold some plots of land from his vast property holdings, and a small "colony" developed. Today, the *Annenhof*, named after his only daughter Anna, is a very valuable and well-frequented summer residence for families from Vienna. I have never been to the *Annenhof* myself, but I know that it charms every visitor, and that a certain tree is always mentioned because it has a table and some chairs set up in its branches. It is supposed to be a nice place to rest, and apparently one can also enjoy a leisurely meal up there.

So Uncle Jacques was in his element. Aunt Lotti approved of her husband's country life in summer or winter, and of his frequent stays in the mountains. She in turn had her own special desires and interests. Since her only daughter Anna was married to the lawyer Dr. Kompert in Vienna, she was no longer tied to the house and could fulfill her long-standing wish to visit distant countries. She took part in several large group tours and was often away for several months. Those journeys stimulated her keen thirst for knowledge.

One night Uncle Jacques was walking alone and had a bad fall. He was far away from houses, could not move, and had to wait with a broken leg until morning. He was found by people who heard the shots that he fired from his gun, and although he recovered, his energy and strength had suffered severely and he died soon afterward. He was mourned by everyone, and in accordance with his wishes he was buried without any religious ceremony. His wife is still very active, but she has not maintained contact with her late husband's relatives.

Klara Schwarz (née Foges)

My cousin Klara Schwarz, the daughter of Moritz and Resi Foges, was an exceptionally competent woman of strong character. Her father was one of my mother-in-law's brothers. She had a difficult and troubled existence, with only a few bright moments, but she took up the challenges that confronted her in life and proved that she was very strong. Whenever fate knocked her down, she always got back up again and fought until the end. I would now like to honor her memory by writing about her life.

Klara was robustly beautiful. Her appearance suggested strength, energy, and reason. She was a likeable person with an open and straight-forward nature, and she provided for herself and her children with earnestness and perseverance.

Her marriage was unhappy because she had fallen in love with and married an irresponsible man named Heinrich Schwarz. Schwarz abandoned himself to gambling and all sorts of pleasures and completely neglected his family. He also neglected his business in Karlsbad (Karlovy Vary) to the point that he was forced to sell it a few years after they married. The buyer, his own assistant, became a very prosperous man. After selling the business, Schwarz did not take care of his wife and children, disappeared, and left his family to their fate.

Klara moved to Vienna with her children at a time when many large businesses manufactured household linen. She was employed simultaneously by several of those firms and received plenty of orders. Gradually she was able to engage a number of girls who could embroider and use the newly invented sewing machines. Her income was not high, but it was sufficient to support her family. She would have been quite content, had it not been for the absence of her husband, whom she adored in spite of everything! Then suddenly he returned, in a sorry state, with his clothes reduced to rags!

Klara, however, was overjoyed to have him back. She provided for his needs and wanted him to assist her by taking over the out-of-town business dealings, the administrative tasks, and calculating the workers' wages. That did not suit him, however. He preferred to remain in bed until ten or eleven o'clock in the morning, play inappropriate pranks on the workers, go for walks, and spend Klara's hard-earned money in coffee houses and other amusement establishments. Klara's tender remonstrations had the effect that he - fully aware of the pain that he inflicted upon her - suddenly left one day and disappeared.

Quite a while later, she was sitting in the horse-drawn tram on her way home to the Leopoldstadt* quarter, when she was taken aback when she realized that the conductor who handed her the ticket was her husband! Reconciliation took place in the carriage, and Schwarz returned to his wife. Unfortunately, he had not changed in the least, and before long he had disappeared again without leaving a trace.

Then Klara decided to emigrate to America with all of her children (I think that she had four or five). She had more than one reason to leave. The most important one was that she was ashamed of her husband, but she also became aware that in spite of her great efforts, she would never earn enough in Vienna to provide for herself and her adolescent children. Furthermore, she was unable to save money for the future. Believing in her abilities, she had no doubt that she would find a more prosperous existence abroad.

When she arrived in America, Klara received support from her Uncle Pentlarge and her cousins, but within a short time she was able to stand on her own feet. At first she worked in a knitwear store, where she was soon promoted to a managerial position. Before long she started a small factory of her own for that type of goods. Her children assisted her, and she was completely satisfied with her success.

But with her happy satisfaction came a renewed yearning for her husband. She paid the costs of his travel, hoping that he would change his ways in America. In the beginning, as long as the language and the circumstances were still unfamiliar, he worked in his wife's business. Later, however, he felt that his position was too subordinate and dependent, and he found himself another employer.

As usual, things went quite well in the beginning, because Schwarz was intelligent and had good manners. But as soon as he had "warmed up" to a position he relapsed into his incorrigible casualness, and Klara repeatedly had to use her money to pay her husband's debts. That went on for years until Schwarz disappeared. It turned out that he had committed a serious fraud and had also involved his wife in it by forging her name.

I do not know the details of that sad incident. I learned only that Klara was obliged to leave New York, to sell her thriving business at a price well below its value, and to move to California with her entire family. There she bought a small piece of property near San Francisco. Her husband remained missing, but she lived to see the happy day when her eldest daughter married an engine mechanic who established a secure existence in San Francisco.

Klara Schwarz died several years ago, and since then I have not had any news from any of her children.

The Birnbaum Family

My Cousin Johanna

After finishing school in Teplitz, my cousin and best friend at school, Johanna Birnbaum, attended the renowned institute of Miss Mayer in Dresden. At the age of sixteen or seventeen, she returned to Teplitz as an exceptionally pretty girl. Her personality was very similar to that of her mother, my Aunt Leni, and despite her young age, she already had her mother's distinguished and dignified manner.

When she was twenty or twenty-one years old, she married Mr. Dominik Strakosch, who owned a factory in Brünn. The wedding celebration was very pompous. Uncle Birnbaum, who liked to show off his wealth and his generosity, held a banquet and ball at Prince Clary's garden salon and sent out two hundred invitations. Half of the population of Teplitz attended!

Dominik and Johanna Strakosch have long since died. He became feeble-minded, and she died during a stay in Karlsbad.

My Cousin Adolph

I shall write only briefly about my cousin Adolph.

As a boy he was already a vain fop and a numbskull. He has remained that way all his life. Even today, as an old man, he dresses in a ridiculous manner that makes him conspicuous to everyone. People in Teplitz, where he lives, call him "Circus Birnbaum." Thanks to his "smart" clothing and his family's name, he was able to wed Miss Reich, a wealthy glass factory owner's daughter. He has long since lost his fortune by gambling on the stock market and betting on horses. It is said that his mother-in-law pays his living expenses. I do not know what became of his children. I was never very interested in him or his youngest brother, Oskar.

My Cousin Oskar

Oskar Birnbaum, who also will never "set the world on fire," fancied himself to be a writer and a poet. He moved to Dresden, was baptized there, got married, and to this day remains a man who in the widest circles...is completely and totally unknown.

LOOKING BACK

George Jeiteles
(My cousin and brother-in-law and his family)

I previously related an episode from George's childhood and described his interesting evolution into a most successful young man. Now I want to discuss his subsequent life.

At a friend's house, George became acquainted with Miss Rosa Strakosch from Brünn. She was a light-hearted and quick-witted girl who found George very much to her taste and therefore desired to impress him favorably. He decided to become engaged to her, although his parents initially did not completely approve of their union. The wedding eventually took place on September 14, 1879 in Brünn.

In time children were born, who brought them great joy, but also much pain. One of their children, little Annerl, was somewhat mentally deficient.

In the town of Gablonz, which was still very small at the time, they were limited socially to a very narrow circle that consisted only of jealous competitors. George could possibly have put up with that, if their envy of his thriving business had not been clad in malicious sympathy and malignant delight with respect to the sick child.

For many years George and his wife endured that painful situation. But the knowledge that they could well afford to live serenely, without cares, and away from such malicious people induced George to leave the company and move to Dresden.

But before that occurred, much irritation and agitation had arisen among the family members. At first they tried to persuade George not to carry out his plan. His two business partners (his brother and brother-in-law) knew very well that his departure would deprive the firm of a significant driving force. They also reproached his wife for insisting that they leave Gablonz for reasons of vanity and self-indulgence. When George insisted on carrying out his plan, however, everyone concerned became filled with hostility and malice that resulted in violent scenes.

All of the fraternal feelings, all of the former love and family solidarity disappeared, and reconciliation did not occur until many years later. George moved with his wife and three children, Siegmund, Vally, and Annerl, to Dresden, although he would have preferred Vienna. Because of his withdrawal from the firm, relations with his mother were not the best, and thus it was only after several years, when many things had been forgotten, that he was able to move to Vienna permanently. Meanwhile, a little boy, Franz-Josef, which was shortened to Josi, had been born in Dresden. Later on, Annerl died in Vienna at the age of about twelve.

During his stay in Dresden, George devoted his time primarily to literary studies and writing, in which he had planned to work professionally. Later he turned to scientific studies and continued to educate himself. In Vienna he continued those activities. He spent his mornings in research and his afternoons taking long walks or playing chess.

I had the opportunity to watch my brother-in-law George's development from his early youth on. I do not believe that there are many people upon whom time and circumstances, and primarily self-discipline, have had as profound an effect as they have had on George. Although the traits that he exhibited as a ten-year-old boy have not completely vanished, at times it now appears as if he were the "tyrannical ruler" of the house, the passionate defender of his current, often erroneous views. But he corrects them without being compelled to do so. Now his selfishness comes to light less frequently and his dogmatic manner has disappeared. He has become the most indulgent husband and father and the most lenient critic of his family. Frequently he even gives the impression that in these things he acts more on the basis of principle than out of conviction.

George is now often somewhat phlegmatic, probably as a result of self-discipline, which reveals the fact that time and circumstances have had a major effect on him. That is the external impression that George makes. Who knows what goes on in his mind? He has experienced many trials and tribulations that have left their mark on him.

With respect to his wife Rosa, who was born on December 16, 1858, I must especially emphasize her kind-heartedness and adaptability. Thanks to those characteristics, their marriage, which was uncomfortable at first, took a turn for the better. Rosa is a most attentive wife and loving mother, who is always anxious to clear away any obstacles that are in the way of family members, and to grant any wish. But she also tries to nip any sign of discord in the bud, to foster reconciliation, and to maintain a peaceful atmosphere in the home. That is not always easy, given the idiosyncrasies of some family members! Her energy, her bright repartees, and her quick wit enable her to achieve that purpose. With those gifts she controls her family, including her husband, who has long since stopped scolding or reproaching his children, perhaps because he fears that it would be useless!

In earlier years Rosa spent her spare time painting, and some of the delightful pictures that she painted can be found in her apartment. Now she has taken up a peculiar but delicate method of coloring old engravings, which consist exclusively of portraits of our imperial family that now embellish her parlor.

Their oldest son, Siegmund, who was born on July 3, 1880, is a distinguished, kind-hearted, and educated young man. His sister Valerie (Vally) was born on August 5, 1882 and was already my favorite while still a child. Her charming personality, her clear and intelligent eyes, and her nice behavior made everyone love her. I had a peculiar attachment to her. I saw her only three or four times a year, but when I thought of her in her absence, she always seemed to me to be a grown-up young lady, while she was actually only nine or ten years old. She completed her education in accordance with her intellectual and artistic talents, and the social relationships that she was soon able to establish in Vienna were in the best circles.

In addition to studying literature and foreign languages, she learned painting from the leading masters in Vienna. Many copies of works in Vienna museums, as well as original drawings and portraits, attest to her ability.

It took a long time for her to find a husband who satisfied her heart and her needs in all respects. Dr. Alfred Jungmann, whom we all love, is the managing director of the health center for lupus sufferers in Vienna. He is a highly regarded personality and is respected by everyone who knows him. His professional achievements are exemplary, and he is even recognized abroad as a leading authority in his field. Their wedding took place in September of

1909. They are the most harmonious and happiest couple imaginable, and their lovely little Elisabeth fills them with joy.

As previously mentioned, my brother-in-law's family increased in size in Dresden in 1893. Little Josi was a particularly handsome child and was also mentally gifted. At the age of six or seven, he spoke perfect English, had an excellent memory, and was his parents' pride and joy. He was intellectually far more talented than his eldest brother, Siegmund, and made great progress in school. His father was especially proud to be able to help him with his Greek and Latin studies.

But the boy received a little too much recognition for his talents and performances and completely lacked any discipline. And because they also catered to all of his wishes and moods, it is understandable that Josi developed a tremendous overestimation of his own abilities and an arrogance that makes dealing with him truly unpleasant.

It must be acknowledged, however, that he is not an insignificant person. This twenty-year-old young man, who has dedicated himself completely to the study of philosophy, has already written papers that have been recognized by highly esteemed experts who have recommended them for publication in the best journals in the field! He publishes his articles under the pen name of "Selety"* and will perhaps assume that name officially in the long run. I hope that the progress and further development of this talented young man meet his parents' and his own expectations.

Among all the characters that "revolve" around Grandfather, Max seems to have been the closest to him. He wrote about him on several occasions, something that demonstrates his interest, his affection, even his admiration, his justified criticism, and his disappointment, all of which finally returns to warm friendship. In the following "obituary" the different aspects of a most complex personality are assembled artificially in an attempt to present a well-rounded portrait of that richly gifted individual.

Max Jeiteles: An Obituary

The middle of March 1914.

The worst of the pain is over, and it has been replaced by a feeling of tremendous emptiness and uneasiness that makes everything seem dull and stale. One more link in the chain is gone. The older I get, the more the circle of loved ones thins out, and the greater the pain becomes whenever dear friends with whom I have shared many years pass away.

Now Max is also gone, and I will miss him very much. We felt great affection for each other for over forty years, not because we were related, but because of our close and warm friendship. He was always a faithful and compassionate friend who was ready to help when help was needed, and there was only one time when we did not have contact for a prolonged period. I will probably say more about that later on, but here I only want to say that it was the result of a combination of sad circumstances.

September 1914

I am writing these lines a few months after his death and still vividly feel the pain caused by his absence. Nevertheless, considering the dismal situation in the world today and in light of the terrible war that now extends across almost all of Europe, I tell myself that it is better for my poor, suffering brother-in-law that he does not have to witness these terrible times.

I knew Max when he was a child, and I can still see the twelve-year-old boy before my eyes. He was small for his age, but fat, with chubby cheeks, and his intelligent and slightly mischievous eyes gleamed with contentment. I also knew him as an idealistic young man of eighteen or twenty, who was fascinated by everything that was beautiful and good. He loved music passionately and always strove to increase his knowledge; nevertheless he met his professional obligations eagerly and very sensibly.

At the age of sixteen, he entered his father's export business in Gablonz, where he did excellent work. Soon his knowledge of several languages enabled him to go on business trips where his extensive technical knowledge made it especially easy for him to establish contact with customers. Over the years he traveled to Spain,

France, England, Italy, Russia, and even the Scandinavian countries, where he quickly achieved very satisfactory results.

But he was consumed by inner struggles, and beginning at a rather early age he became one of those people who are never satisfied with themselves, with the people around them, or with fate, and who do not appreciate the good things that have been given to them. Thus Max undervalued his business successes and believed that his true vocation was that of a composer! In order to ascertain the truth for himself, he sent one of his compositions to a famous musician for evaluation and enclosed a letter that stated his doubts. The expert replied with praise for his composition, but also advised him not to give up his current profession and not to begin a career as a composer.

Of course, Max remained a passionate music lover. He played the piano and the organ brilliantly and always had attentive and grateful listeners.

Max had a nervous disposition. As a young man he already had to take cures every year in order to strengthen his nerves. Unfortunately, he also had a tendency to harbor prejudice and voice strong criticism of other people.

Nevertheless, he had an extraordinarily passionate and unbounded love, for example for France, and for Paris, where he had lived for many years as a bachelor and later on as a married man. He would approve of the chauvinism and all of the superficial characteristics of the French and even defend them!

How unjust he was, however, in his attitudes toward Austria, toward Vienna, toward the *Neue Freie Presse*,[*] and even toward Berlin! And how he denigrated the young people of today! Even though some of his attacks were admittedly justified, he often had antiquated and biased points of view with which I really could not agree.

I should not omit the fact that Max sometimes acted without the necessary caution and consideration, even when it came to very serious matters. He was engaged twice before marrying; the first engagement lasted twenty-four hours and the second lasted two weeks. He was among those people who see everything in a rosy light at first, but who require more time to make accurate judgments.

On November 20, 1887 he married Miss Jenny Lismann from Fürth in Bavaria, whose kind and winning manner made a favorable impression on everybody. I was delighted to have such a charming lady for a sister-in-law.

During the first years after their wedding, the young couple lived in Paris. Influenced by their happy marriage, the birth of their son Alfred, and his great love for France and Paris, Max experienced satisfactory health. But then his older brother George retired from the company in Gablonz, and he was forced to replace him there.

From Paris to Gablonz - that was a stark contrast! The small-town atmosphere and the lack of cultural stimulation inevitably had a negative effect on Max's health and disposition. He ran the business in an excellent manner, and it brought him substantial profits that he generously shared with the poor and the needy. But he saw it as a chain that bound him to the place and would much rather have left the business as his brother had done!

For a long time he was at odds with himself about it. He was depressed by concern for the wishes of his mother, who warned him not to leave the business, and with the thought of burdening his only partner and brother-in-law Schwenk with the responsibility for running the business in both Gablonz and Paris. Nevertheless, in 1904 he carried out the plan that he had entertained for a long time and finally moved to Vienna.

Max was now a man of independent means. His wife and his two children Alfred and Grete were soon at home in Vienna. He had an exquisitely furnished home that became the meeting place for the entire family. He was very popular with young and old. His nephews and nieces enjoyed his visits because he always brought plenty of presents and little remembrances. His entire nature was delightful and did everyone good.

He was a pleasant conversationalist, knew how to tell stories well, and had an excellent memory for good jokes that he always told at the appropriate time. Yet it was also possible to have long and serious conversations with him, conversations that were always stimulating. Nevertheless, we did not always agree with each other, especially when it came to the rearing of children in general and the character and traits of his offspring in particular.

He was dissatisfied with them. His ideal was still that of the "good old days," when young people had to follow their parents meekly and blindly, were not permitted to have their own opinions, and did not dare to contradict. He did not want to recognize that those days had long since passed away and that the reasons for the change lay in the social environment and in the behavior of parents who now spoil their children at an early age and make them the focus of the family.

He denied his children affection and love, although Alfred and Grete were very kind-hearted, serious, and eager children. They were intimidated by him, because he had only criticism and unearned reprimands for them and seldom gave them words of acknowledgment or love. Naturally, they were shy and frightened in his presence, while on the other hand they were the best of children and very affectionate toward their mother, who treated them lovingly. Max was slightly jealous because of that, but not enough to change his approach.

He believed that he gave his children signs of love and affection sufficient to warrant their full trust, but he was deceiving himself. Rather, he frightened them away with his constant reproaches and corrections.

The following story gives evidence of that fact:

A few days before his departure to St. Moritz, Max read me a sweet and touching letter that had been written by his daughter Grete, who was attending a boarding school in Paris. There she thanked him in a moving way for some praise that she had received from him in his latest letter. The letter read approximately as follows:

"I cannot describe, dear father, how happy your compliments have made me. Although I believe that I have always done everything that I could to obtain your approval, I have hardly ever received your praise. Now I ask you, dear parents, to allow me to speak openly and honestly to you today, while I am in such a happy mood. I know that until now I have not always been entirely frank and trusting towards you and that I actually had to force myself not to show my love for you - but I could not do it!

"You have shown me your discontent and your displeasure so many times on occasions when I did not always deserve them, that I have developed a certain degree of caution, even fear towards you! I would ask you, dear parents, to let that be different in the future. Please let me be the person that my heart wants me to be, and you will make me happy."

This letter is characteristic for the heart and nature of the seventeen-year-old girl, but also for the behavior of her father up to that point. As a matter of form, the letter is addressed to both parents, but it is really directed only to the father.

In his childhood, Max had still witnessed the performance of rites and ceremonies from the Old Testament. His grandfather, Koppelmann Foges, clung to the old traditions. For instance, every year before Easter he signed a mock contract with their Christian maid, in which he "sold" her all of his leavened provisions for eight days. The Feast of Tabernacles was always celebrated in his own bower, which was set up in the attic of the house. For eight days all family members had their meals up there, and they strictly observed the traditional ceremonies.

Max had retained many joyous memories of those times, but his own household was run in a modern, up-to-date fashion, and none of the Jewish religious rites were observed. Yet it cannot be expected that children who have never seen anything that would lead them to piousness will develop religious inclinations as young people and suddenly become devout Jews who fast for twenty-four hours on Yom Kippur.* That, however, was what Max demanded, and he felt hurt when his children did not comply with his wishes.

In 1909 and 1910 Max made two pleasure trips to very distant locations. His desire to see the world led him to cross the ocean and visit the United States of America, and the next year his predilection for scientific studies took him into the far North, toward the polar region. During the latter journey he had good reason to be worried about his health. He suffered from shortness of breath and cardiac distress and had very bad nights.

Back in Austria he could not tolerate the climate of Vienna. On his doctor's advice, he spent most of the subsequent winters in the South and the summers in various health resorts. But neither the doctor's recommendations nor the medical treatments brought much improvement. And yet he bore his sufferings patiently and could even look cheerful when in stimulating company. On his silver wedding anniversary, which was celebrated on November 20,

1912 in the close family circle, we were relieved to see him full of wit, lively humor, and warm feelings once more.

At the urging of his doctor, in December of 1913 he spent some time in St. Moritz in Switzerland, and the reports that we received from there were initially quite reassuring. Max wrote cheerful letters in which he told us how pleased he was to be free of the troublesome attacks. He was in a good mood.

You can therefore imagine our shock a month or two later, when we received word by telegram that Max had fallen seriously ill, would have to undergo an operation, and that his son Alfred was to come immediately.

Then we finally received the message that the dear man had passed away. On Sunday, March 1, 1914, the cremation took place in the crematorium in Zurich. The following day his wife and children arrived in Vienna. On Tuesday, the third of March, the urn was buried without any religious service in the central cemetery here in Vienna.

In accordance with Max's desire to have one of his friends or family speak a few words of farewell, my son-in-law Robert gave a short speech in which he described the kind-heartedness, the generosity, and the noble character of the deceased in heart-felt words, and said good-bye to him in the name of the family.

Max is sincerely mourned by his wife and children. His son Alfred, who already has a doctorate in law and will become an attorney, has all of the characteristics of a kind and valued man. His daughter Grete is a beautiful and talented young woman. I wish with all my heart that both of them may find more happiness and contentment in life than did their father.

Finally, I want to return to the comment that I made in the beginning, that it may have been good that Max did not have to witness the current difficult time of war. Apart from the worry and the pain that abides in almost every family now, and under which Max would have suffered severely, he would have been in violent conflict with himself. He loved France above everything else, and her possible defeat by the Germans would have hurt him deeply. Then again, he hated Russia and would have begrudged the Russians any victory. He thought highly of the Germans without really liking them. He would never have wished for Russian barbarity to replace German culture. Despite his frequent carping and criticism, he did, of course, have warm feelings for his Austrian fatherland. Those are enormous contradictions that Max could hardly have coped with, given his nervous state, his overly sensitive personality, and his irritability. Perhaps fate was being gracious in not letting him experience our current difficult times.

We have become acquainted with Grandfather's wife Auguste as she was in her youth, as a young, happy wife and mother. Grandfather remains noticeably quiet about later periods. Then suddenly, toward the end of his memoirs, a few lines appear.

Auguste: A Very Personal Depiction of a Broken Marriage

I now want to reminisce, objectively and without resentment, about a time when the friendship between Max and me was disrupted for more than two years.

I had always acknowledged and greatly appreciated the excellent qualities of Auguste, my wife and Max's sister, but over time she became so severely hysterical that living with her, and even everyday dealings with her, became extremely difficult. Out of the blue and without any provocation she threw the most terrible tantrums. Those episodes caused me to suffer dreadfully, and they affected my youngest daughter Agnes even more. My other children and my wife's brothers and sisters were also filled with consternation.

No matter how much I tried to drive away the thought, after years of inner conflict it became clear to me that a life with her under such sad circumstances was impossible, especially for Agnes. My conviction was strengthened even further by my wife's repeated expression of her desire to leave us. So the necessary arrangements were then made between us, and I discussed all of my steps with her brothers George and Max. Both of them agreed to and supported each of my decisions. At last, while Auguste was on a vacation trip to Rome and Naples, Agnes and I moved into temporary accommodations at the *Hietzing Park Hotel* and left the apartment at *Piaristengasse* 34 to my wife, as she herself had requested.

Max was a great help to me during our move. He lent me suitcases and boxes and repeatedly came to see me in our new home. Our friendship was as good as ever.

Several weeks after moving into the hotel I received a letter from Paris. My brother-in-law Adolph Schwenk, my sister-in-law Tony's husband, urgently requested that I return and live with my wife again. I explained to him in detail why I could not do that. I gave him my reasons and also mentioned that Auguste herself no longer wished to live with us, in spite of her sister's admonition. She had received a similar letter from her sister in an effort to influence her. In spite of the rejections from both parties, my brother-in-law Max received explicit instructions from Paris to do everything possible to change my mind.

Tony had always had a strong influence on Max, to the point that she was able to get him to change his mind and his opinions completely. This situation was no exception.

Max came to see me one day and surprised me by asking me to forget everything that had happened in the past and return to my wife. When I told him that it was impossible and expressed my surprise at his complete about-face, Max became more and more insistent. Finally he played his last trump, which he thought should and would convince me.

When I had first started my export business, Max had loaned me a considerable amount of money that he himself had called a permanent loan at the time. He now insisted that the money be repaid immediately. I was as shocked at the fact that he was capable of doing such a thing to me as I was at the request itself. But most of all I was deeply disturbed by the thought that he believed me capable of changing my mind for financial reasons. If anything at all could have moved me to return, it certainly would not have been material considerations.

I was so deeply hurt by Max's action that I am still unable to describe my feelings. It was even more painful for me, however, a few days after that incident, when Max ironically declined to accept deadlines for payment that I had requested by letter and that would not have affected me as severely.

I would have thought that Max would have reconsidered his behavior toward me, and that he would have come to see the matter more clearly. But that was not the case.

I fully met my obligations to Max, but for two years we had no contact whatsoever. Only when the death of my wife led him back to me in 1911 did he offer me his hand in reconciliation. Under such sad circumstances I could not and did not wish to refuse it. From that day on, Max made great efforts to reestablish our former friendship and behaved in a particularly obliging and cordial manner. I was prepared to forgive, if not forget, and our relationship was soon back on friendly terms.

It was a sad incident that had separated us. One that was deeply painful for both of us brought us back together. I believe that following those events we were closer than we had been before, if that is possible. I also believe that we had both missed each other's company during that time, and that we both had reason to judge each other's behavior leniently.

GREAT WORRIES...SMALL PLEASURES

The Brioni Project

December 11, 1913
Alfred, my son-in-law, who is the husband of my daughter Agnes, had previously been head physician at Dr. Konried's clinic in Edlach.* With the cooperation of a number of friends, he now began to promote the establishment of a new clinic that he wanted to operate in Brioni.*

The owner of the Brioni Islands, Director General Kuppelwieser, was very much in favor of the idea and participated in setting up a committee for the completion of the project, which had not yet received ministerial approval.

The day before yesterday, on the evening of December 9th, Agnes brought me the great news that the project had been approved by the minister of war. I was all the more pleased because the odds of gaining that approval had not been very favorable. The application had been made much earlier, and everyone feared that it would be rejected.

The project has now been approved, but so far the available funds for construction and equipment cover only half of the cost. As long as all of the required capital has not been secured, the construction of the clinic cannot proceed.

At the moment, the general world situation is rather unfavorable, and that will likely make raising funds more difficult. But the idea itself seems to be such a good one that the realization of the project will probably occur in the foreseeable future. My own personal feelings with regard to this enterprise are quite mixed. On the one hand, it pleases me greatly to see the material future of my children secured by the project in Brioni, and although Alfred's position as chief physician at Edlach is quite satisfactory, it cannot be considered to be completely secure. On the other hand, I will rarely have the pleasure of personal contact with my children once they move to Brioni.

Agnes is my youngest daughter. She grew up at a time when my two older daughters were already married. She was my constant companion and devoted caregiver for many years, in Vienna and during all of my travels. And even now, after her marriage, we remain in constant contact with each other. During the summer months, from May to September, she stays with her husband in Edlach and I go to visit them regularly. From October until the end of April, she lives in Vienna and we see each other every day.

I have grown very fond of my son-in-law Alfred, and Otto, my youngest grandson, is a charming, sweet little boy who seems to return his grandfather's love.

Therefore, I will very much miss the contact with my children and grandchildren when they are in Brioni. The season over there lasts the entire year, and it is questionable as to whether I will be able to make the journey to Brioni at all, let alone often. I am almost seventy-two years old today, and the clinic there will not begin to operate for another two or three years. By that time I will be even older. But I push away all of those thoughts knowing that my children will have a secure position in life, and I hope for a speedy and happy conclusion of the project.

My Grandson Otto

December 14, 1913

The first step in a person's life is always meaningful and deserves special attention, even if it is that of a young man of only thirteen months. Yesterday my youngest grandchild Otto got up from his porcelain throne all by himself and followed his father all the way into the anteroom without being noticed. His parents did not notice him until he was standing right behind them, and their joy and surprise are easy to imagine. I hope that the first walk of the darling boy's life will be followed by many, many happy others!

> Otto is a sweet little boy - his parents have much fun with him,
> But it grieves his mother very much that he is still quite often wet.
> "Where shall I get all those pants from, you naughty boy?
> If you don't tell us in time, you'll get a good hiding!"
> Otto puts on a serious face and looks surprised,
> "Mother asks too much of me, I'm still so little after all!"
> "No matter how much you look at me, it will do you no good.
> You will now sit on your potty for two hours."
> So now he sits on his potty and looks around the room,

But everything is far too boring and he knocks the potty over.
He has, however, done his duty, the carpet is terribly wet.
The fact that his pants stayed dry pleases his mother greatly.
Then one day Otto told himself: "I want to try it once,
To get up from the little pot all by myself, to march on my own."
The little boy did manage it, he had no accident,
And may his walk through life be similarly happy and blessed!*

Changing Moods

December 24, 1913

I have had to remain in my room for the last two weeks with coughs and sneezes, but I did not have a fever and was thus permitted to move about indoors. I have not suffered from boredom during this period of confinement because of my earlier decision to write down not only my own life story but also whatever I knew about all of my close and more distant relatives and friends.

Accustomed to serious work since my very early days, I thought that I would simply have to find another occupation. My nature still drives me to work rapidly, and therefore I do not experience boredom. Thus I give the impression of being a person who has happily withdrawn from his former activities and seems to spend his time in a calm and pleasant way. My children also believe that and are pleased about it, so I do not contradict them.

In reality, however, I do not like my current life very much. I still have too much energy, too much vitality to fill day after day with nothing but eating and drinking, sleeping, reading, and writing. Nevertheless, I have to try to put up with it, whether I like it or not. When I ask myself if it would have been better to have continued "pulling the cart," I remember that during those last days of my involvement in business the cart had become a bit too heavy for me and that it was time to let go. I am getting older and perhaps more settled, and if I get into a mood of dissatisfaction every now and then, at least I have my daughters to lift my spirits by coming to visit me frequently. I see Grete and Agnes almost every day. That is a welcome interruption of my rather uncomfortable mood, particularly when I have not spoken to anyone all day.

It is terrible to be alone all day. The thoughts that arise and want to be heard are not always the most pleasant ones, and they also have a habit of being insistent and refuse to be turned away. But Grete and Agnes are clever. They know how to do it.

New Year's Day 1914

Today I feel quite content. My children and grandchildren were here with me at lunchtime, and that is always a great joy for me. Their cheerful mood reflects back at me, and I am grateful to my Creator that I have been blessed to see my children turn into fine, well-respected people, and to have my grandchildren around me, filled with promise.

I also take pride in being the host and am pleased that my guests feel at ease in my home and that they heartily partake of what is offered. "Aunt" Lori (i.e. my cousin Lori Jeiteles) and my nephew Dr. Alfred Jeiteles were also at today's lunch, and they all stayed until after five o'clock and had a pleasant time together. Such days make up for all of the lonely ones that are yet to come.

But nothing is perfect, and even in this case there is something that could be improved. As often before on such occasions, I had to do without the presence of my eldest daughter Alice, her husband, and her son. For reasons that are totally strange and incomprehensible to me, my son-in-law Josef Kanitz has no feelings of friendship for me. Our contact is restricted to two or three visits a year. Alice comes to see me every eight or ten days, but my contact with her and my grandson Erni (Ernst*) is not as intimate as with my other daughters. I believe that Alice feels awkward about it as well, but she is powerless to change it. I would also have liked to resolve the misunderstandings that have persisted between Alice and Grete for quite some time now.

January 27, 1914

After being in a contented mood for a while, I suffered another setback. Being alone with my industrious idleness does not benefit my mood, and when there is reason for worry, I feel it twice as much because of my generally pessimistic outlook. But I cannot speak to anyone about my worries, not even to my children, because I do not want to dishearten them.

January 28, 1914

Today my son Konrad told me over the phone that he had returned to Vienna and that he was quite desperate. He had taken a few good photographs while on his journey, but in the meantime his assistant in Vienna had spoiled quite a number of them, and that was the fault of Professor Lainer's photographic paper. Because of that and for other similar reasons he was close to despair.

With a person like Konrad, who is quite insecure, that is not surprising. He is totally at the mercy of temporary external influences and is apt to act precipitously before thinking things through. As a result, he can unfortunately be expected to make the biggest mistakes and blunders. In spite of his thirty-eight years, he is incapable of thinking clearly, of proceeding according to a plan, and he is guided purely by chance.

He is extremely competent in his own field. He has made a name for himself in landscape photography,* both in this country and overseas, but that is all. He does not know how to take full advantage of his talents.

Unfortunately, his effusive mood swings and feelings of despair continue to repeat themselves. They are not new to me, but they do leave me in a most unpleasant mood.

May 8, 1914

It is my birthday today. I have completed my 72nd year, and for the first time in a long while I again feel like putting some of my thoughts down in writing. I am also in a slightly better mood today than I have been for quite a while. I attribute that to the many signs of love and affection that have been shown to me today by my children and those who are close to me. I also want to rejoice in the fact that despite all of the pain and worry, the misfortunes and the emotional suffering, I am still in such good condition that outsiders would describe me as "in perfect health, both physically and mentally." I do not wish to argue today and will only say: "I know better."

In reality, however, my birthday is a big surprise for me and has been for many years. With all of the many serious illnesses that I have endured, I never expected to grow so old. I would simply wish that whatever time remains to me will be happy in the main, that my children will remain healthy and happy, and that sadness and worry will keep their distance, so that my last years will compensate for the pain that I have suffered all of my life.

May 16, 1914

I am very worried about my son-in-law Alfred's future. His contract with Dr. Konried in Edlach will run out at the end of 1915, and the negotiations regarding Brioni are making only very slow, sometimes even negative progress. What is more, the required capital cannot be raised. Alfred's position in Brioni would offer him not only great influence and honor, but also great financial satisfaction. Knowing that fills me with joy, but it also creates new desires and hope that the enterprise in Brioni will enjoy the success that many insiders and outsiders predict.

June 21, 1914

These past weeks have brought me nothing but worry and excitement. On May 16th I was able to express my hope that the completion of the Brioni project was assured. But today it looks very doubtful, and I am not even certain that I should wish for its realization.

To judge from our experience so far, Kuppelwieser seems to be a very bad neighbor, and it will not be easy to work with him. The question is therefore justified as to whether or not, even if he were to give in, it would be in the project's and in Alfred's own best interest to hope that arrangements will be finalized. That is the current state of affairs, and we will just have to wait for Kuppelwieser's answer and see how the whole thing develops.

"Jour Fixe"

Three anecdotes about "modern" education from the year 1914

I established a so-called *jour fixe* at the beginning of the winter. Up until then all of my time had been taken up by my job, and friends and acquaintances knew that they would not find me at home. That has changed now, and I always look forward to having dear friends come to see me on Fridays. I want to write down some of yesterday's *jour* conversations here, because they reflect our current era and circumstances so well.

One of the ladies who were present told the following "nice" story: With the permission of their parents, the children of a family that we are well acquainted with - that of the assistant professor Dr. F. - started a club for the purpose of perfecting their command of the German language, but primarily to practice public speaking. At first the meetings took place at Dr. F.'s house, but the club soon expanded to sixty or seventy members, consisting of both boys and girls between fourteen and eighteen years of age, and they were forced to rent a separate place. After that the nature of the meetings changed significantly. The club for public speaking and perfecting their command of the German language became one with the motto: "Away from the parents." The idea, however, was that the parents were still obliged to care for their children as before, but that in a "spirit of true independence from their parents," the children should be completely emancipated with regard to their actions. These views were expressed and reinforced by the club's leadership in frequent newsletters, and were accepted and applauded by its members.

Naturally, the parents prohibit their children from attending the club anymore, as soon as they discover its true nature. Yet whether or not they are obeyed is questionable. In any case, for every member who leaves some new ones will seek membership.

A second lady told another "pretty" story. One of her friends recently held a ball at her home. A few days later she ran into the mother of one of the invited young ladies. The mother felt obliged to express her thanks and to mention how well her daughter had been entertained and how much she had enjoyed herself. The lady who had given the invitation was quite stunned, because the young lady had not appeared at the ball. She quickly recovered, did not wish to cause any consternation, and received the thanks calmly. But where was the young lady that night? Who can say?

Then a third lady also told a story. She had just spent several days in Gösing, a mountain town that is now very popular because of its excellent location and its great ski slopes. It was a two-day public holiday and the rooms at the hotel were fully booked. In order to accommodate the large number of late and unexpected male and female guests, beds had to be prepared for them in the hotel's common room and on the floors of various barns. The young people found that quite hilarious and probably spent the night very quietly and honorably, since nobody there would have dared to say otherwise! The lady who was visiting me explained that on the second evening at around nine o'clock she remembered that she had forgotten her book by the window of the common room and wanted to go and get it. When she got there, the room was illuminated only by a small flame and at first she could not see anything at all. As she went further, she realized to her surprise that the room was filled with boys and girls and that she had startled them out of the most intimate positions. She went to get her book and left.

These three stories reflect the current conditions among our youth and their parents. The latter are the ones who should be most harshly judged. By bringing up their children improperly, they plant a bad seed at a very early age, one that bears fruit in so much damage later.

Then come the school years, a time when children are supposed to become somewhat acquainted with the seriousness of life. What do parents do then? If the child comes home with bad grades, it is usually the teacher's fault, since the child, of course, is smart and has very good comprehension. If the child is forced to repeat a year, a remedy is found immediately. The child is given private lessons so that he or she will not have to put in too much effort. What the parents do not think about is the fact that with a bit of effort the children may well be able to help themselves, and that in their younger years children should acquire the habit of overcoming obstacles and difficulties on their own and increasing their energy in order to prepare for the struggles of life.

The children get older and the tenderness and affection that parents continue to give them cause them to become more and more demanding. They often respond to their mother's caresses with unkind rejection, and it is not the children who make an effort to keep their parents in a contented and kindly frame of mind, but the other way around. If the parents do not succeed, they just shrug their shoulders and think: "It will turn out all right eventually." The children grow up in the habit of receiving everything they want from their parents, and their expectations are neither modest nor appropriate! The parents would like to protest but are no longer able to do so. They have long since relinquished their authority, are eventually no longer even asked for permission, and the children do whatever they like.

And that is why we now have a club with the motto: "Away from parents," why a daughter spends a night God knows where, instead of at a ball at a family friend's house, and why young girls wear "flattering and chaste" ski pants and stay away from home to spend nights with young men in hay barns. Such girls are supposed to become wives and mothers. Such young men, who are spoiled from the start by the good life and too much license, who have no moral basis and lack firm character and resilience, are supposed to become pillars of families someday.

But who is more to blame? It is definitely those parents who do not know how to raise their children properly. Thank goodness there are still exceptions. In some families the mothers, who are mostly well-raised daughters themselves, make an impression on their children and know how to maintain decency and propriety in their homes. But they and their children have acquired the reputation of being old-fashioned and dated and are no longer accepted as valuable members of society.

This sad state of affairs must come to an end. But before that can happen, a number of other changes must take place. What we see in the theater, what we read in books, our tastes, our thinking and feeling simply must change. Otherwise things will not improve.

WRITTEN DURING THE FIRST WORLD WAR

Dated Writings

August 4, 1914

I was unable to carry out my plan for the summer! It is true that I have been staying in Edlach since the 8th of July, but I was unable to fulfill my other wish and go to Ahlbeck* to meet my daughter Grete and her children. I already had my ticket and had reserved a sleeping compartment for the 16th of July, but I could not use it because unexpected and unpredictable world events made long-distance travel seem unwise.

So I am still here in Edlach, deeply worried and out of sorts. Up to now I have worried incessantly about my children's livelihood. Brioni and Edlach have filled all of my thoughts. But today I cannot help realizing that many things that seem great and meaningful, that dominate our thoughts, worries, and striving, things that trouble us day and night can turn into nothing and lose their substance very quickly, while all of our hopes and expectations now culminate in prayers for health and life for all of our loved ones.

As I mentioned before, Brioni had caused months of serious difficulties. There were troubling times, but eventually a satisfying certainty seemed to come. Dr. Alfred Neumann, my son-in-law, found some friends who would put up enough capital for Edlach, and a decisive letter that rejected the proposal was written to Director Kuppelwieser. On Sunday July 26th a contract was discussed by the owner of the Edlach nursing home, the imperial councilor Dr. Konried, and the representative of the newly founded company *Edlach Sanatorium*, Dr. Robert Heller. It was agreed that the contract would be completed and signed by the two parties within a few days.

That was on Sunday, July 26, 1914. A day earlier, on Saturday, July 25th, late in the evening the news had arrived that Serbia would not accept the conditions that were set by the Austro-Hungarian Empire following the assassination in Sarajevo. Everyone hoped that the contention between the Serbs and us would remain localized. As a precaution, however, the clarified world situation was taken into consideration in the agreements with regard to Edlach.

Only nine days have passed since then, and it now seems to me that all of my worries about Brioni, Edlach, and my children's livelihood were insignificant trivialities. Much larger and deeper apprehensions fill me now, because as a result of the war my son-in-law Alfred has been called up to serve as a physician at the field hospital in Posada-Chyrowska near Premyzl in Galicia.

He departed from Vienna on Sunday, August 2, 1914. Agnes accompanied her husband to Vienna and helped him make all the necessary purchases and preparations for the journey. They both demonstrated their great strength of character by steadfastly keeping their composure as they said good-bye. Their great love for each other made that all the more difficult. They outdid each other in showing their strength and willpower as they each attempted not to make the farewell even more difficult for the other and separated with seeming calmness and composure.

Agnes is back in Edlach now, and I am staying with her. Our only joy and distraction is our little Otto. Otherwise we are understandably very depressed.

For the child's sake we intend to stay in the country for as long as possible, despite the fact that we are practically cut off from the rest of the world. Postal, telegraph, and telephone services are extremely limited. As a result of the mobilization, the rail services have come to an almost complete standstill, and we are both endlessly impatient until six o'clock in the evening, waiting to see if there is anything in the only mail that does get through, and if so, what it might be.

August 6, 1914

My daughter Grete and her two sons Heinz and Paul have finally returned to Vienna from Ahlbeck, after a very long, uncomfortable, but extremely "interesting" journey. For a long time I have heard nothing from my son Konrad, who made a trip to Sweden, but we have received some postcards that were mailed along the way by my son-in-law Alfred. I also just learned that Dr. Alfred Jungmann, my niece Vally's husband, was called up to serve at a military hospital in Zenika in Bosnia, even though he is the senior physician and head of the lupus clinic in Vienna. Owing to a bad case of influenza he was allowed to take eight days of leave. Both sons of my brother Julius, two sons of my sister-in-law Erna, my nephew Siegmund Jeiteles, and the son of my niece Sophie Weishut have enlisted. My son Konrad must report for duty on the 6th of September.

But I also have brothers and sisters-in-law, as well as a nephew, Victor Schwenk, in Paris. They are all naturalized French citizens. My nephew is definitely eligible for military service. I think that he is even an officer, and he will certainly be in the army. It is quite possible that he will have to fight the brother of his own wife, a young woman from Alsace, whom he married two years ago. Her brother enlisted in the German army and is therefore Victor's "enemy."

This horrendous war is bound to plunge thousands of families into misery and untold grief.

August 11, 1914

On the ninth of this month my daughter Grete wrote the following: "Alfred Jungmann left yesterday morning. Since he suffered from influenza and sinusitis, he looked very ill, and I am not sure that he has quite recovered. He and Vally were very brave when they parted. Konrad has arrived safely. He looks fabulous.

August 13, 1914

On the eleventh of August my brother-in-law Georg Jeiteles wrote that he had received good news from his son-in-law Alfred Jungmann from along the way, and that his son Siegmund is stationed at Theresienstadt* for the time being.

August 19, 1914

We are all inconsolable about the dreadful loss that Vally - and our whole family with her - suffered in the death of our dear Alfred Jungmann.

The way that fate caught up with him is really tragic. He departed from Vienna on the eighth of August with his health not fully restored. His wife and family entreated him to apply for an extension of his leave, but his sense of duty drove him to leave. It seems that he survived the journey quite well and arrived safe and sound at his destination, Zenika in Bosnia. From there he sent comforting reports home, with the cheerful message to his wife that upon his arrival there he had received official orders to leave for home immediately and return to his post as head of the lupus clinic, where he was the driving force. He was going to rest at Zenika for one day before starting the journey home. But those reports did not arrive in Vienna until he himself was no longer alive. On the journey home, he became dangerously ill and arrived at Fünfkirchen (Pecs, Hungary) nearly unconscious. He was met there and taken to a hospital by doctors who had been notified by telegraph on the 14th of August. He died there the next morning, on Saturday, the 15th of August.

On Sunday, the 16th of August, at six-thirty in the morning poor Vally received the terrible news by telegram. It instantly crushed her. However, her personality and energy did not permit her to remain overcome with grief for more than a short time. She hurried to various administrative offices, partly in order to find out additional details, but primarily to acquire the necessary papers and authorization to travel to Fünfkirchen immediately, in order to be present at her dear husband's funeral. She also had enough composure and presence of mind to ask for travel authorization for her father, George Jeiteles, at the same time, because she was certain that he would want to accompany her on the trip. They both left Vienna at midday on Sunday.

August 25, 1914

Yesterday I arrived in Vienna with Agnes and her little boy, Otto. Our stay in Edlach had become quite intolerable. The reports from Alfred that we had so fervently longed for were experiencing terrible delays, and our desire to return home in order to be closer to events could not be repressed any longer. So we arrived in Vienna with all of our worries, our pain, and our hope.

My first visit was to poor Vally. She had just returned from Fünfkirchen with her father. There she had seen her dear husband one last time and had been present with her father at the funeral. They were supposed to leave the next day, but due to all the turmoil she had a violent attack of vomiting and diarrhea. My brother-in-law was happy to be able to postpone their return trip until the next day.

I have seen her now and cannot find words for the grief that she is suffering over the loss of her dearly beloved husband. May time gently help her to overcome her sorrow! The untimely death of a man who was held in such high esteem and so competent in his field is an irreparable tragedy. Alfred's old mother deeply mourns the loss of her son. He was everything to her, her pride and joy. And Vally's parents are also grieving deeply.

October 9, 1914

We live in a time of constant excitement. If we took the time to reflect calmly, we would be surprised that we are able to bear it all. Is it reality or a dream that such a terrible war is going on, one that brings misery and worry to each and every family and has no end in sight?

Just over two months have passed since nearly all of Europe was thrown into a state of war. What varying impressions have taken hold of us during that time! First we felt outraged at the impudent rejection of the demands that were made after the horrible assassination in Sarajevo. We were indignant that Russia sided with those who had committed regicide and promised to support them. We were shocked by England's shameful dealings, which, under the guise of mediation, were largely responsible for the outbreak of the war. But we were also worried that those three great powers, England, Russia, and France, together with Belgium, Serbia, and Montenegro, would unite against Germany and us.

And as if that was not enough, they have even called on the Japanese for help. All colonies are required to send whatever forces they can spare to fight against us, and there are brown, yellow, and black soldiers mustered against us.

We find consolation and support in our awareness that Germany is on our side and that there is a strong tie of unalterable loyalty between us. There is also the conviction that we are fighting for a just cause and that we have been forced to take up arms. But we must not forget that the continual armed insurrections and political crises of the last few years became so intolerable that a radical resolution of the situation was absolutely inevitable.

Initially, after the declaration of war by Austria, when all men who were fit for battle were called up for military service, we were all iron-serious and rock-calm. We could see that our loved ones were heading into an uncertain, dangerous future, but we kept our strength and faith intact. But soon the seriousness was joined by hope when the powerful forces of the German army and navy brought us unexpected early victories.

Another important event also contributed greatly to our reassurance. In 1908, after the annexation of Bosnia and Herzegovina, we had discovered that our Slavic nations did not support our determined course of action against Serbia. Some military units even refused to move to the border. Even worse could be expected now that we were fighting not just against Serbia, but against the "beloved, holy Russia."

Then the Slavic parliamentarians, first and foremost the Czech Kramarz, had openly and candidly voiced their disapproval in the sharpest manner, in both the Imperial Council and the parliament, and had demanded that we receive Russia with open arms. All Slavic party organs had spoken with great spite and agitation against the traditional German cultural influences in Austria. Their proclamations bordered on high treason.

For decades our government had pampered the Czechs and Slavs and - ever since Belcredi* and Taaffe* - strengthened their megalomania. No wonder they were doing all they could to employ the catchword of equality to suppress everything German in Austria. We now had real reasons to fear that events similar to and far worse than the ones in 1908 would arise, and that internal unrest would be added to the outward threat of war. We were very much aware that our enemies were counting on the destruction of Austria by inner conflict in the face of a war with Russia.

Yet the exact opposite occurred, and the populace's healthy common sense came to the fore, in contrast to the criminal activities of the people's representatives and the demagogues and their institutions. The state of war prevented the Russian emissaries from continuing their covert activities. Some of them were even put behind bars. But the people went their own way and there is now total harmony among all of the nations in Austria-Hungary.

The Czechs fraternize with the Germans. In Prague representatives of both nations unite for ovations in front of the German consulate. Our soldiers of all nationalities go to war together, ready to fight, and everywhere in Austria there is harmony that has not been seen for a long time. The same is true of Hungary, where

Romanian, Serbian, Croatian, and Slavic nations form one people and loyally serve the "Emperor and the Fatherland." And let's not forget the Bosnians and the Herzegovinians, who are also loyal to us.

Let us hope that this war will not just bring victory, but that it will also succeed in bringing peace and unity back to our beloved Austria, and that we will achieve strong and healthy development in the future!

The mood in a very nervous Vienna reflected the events of the war and changed accordingly. The terrible anxiety that dominated everything initially was soon followed by great hope. Several positive reports arrived in quick succession, and people began to believe that more great victories could be expected every day and every hour. Thousands of people constantly besieged the Ministry of War, where the crowd did not disperse until long after midnight and was disappointed not to be able to bring home news of another great victory. But when more good news did arrive, the jubilation went on forever. The national anthem, *"Die Wacht am Rhein,"* and other patriotic songs were sung with enthusiasm, and young and old, rich and poor were united in their elation.

But soon enough a time came when we heard little or no news from either our own or the German army. That left a lot of room for speculation. The most unbelievable and pessimistic rumors were spread. One person had heard "it" from an officer friend, another from a cousin, or from an influential official in the Foreign Ministry. A third was even present when it was read aloud in the mayor's office, and people believed it all and told "it" to the whole world "in confidence." Many otherwise sensible and calm individuals lost their heads and rushed off to obtain passports in order to be able to leave quickly, if necessary.

Times of war often produce such great "strategists," who boast of their knowledge in coffee houses and at family gatherings, as well as politicians and "diplomats," who impose their "total conviction" on everyone while explaining what really should have been done and how obvious it was that the applied tactics were completely wrong. Such people also predict what will happen now because of mistakes that have been made. Given the national tendency toward pessimism and negative criticism, these know-it-alls find willing listeners and have the satisfaction of having produced feelings of fear.

At a point when there was no news, a carelessly written official communiqué* appeared, one that could be interpreted in different ways, just not in a manner that put people's minds at rest. As a result, everyone was terribly worried, and the people who spread the worst rumors were readily believed.

Things have improved now that our army's great success has revived people's sense of safety and trust. Even the Russian siege of Lemberg (Lvov) was taken relatively calmly. The invasion of the Carpathian Mountains and of Hungary did not cause any great unrest, because the enemy was soon beaten back and suffered great losses. The situation on the eastern and western fronts can be viewed as favorable. We are all filled with hope for a quick and happy end to this unique world war, and by the desire to welcome our loved ones home again. That is all that we pray for.

So far we have received reassuring reports about our close family members. At long last we received a letter from Alfred. He worked for a long period as chief physician in the field hospital at Chyrow-Posada and seems to have been very popular there. We learned that fact from the wife of one of the officers who were stationed in Chyrow. She had been forced to leave because of the Russian advance and came to see us in Vienna. According to Alfred's description, his stay in Chyrow was apparently quite interesting, particularly in the beginning.

He had never been in the army, and life as a soldier was quite new to him. As chief physician he held the rank of lieutenant and was initially surprised when the other officers addressed him with the familiar form "*du*" and he was forced to do the same. He was received in a friendly manner, which is hardly astonishing in light of Alfred's personality and character. He was asked by the officers to accompany them on visits to the surrounding countryside and ended up traveling a fair distance on a locomotive. Another time he rode a horse for the first time in his life, after first finding out about all of its peculiarities.

At the beginning of his stay in Chyrow he had very little to do. Together with another officer he lived in the first-class waiting room at the train station. His sleep was always only very brief because the waiting room also served as an office. Interviews with spies and other suspicious individuals were conducted there until late into the night.

Later he was given a small apartment at the hospital. He had it disinfected and renovated because he intended to have his wife come and work with him as a nurse. But the events of the war prevented that. Nevertheless, Alfred had the place furnished as comfortably as possible, took his breakfast and evening meal there, and made it his home.

But there was soon hard work for him to do. Trains full of injured soldiers arrived day and night. He examined them all, and some of them were sent on for treatment while others remained there for him to treat. After Alfred had been in Chyrow for a good month and a half, he received an order by telegraph to arrange everything necessary for an immediate departure to Homona (Hungary). From six in the evening until two the next morning he packed his furniture and medical equipment. The next morning he began the journey to Homona with his staff and the luggage, which filled two railroad cars. The distance from Chyrow to Homona is about ninety or a hundred kilometers. Under normal circumstances an ordinary passenger train covers the distance in just less than three hours, but this trip took all of sixty-five hours!

The journey was an extremely tedious one. *Before* each station there was a delay of several hours, sometimes as much as twelve hours. Fortunately they were able to pick up some canned food along the way. Otherwise his poor soldiers would have had to suffer from hunger as well as from cold during the trip.

At one of the stations, after the train had been standing there for more than three hours, Alfred was asked by an official to leave the train and go with him to the stationmaster, who intended to detach Alfred's railway cars from the train and attach them to the next one. Imagine Alfred's shock, when barely half a minute after he had disembarked his train left with his two railway cars!

Fortunately, another train departed in the same direction a short time later. Alfred hoped to catch up with his train at the next station, but the train that he now rode also stopped *before* each station. He therefore had to make a phone call from a gatekeeper's house and ask that "his" train wait for him. After a two-hour walk he was finally reunited with "his" staff and luggage.

Alfred found pleasant, clean quarters with some nice people in Homona. He felt very comfortable there. The tidy little town had electric lighting, concrete sidewalks, a nice coffee house, and compared with Chyrow it seemed like a big city. He even happened to meet some physician friends and spent a few quiet, pleasant days waiting for new orders.

He was first sent to Eperjes (Hungary) and then on to Magyar-Pleszkawicza. Today we received the news that he was sent back to Homona, where he will probably find some professional work waiting for him.

March 9, 1915

After a long period of time I once again want to write down my thoughts and account for how the times have affected me, how I have lived, and what I have thought and felt.

People always say that the present era is a *great* one. Perhaps that is also because we have great worries and great tasks to accomplish.

I also wish to point out the *great* willingness to make sacrifices that has been demonstrated by men who are fit for battle. They go to war and fulfill their duty faithfully. But the big question is: How many of them follow the flag out of pure enthusiasm, and how many of them do it out of a sheer sense of duty, because they have to?

There is also a *great* willingness to sacrifice among all classes in the general population, young and old - with the exception of a large part of our high nobility, our high clergy, and our nationalistic populace in Bohemia. The voluntary donations to lighten the load of all those who have enlisted and all who have been affected by the war are reaching astronomical heights. The contributions of love, the welfare institutions - all of these things show a nearly boundless willingness to sacrifice. In particular I want to point out the active contribution of our women and young girls. They work day and night in selfless devotion, some of them at the sickbeds of injured soldiers, others sharing the countless tasks of help and support that contribute to the welfare of everyone.

But this era that is celebrated as "great" must also be experienced by every thoughtful and feeling person as an incredibly great disappointment. Nine months ago, who would have thought possible things that have become cruel reality today? We live in a time of the most splendid discoveries in the areas of hygiene, technology, and many other fields, discoveries that astound the whole world, a time when the most strenuous efforts are being made to prepare for peace in the entire world. We live in a time when all nations that claim to be civilized established and expanded the peace conference in The Hague. Then suddenly a catastrophe breaks over us, one that everyone would have thought impossible, would have expected to be utterly unthinkable, a catastrophe that surpasses by far any brutality and cruelty that was ever committed in the Middle Ages.

This slaughter of millions of people has now lasted for more than seven months, and the whole world watches the spectacle with a fatalistic calm that is utterly incomprehensible.

It was different at first, of course. Then our nerves vibrated in feverish excitement. Day and night we waited for reports of a decision. Each victory created the highest expectations, each defeat the most profound pain. But now it is all different, because the larger and smaller successes that are achieved by our side make only a passing impression. The enormous numbers of soldiers in the enemy armies do not permit us to expect a final result any time soon. Hindenburg alone captured more than 200,000 Russian prisoners. And what good did it do? Russia continues to send more and more troops. A large portion of France and Belgium is occupied by German troops, but France and Britain are a long way from having exhausted their resources. The same hope for victory that we entertain also keeps our enemies fighting. Under such circumstances, how can we take pleasure in the daily news of small successes?

What is more, in these seven months it has gotten to the point that trade, industry, and general prosperity in the whole world are severely threatened. Worst of all is the fact that almost all of Europe has had to be put on meager rations. Noble Britain plans to starve both us and Germany.

Hypocritical France, once a representative of human rights, now sides with one of the most brutal and cruel countries of all, Russia, and together the two of them hope to wipe out our culture. Why? To what end? The answer must fill each thinking and feeling person with fury and disgust: Common envy, greed, and revenge are the causes of all of the misery that we have thus far endured and are likely to endure for quite some time to come.

We did not threaten England, France, or Russia. Trade, industry, and prosperity flourished in all of those countries. The most despicable emotions caused the beginning of this war.

Now I ask myself when and how this war will come to an end. My answer is not very comforting, because in my view none of the warring parties will give in as long as they have not been utterly defeated, both physically and materially. And that could take a long time. But I hope for an unexpected event that will break over us with vehement force!

As for me, at the moment I live through the days from the morning paper to the evening paper, but the hours actually pass by rapidly for me. That is probably because my hopes and desires are directed towards certain goals, but not within a certain timeframe. One week passes after another and life winds away uniformly and uneventfully. My one great joy and distraction is Otto, my youngest grandson, whom I have taken into my heart completely and with whom I spend a lot of time.

May 30, 1915

On the 22nd of April my son-in-law Alfred wrote that he had fallen on the third of the month and sprained his foot. He had been in the hospital since then and was due to arrive in Vienna very soon to recuperate completely. We did not worry about him and believed his words, because we had previously always received good reports from him.

He arrived in Vienna on the 25th of April, and we learned that it was not a fall and a sprain, but rather a shot in the leg that had caused his injury. It was no enemy's bullet that injured him, but rather the foolishness and inattention of a fellow officer.

On the evening of April 3rd, Alfred had been sitting around with a number of officers. Some of them were playing cards and Alfred was watching the game. One of the officers, named Ronay Aladar, took his pistol apart. After he had cleaned it and put it back together, a shot was fired. It was no accident. With a number of officers present, Mr. Ronay saw fit to try out his pistol inside the room. That practice shot hit Alfred in the right thigh. He was taken to the hospital the next day, but before that the commanding officer, who was present during the whole event, made out a report about the incident.

This is what the report said:
Royal and Imperial Ammunition Depot Division Number 38, Extra H 79 - K1915
Report
Present: The persons mentioned.
Report about the injury of Dr. Alfred Neumann, Assistant Physician, stationed at Ammunition Depot Number 38.
On April 3, 1915, in Matkow, the above mentioned person was wounded in the right thigh by a pistol that was shot in the presence of the undersigned. Due to the inattention of an officer, the pistol was accidentally discharged during cleaning.
Matkow, April 4, 1915. Witness: —
Name of the offender: Ronay Aladar
Commanding Officer's Seal

The remarkable thing is that the same Ronay Aladar is known to have committed a similar act of foolishness in the past. In addition, several reports of maltreatment were filed against him by soldiers. Those will probably not be investigated until after the war.

July 30, 1915
Alfred's wound has healed well. Even though the bullet is still lodged between flesh and bone, he has no difficulty walking. He had to report back on the eleventh of July. As a consequence of the investigation that occurred, he can serve only in a hospital, not in the field.
Alfred's wife and son stayed in Edlach during the summer, and I also spent several months there.

November 15, 1915

I also want to mention that at the beginning of October Alfred was awarded the Golden Cross of Merit with the crown on the ribbon, with the medal for bravery attached.

We received only unofficial news that my brother-in-law Adolph had died in Paris on the 5th of October.

Just imagine the worries and depression that every foreigner living in France must feel.

Adolph Schwenk and his wife were born in Bohemia, but they lived in Paris for more than forty years. They are naturalized French citizens, but they did not dare to write even a single line to their Austrian relatives.

December 31, 1915

The Operation

Tomorrow is New Year's Day. Three days ago I returned home after spending nearly two weeks in the hospital in order to undergo an operation. For the doctors it was only a minor one, and everyone who wanted to make it easier for me said the same thing. My children and I, however, worried about the outcome. After all, for a man of nearly seventy-four years, whose heart no longer functions normally, and who has suffered from bronchial catarrh for years, any operation is serious.

The whole thing came out of the blue like a flash of lightning. I had been confined to my room for a while with a fever and a cold, but had begun to feel better. Then, on the tenth of December, I noticed a sizeable lump in my groin, which had not been there before. Since it did not hurt at all and did not bother me, I thought that it was just a temporary swelling, but I did call my personal physician anyway.

He came to examine me and found that I had a hernia. He told me that I would have to wear a special bandage, but that he could not give me any more details until the next day. The next morning, after a thorough examination, Dr. Pollak told me that he did not wish to make a diagnosis on his own, but that he wanted to refer me to a surgeon. That same evening Professor Schnitzler* came to my house with my doctor. After examining me thoroughly they said that an operation was imperative, albeit not immediately. That notification understandably made me rather nervous.

The next morning, on a Sunday, I was quite calm and composed again. I reflected on the fact that I had actually reached the ripe old age of nearly seventy-four, that I had already exceeded the average human age, and that everything in the world had to come to an end. At least I would not have to face the final end a second time if something went wrong with the operation.

For quite some time I have been aware that even on reasonably healthy days my mood is troubled by the fact that I am not satisfied with what I do or do not do. I still have too much energy for my age but am forced to spend my days in more or less busy idleness. I no longer have any ambitions, but on the other hand I also know that I am not physically strong enough for any serious occupations. I do not sleep well. My digestion is not good, and I have a sore foot, which makes walking difficult. Those are all reasons for my dissatisfaction, and those considerations caused me to begin settling my affairs as if I knew that I had to say farewell to life that Sunday morning.

I sent word to my daughter Agnes, who is currently staying in Hermannstadt (Sibiu, Romania), my son Konrad, who is doing military service, and my brother Julius in Teplitz. My eldest daughter Alice was prevented from coming to see me because her son had just developed scarlet fever and she was busy looking after him.

On the evening of Wednesday, the fifteenth of December, my daughter Grete accompanied me to the *Fürth Clinic*. Up to that moment I had been calm and composed. But then at the hospital I was overcome by a sudden nervousness that revealed itself in an irregular heartbeat. The tension of the situation and the awareness that I was about to take a serious step affected the state of my health. My daughter's presence, however, had an extremely calming effect on me, and when Dr. Pollak came to give me a sedative, my equanimity returned. I had a small but delicious supper, spent some time talking with my daughter Grete and my son-in-law Robert, and went to bed at around nine o'clock.

After that, Grete spent three days and nights with me, even though I had my own nurse looking after me as well. I cannot thank her enough for her selfless devotion. I had quite a good night's sleep and awaited the operation without apprehension. It was due to take place on Thursday morning at just after eight o'clock. Robert came back to see me early in the morning, and my children's presence contributed much to my feeling of calmness.

The head physician at the sanatorium, Dr. E., gave me a morphine injection at half past seven. I felt its effect right away. First my right hand went numb, and soon after that I felt my whole body slacken, and an indescribable weariness came over me. Nevertheless, I saw and heard what went on, but with a feeling of great detachment.

First Dr. Pollak arrived, then Professor Schnitzler, followed by two helpers who moved me from my bed to a gurney, then into the elevator, and from there to the operating room. Even there I knew exactly what was going on and what was being said. On the one hand the morphine injection made me drowsy, but on the other hand it was not a strong enough anesthetic to put me to sleep completely. Then I was lying on the operating table and the anesthetist asked me to count. I got as far as thirty-five, at which point I felt a sensation as though someone were making two pencil marks on the spot where I was to have the operation. Then I lost consciousness altogether.

After a short while I regained a somewhat dull consciousness. On the way back to my room from the operating room I already expressed my satisfaction at how totally painless the operation had been. From the look in my children's eyes, I could see that the operation had been a success, and I was pleased about that for their sakes as well as for my own.

The first few days after the operation were quite unpleasant. First I experienced nausea caused by the anesthetic, but that lasted for only a few hours. Then my mouth and my throat felt very dry, and that was alleviated only by repeated gargling with ice-cold soda water. Last but not least, I was forced to remain immobile in bed for days with a heavy bandage. But the worst thing about it was a strong urge to cough. I refused to give in to it because each time I coughed I felt a sharp pain in my incision. The fact that I had not eaten for nearly two days did not bother me at all.

On the third day after the operation the bronchial catarrh came back, and the faces around me were looking a little more serious. The doctors instructed me not to suppress the coughing, no matter how much it hurt. I was given several injections of pine essence and had to inhale some oxygen as well. The effect of all of that was that the bronchial catarrh disappeared after two or three days. The doctors and my children were very pleased about that, but *only I* was aware of the pain that I suffered due to the coughing! Three days after the operation I was given the first little bit of food, and after that I had nothing at all to complain about with regard to food and drink. I was given more than I could consume.

On the fifth day the bandage was removed. The incision was healing well. I was bandaged again more lightly and a little more freedom of movement was allowed. On the sixth day I was able to spend a whole hour out of bed in a lounge chair. By then I also knew that I had survived the operation and I imagined the enormous relief that a younger man must feel, one who still must work and provide for his family, when he returns to life after surviving the danger. I kept my state of mind even and calm, as befits a seventy-four-year-old. But the sympathy that I received from friends and family did me a world of good. I was particularly pleased that my brother Julius and his wife came from Teplitz to see me. By then I was already out of bed to receive them.

I stayed at the sanatorium until the 28th of December. For the last two days my mood was very much affected by the huge bill that they handed me, but it had to be paid.

My daughter Grete had taken me to the sanatorium, and it was also she who took me back home. A wave of contentedness came over me when I crossed the threshold.

Tomorrow is New Year's Day. Let us hope for peace in the world and the best for me and my family.

A Strange Coincidence

A hilarious story comes to mind that I have not yet reported. It happened to me a long time ago, when I was a young man and traveled regularly to Paris and London.

I remember a very peculiar incident. In those days we had a commissioner in Paris, a certain M. Hirsch.* There would not be much to say about that man, and certainly not a lot of good things, but his wife Helene was Heinrich Heine's niece, the one whom the poet called "his blonde Lene"! Her maiden name was van Embden-Heine, and as far as her upbringing and education were concerned she was absolutely unsuited to her husband. She was not pretty, but very eager to please.

It was the era of Napoleon III, when "all of France" led a very easygoing life and the German Jews who lived there thought that they had to keep up with that lifestyle. Hirsch introduced me into several French-German households. I found excessive luxury and a happy-go-lucky attitude there, but that did not mean that we were not very well entertained.

That kind of lifestyle had an effect not just on the master but also on the mistress of the house. There seemed to be extremely "free and easy" behavior in their house. The wife did not take her husband's affairs too seriously and liked to chat with Monsieur Flachfeld, her husband's former associate, who was an elderly bachelor.

I was often invited to the Hirsch home because our professional ties were close and we were on friendly terms.

I want to describe two experiences here.

One afternoon I arrived at my hotel in Paris after a very unpleasant crossing from London, during which I had successfully "conquered" my seasickness. There was a letter from Hirsch waiting for me at the hotel. He knew that I would be arriving and invited me for dinner that same evening. It was his wife's birthday, and he had invited a few friends to the party.

I decided to accept the invitation. I freshened up and changed my clothes appropriately, went out to buy a nice box of chocolates as a present for the lady of the house, and arrived at the appointed time.

Several guests were already there, and I was delighted to find myself sitting at the table next to some beautiful and charming ladies, with whom I conducted a lively conversation. First the soup was served, followed by the cold cuts, and we all ate with relish while chatting cheerfully. But after that - oh, what a shock - a huge fish was served. The strong odor made me feel quite squeamish as soon as it was brought into the room. But when I finally had a piece of it on the plate in front of me, my insides rebelled so much that everything that I had held back at sea now pushed its way out with enormous force. I jumped up from my seat in horror but did not manage to leave the room before my pain had "expressed itself"!

What a frightful experience! Everyone there was horrified. The host rushed to my side, but I hurried back to my hotel room, filled with pain and shame, and spent a sleepless night there.

That is what happens when you try to demonstrate your ability to conquer the elements. Had I been more compliant, I would have spared myself such a disgrace.

All that happened in 1869. In May of 1870 I was in Paris again for the last time before the Franco-Prussian War, but there was no mention of war then. That was the last time I saw Hirsch. All Germans were expelled from France because of the war, but afterward I heard only unpleasant things about him. The war, or his expulsion, to be precise, apparently suited him quite well. Life in Paris had become a bit too precarious for him anyway. Debts that he could not pay continued to mount up. That way he escaped from them and moved the scene of his shady business activities to Berlin. He apparently died there not much later.

In 1913, I spent the summer holidays with my children Robert and Grete and their sons at Ahlbeck on the Baltic. One day we decided to go on an excursion to a place called Swinemünde, which was not far away. I went there in a horse-drawn coach with my grandson Paul and his cousin Etienne* (the grandson of my sister-in-law Tony Schwenk in Paris), who was visiting us at the time. Robert, Grete, and Heinz followed us on foot. Even before we arrived in Swinemünde, a great thunderstorm struck, culminating in a tremendous downpour. When we arrived in Swinemünde, there was no room in the café where we had arranged to meet, because it was filled with people in search of shelter.

As we tried to find seats to sit down, I saw a table where a group of ladies were sitting together, but where there was still some space for the three of us. The ladies moved a bit closer together and we were able to sit down. My grandson Paul ended up sitting next to a very old lady. She asked him how it was that he was still on vacation, since school had already started in Germany in the middle of August. Paul replied that he was Viennese. The old lady then turned to me and asked me if I was from Vienna as well. Then she told me that she had lived there herself for several years, that she had excellent memories of it, and that she still corresponded with her relatives there. When I asked for the name of her relatives, she named the Heine-Geldern family. Puzzled, I asked her: "Did you know a Mrs. Helene Hirsch, née Heine, and could you tell me if that lady, whose house I often visited in Paris, is still alive?" The old lady looked at me in surprise and said: "Just who are you? I am the woman whom you are asking about." Touché!

Together we reminisced about the old days. She told me that all of the ladies at the table were her daughters, granddaughters, and great-granddaughters. During our conversation she also inquired about Monsieur Jacques Flachfeld, and we finally ended up talking about that unfortunate evening that we both remembered so vividly!

May 9, 1917 - My 75th Birthday

This terrible world war makes us bitter. It spoils our pleasure in everything. Even people who do not have any other duties find it hard to summon the energy to do things that once gave them great joy and pleasure. Thus I, too, have not touched this book for nearly a year and a half.

Today, however, stirred up by my birthday, which was yesterday, I feel the urge to write down my thoughts and feelings. I completed my 75th year yesterday, apparently "in good physical health and mentally alert," as they say.

But the reality is quite different. I can feel my mental powers wane. I am getting forgetful and act like I am in a dream. I notice that I can hardly remember things that took place a couple of hours, a couple of days, or a few weeks ago, and if I do, it is all so vague. But what I find most strange is that events from my youth, things that happened a very long time ago, are firmly lodged in my memory. That is evidence that my mental powers are fading, and it demonstrates the effect of the years. And as far as physical well-being is concerned, almost everything pertaining to it continues to fade. My body has shrunk; my weight is incredibly low; sleep and digestion leave a lot to be desired. Irritation, weariness, and lack of energy are taking over. So much for my physical condition! Still, I have little to complain about. Despite all the sadness and great sorrow, despite the frequent and serious illnesses that afflicted me, I was blessed to be able to celebrate my birthday in seemingly good physical condition and mental alertness, surrounded by those who are dear to me. Seventy-five years have passed, and the time that is left to me by human estimation is presumably short. All I can wish for in that span of time, and far beyond, has to do with the well-being and happiness of my children and grandchildren.

Children and grandchildren, brothers and sisters-in-law, and my nephews and nieces all came and brought me their congratulations yesterday. The so-called feast was a simple afternoon coffee. The war, the general hardship, and the inflation make it impossible to celebrate even a rare feast day in any but the simplest manner. Even the many gifts that I received bore the marks of war and difficult times. They gave me great joy, however, because they were exactly what I needed most urgently and what I wished for most.

To be sure, on my 70th birthday I was offered gifts of a different kind: rugs, paintings, flowers, and all sorts of beautiful things that we can live without. Yesterday was different: flour and beans, sugar, cocoa and chocolate, eggs and potatoes, condensed milk, canned food, and all kinds of other food items covered the table that I contemplated with great joy and contentment. Times have changed enormously. Who would have thought five years ago that anything like this was possible? Who would not have expected such presents to cause offense? But still, such times have occurred before, and "there is nothing new under the sun."

During the time of Napoleon's reign there was great hardship in Germany. Food items were the most popular gifts and were received just as gratefully as they are today. My children's and relatives' gifts of love relieve me of the effort of having to go out and obtain foodstuff for a while, and that is a great advantage for a man who lives by himself these days.

Heller & Thewett Exports

Through my long years of business dealings with the company *Ed. Kanitz & Co., Exports* in Vienna, I was acquainted with Mr. Louis Thewett, its managing clerk. One morning he came to see me with the proposal that we join him in starting an export business in Vienna. I knew him to be a competent businessman, an expert in his domain, and well liked by most of his clients - or rather, those of *Kanitz & Co*. Nevertheless, I asked for time to think about it and made inquiries, the results of which put my mind at rest. Since I did not have a business of my own at the time, soon after that, in the summer of 1888, our company, *Heller & Thewett, Exports*, began to operate.

Our main markets were in North and South America, England, and France. Within a short period of time our firm developed so well that after a few years we were one of the most important companies in the field and operated with great success.

In 1889, Mr. Thewett made a trip to North America. It turned out to be very successful because he established contacts with a number of prominent import businesses.

Our company grew. Russian, British, and French establishments turned to us of their own accord, and we felt great satisfaction in seeing our efforts well rewarded. But the way in which we worked would not be possible today.

We and all of our personnel stayed at work from seven o'clock in the morning until midnight, summer and winter, taking only a short break of two hours for lunch. Sometimes we thought that we could not cope with it. But we had in mind the acquisition of more trade relations that were based in New York. For that purpose, Mr. Thewett decided to travel to North America once more at the end of 1896. He never came back from that journey.

He boarded the steamship *Elbe* in Bremen on January 5, 1897. The next morning at five o'clock it collided with the Dutch coal freighter *Creytby* in the Channel and sank. Only sixteen people, most of them sailors, were saved. Thewett went down with the ship.

His death came as a great shock to me. Thanks to his long years of experience, his many personal contacts with clients and manufacturers, and his thorough knowledge of products, Thewett was definitely the most important person in the company, and it was largely due to his competence that we were so successful.

My contribution was mostly limited to correspondence and bookkeeping. Thewett always seemed to get irritated whenever there was more than a fleeting contact between me and a client. He was petty and jealous and seemed always afraid that I would turn into a competitor.

Now he was dead. The company had lost its main driving force, and I saw a huge task ahead of me in keeping it afloat. After

I had gotten over the initial shock, I came to the conclusion that I was quite capable of carrying on, if I would just put all of my effort into it and set out with confidence. Even though the extent of my involvement had been limited to internal work until then, I had still kept a constant eye on the transactions. I can state with great satisfaction that our enterprise continued to grow, even after Thewett's death, that our former clients took a liking to me, and that a large number of new ones came to us and put their confidence in us.

Thus *Heller & Thewett* still exists today (1917). I retired from the business on December 31, 1912. My advanced age and my poor health were the reasons. Two employees who worked at my side for almost twenty years own the company now. At their request I gave it to them in exchange for a moderate pension that was calculated on the basis of four years' sales. During the first year of their independent operation (1913) the company was quite successful. Unfortunately, the disastrous war broke out during the second year and brought the export business to a complete standstill. Then, however, the skill and perseverance of the new owners gradually enabled them to find a substitute market and they achieved quite respectable results.

I personally suffered a rather substantial financial loss because of the war. The amount that the new owners were to pay me as compensation was calculated on the basis of a fixed percentage of the sales over four years. But those sales dropped drastically and brought me a much smaller income than I had anticipated. But I have no regrets, considering what it would have cost me if I had still been the owner during the war.

For me, as an elderly, ailing man, it would have been extremely difficult to break new ground. I would have had to continue paying the salaries of all of my employees, especially the high wages of the present owners, Tichy and Klein, and that would have been extremely troublesome for me.

I must view the choice of a favorable moment to transfer my business to others as a very advantageous decision for me. With that, my commercial activities, which began when I was an eleven-year-old boy, came to an end, and I am now able to look back on an honorable past.

THE DOCTORATE OF DR. JONAS JEITTELES*
AT THE UNIVERSITY OF PRAGUE

May 25, 1918

At the house of our friend Hermann Weinberg, I met Mr. Adolf Jellinek, whose company I then often enjoyed. Mr. Jellinek was born in Moravia. He is now eighty-four years old and can look back on a most interesting and successful career. He is a highly intelligent person who is gifted with an admirable memory that allows him to recall events from the distant and the more recent past with incredible accuracy, despite his advanced age. When I was in his company, time passed very quickly and pleasantly.

I now want to relate a very interesting story that he told me, one that dates back to the second half of the eighteenth century. He heard it from his close friend, the late court councilor, Mr. Richard Jeitteles, a senior civil servant, and for many years the managing director of the Ferdinand North Railway. The central figure is a certain Jonas Jeitteles, a great-uncle of Mr. R. Jeitteles.

During the eighteenth century, Jews in Bohemia were not allowed to undertake any medical studies or practice as doctors. They were allowed to go as far as being barbers, to run barber shops, and to apply leeches and suction cups, but they were not permitted to practice legitimate medicine, even if they had acquired the necessary knowledge.

In those days, the above mentioned Mr. Jonas Jeitteles lived in Prague. He was allowed to bear the title of *barber*, but that did not satisfy him. So this highly intelligent man went to Halle in Saxony to attend the university there and complete his medical training, something that was prohibited in his home town and made impossible by the legal situation.

Jeitteles attained his goal, became a medical practitioner, and brought home not only his diploma but also all of the documents that attested to his excellent qualifications. Nevertheless, practicing medicine in Prague was still out of the question, because the degree that he had obtained in Halle was not recognized by the University of Prague. Jeitteles therefore resorted to submitting a petition directly to His Majesty, the Emperor Joseph II, in which he described the prejudice against Jews at the University of Prague. He enclosed his degree and certificates and begged His Majesty to put pressure on the University of Prague to recognize his medical qualifications and no longer prevent him from practicing. He argued that his religion should not deprive him of the right and duty to put his skills and knowledge at the service of suffering humanity.

It was not long until a decree was sent from the Imperial Chancellery to Doctor Jeitteles and to the University of Prague. It was signed by Emperor Joseph himself and said: "...that Jeitteles the Jew, whose degree and excellent qualifications have been submitted to His Majesty, must be given his medical accreditation by the University of Prague. He is not to be prevented in any way from exercising his profession as a medical practitioner and must be treated in exactly the same way as, and as equal to, all other medical practitioners that have received the doctorate at the University of Prague, regardless of their faith..."

That was a severe blow to the rector and the professors. There was great consternation. Long and detailed discussions took place about whether His Majesty's order was to be followed, or how it could be circumvented. After lengthy deliberations, they finally decided to send a strong appeal to His Majesty's secretary, saying: "...that the University of Prague is a Catholic university. Allowing a Jew to obtain a medical degree here would cause not only great excitement but also unrest on the part of the students and the general population, and that following His Majesty's order would call into serious question the reputation of the Catholic University of Prague." In conclusion the main argument was presented: "...that the possibility of granting a medical degree to a Jew is totally out of the question, simply because the person would have to take an oath on the cross, which the Jew Jeitteles would not agree to do, and which the rectorate of the University of Prague would not allow."

After that, the appropriate circles fervently hoped that the submitted arguments were persuasive enough to cause the Emperor to withdraw the decree.

But they were mistaken! The answer from the court was not long in coming. Its contents read: "...that the ceremony recognizing the medical degree of the Jew Jeitteles will take place at a date and time appointed by me. It will be done with the pomp and ceremony that is customary on such occasions. The argument that the University of Prague is a Catholic university is unjustified, if only for the reason that anyone possessing the ability to alleviate suffering should not be excluded from doing so, no matter what their religious confession may be."

It also stated that: "...care must be taken to ensure that the cross atop the rector's staff, on which the oath is to be taken, be removed. In its place, the imperial double-headed eagle shall be attached forthwith.

"With respect to the fear of any possible unrest during the ceremony, caused by students or the general population, the Imperial Chancellery has taken the following precautions: Simultaneous with the issuing of this decree an order is being sent to the military headquarters in Prague. On the day of the ceremony, they are to send a military detachment accompanied by musicians. The detachment is to be of a size appropriate to ensure that order is maintained inside and outside the university by whatever means are necessary."

The decree ended with the notation: "...that the Jew Jeitteles shall receive a letter to the same effect, and any counterargument by the university will be disregarded."

That is how the Jew Jeitteles was awarded his medical degree under the protection of military forces. It was a most solemn ceremony and proceeded without any disruptions on the day and at the time appointed by the Emperor's chancellor. Thus Jeitteles was the first Jew to have a medical degree recognized in Prague and to have all privileges of a medical practitioner conferred upon him. That paved the way for many "scientific luminaries" of the Jewish faith to serve suffering mankind.

EPILOGUE

Our grandfather's notes go as far as May of 1918. How can we finish this book? Only with suppositions and reflections on the period immediately after the war. Our parents undoubtedly did everything within their power to make their dear ailing father's last years as comfortable and as warm as possible. His youngest daughter Agnes, our mother, had cared for her father at all times, had even accompanied him during his travels, and must have been very attached to him.

When the Austrians had to endure the breakdown of the Monarchy at the end of the war, when the foundations of the state were shattered by political upheavals followed by inflation and - particularly in Vienna - a period of starvation, our parents took the lonely old man with them to the country as a matter of course.

In those days our father, Dr. Alfred Neumann, *was the chief physician at the* Konried Sanatorium *in Edlach, a mountainous area. He later practiced at the* Friedmann Medical Bath *at the well-known thermal spa Vöslau-Gainfarn in the vicinity of Baden, near Vienna in the southern Vienna Woods.*

Our grandfather ceased writing at that time, but we can imagine the thoughts and fears that those upheavals produced in him. If he had written them down, it would have made his children "fainthearted," as he himself put it. He did not want that, and so he kept his worries to himself. He maintained his composure in the face of the inevitable.

For a few years he lived quietly in the house of his daughter and her children - my brother Otto and me - under the medical supervision of our father, to whom he had become very close. Those peaceful years were the best that he could have hoped for under circumstances that were difficult to endure, even out in the country.

Naturally, I did not know about any of that. All I remember now is that I went for walks with him in those days, when I was about three and a half years old. I also remember climbing up on his bed each morning to give him a little kiss...and that one morning, when I did that, I was surprised that he did not open his eyes...something that I, of course, could not understand....

Antonie Neumann

APPENDIX

Even though the following story is not a part of the family history as such, it was still an extremely strange experience for Grandfather, a mystery that made such a lasting impression on him that he dedicated a long chapter to it. It therefore seems important for us to include the episode, especially since Grandfather mentioned other inexplicable events earlier (the waxed canvas and the shipwreck).

While doing some research, we managed to find an extensive article on the clairvoyant B. Reese (1851-1926) in the Encyclopedia of Occultism and Parapsychology *(4th edition, p. 1083). It quotes the text that Grandfather copied and mentions other very amusing anecdotes from Reese's life. The article also presents confirmation of the unique powers of this "phenomenon" from eminent scientists such as Thomas Edison, Hereward Carrington, Charcot, and several others. They all thought that Reese was one of the most amazing personalities of his time.*

MEMORIES OF INEXPLICABLE EVENTS

Professor Berthold Reese

An enigmatic, mysterious person or a charlatan?

Summer 1913

My friend Weinberg recently asked me to tell his visitors about my experiences with Professor Reese as well as anything else that I might know about him. I complied with his wish.

On that occasion, just as it is whenever I talk about that man, the majority of my listeners responded with skepticism and expressions of regretful astonishment. They also expressed surprise that something like this could be interpreted as anything but fraud. Nevertheless, I have also met eminent, brilliant people who believe that Reese had a rather exceptional special talent, and who reflect a certain restrained approval when assessing what I tell them. For my part, I think that my encounter with Professor Reese and everything that I know about him are interesting enough to be recorded here.

It may have been in the summer of 1905 or 1906, when two of my American business acquaintances from New York, Mr. Maasbach of *Bloomingdale Brothers* and Mr. Louis Steiner of *Steiner & Co.*, were staying in Vienna. We had made arrangements to spend one Sunday afternoon together. I went to meet both gentlemen at the *Grand Hotel* at the appointed hour and found them both in a very excited state!

Seeing my surprise, they told me that they had just become acquainted with a German-American, Professor Berthold Reese from Chicago. They had never seen the man before, and he had certainly never met either of them. Nevertheless, he told them enormously surprising things about their lives and their past. He had just told Mr. Steiner in what year he had started his company and when he had had his best and worst annual profits, quoting the exact figures. He also told him what ailments he had, which German and American doctors he had consulted, and other similarly astonishing things.

Mr. Maasbach was told how long he had been married, how many children he had, and when he had begun working at *Bloomingdale Brothers*. The man also named the physicians that he and his wife had consulted.

I reacted to those revelations with a skeptical smile, even though I could not explain how Reese was able to make such statements. But my friends said, "Just a minute. Professor Reese is staying here, too. He will be down in a moment, and you'll have the opportunity to meet him yourself."

He came and was introduced to me.

Now let me describe the man's appearance. His face seemed rather insignificant to me. He was pale, clean shaven, puffy, strong, with bushy eyebrows. His head was almost completely bald with just a few graying hairs. The man himself was quite fat. All in all he had an appearance that did not make a strong first impression, let alone have the power to command attention.

We sat down in the foyer of the *Grand Hotel*, and I expressed my surprise at what my friends had just told me. Professor Reese said that he was not at all surprised and told us in passing that he had met most of the European royalty. He said that he had been asked for advice by many of them and mentioned that he had met the King of Belgium and the Russian Czar a few times. He also said that he was banned from the casino in Monte Carlo, as well as other casinos, because he had broken the bank several times. In addition he told us that at the beginning of the war between Russia and Japan, the Russian Czar had asked him to come to St. Petersburg so that he could ask his advice, but that the American government had refused to let him leave. Then he told us that he was invited to the *Hotel Imperial* the next day, where a large group of industrialists and bankers from Vienna would be waiting to meet him.

Reese spoke about all those things quietly, naturally, and without any pathos. He exhibited complete self-confidence, and it was obvious that he cared little about whether or not people believed in his "abilities."

That only intensified the curiosity that we developed with regard to the man, and after a while I ventured to ask him if he would give me a small demonstration of his talent as well. He looked at me and said, "I am a little tired now, but if one of your friends will let us use his room, I'm ready to do it."

At that moment, an elderly lady approached us. She must have been sitting near us, but we had not noticed her. She introduced herself as Baroness Puttkammer, née Baroness Popper. She apologized for eavesdropping on our conversation, but said that she was completely captivated by what she had heard and begged us to allow her to accompany us.

When we arrived at the room, Professor Reese told us a few more surprising things. Eventually he said that he and my two friends would briefly leave the room. Baroness P. and I were to remain there alone and cut a piece of paper into two halves. The baroness was to write the name of her son-in-law and I my late mother's maiden name in pencil on our halves of the paper and fold them up. When we had done that, we were to call him and the other two gentlemen back.

The baroness was just as surprised that Professor Reese knew that she had a son-in-law as I was to hear him speak so specifically about my *late* mother.

We deliberately penciled the names faintly on the pieces of paper. After folding them many times, we carefully placed them in an empty glass in front of us. That way neither of us knew who had written on which piece of paper. We then asked the gentlemen to come back into the room.

Professor Reese immediately picked up one of the pieces of paper and placed it against his temple without even so much as looking at it. After a little pause he said, "Your late mother's maiden name was Sophie Jeiteles." A moment later, after the same procedure, he also correctly named the baroness's son-in-law. Until then, Professor Reese had not known anything of my existence or my late mother, nor of the baroness and her son-in-law. In fact, he had known just as little about us as he knew about my friends Maasbach and Steiner and their relationships.

I cannot describe how surprised we were, and we asked ourselves and him how these things were possible. His response was a shrug of his shoulders and a smile. Nevertheless, our astonishment seemed to have amused him and he said, "Wait a moment. I'll go to my room and get a book that will entertain you." He then brought in a rather large scrapbook that had a lot of newspaper articles glued into it, complete with the date and the name of the newspaper.

In those clippings men like Gould, Vanderbilt, Edison, and other well-known people confirmed that Mr. Reese's fabulous abilities were a great mystery to them. One of those articles claimed that Reese, while visiting a lady in New York, said quite out of the blue: "While we are talking here, death is catching up with your brother, who is attending the *Grand Prix* on the *Longchamp* in Paris." And that is exactly what happened.

All this, of course, increased our amazement, and we felt that we were in the presence of a man whose abilities were quite exceptional and admirable. From the way he spoke and from his behavior we could tell that he had to be quite wealthy. He and his wife had taken lodgings in three of the best rooms on the second floor of the *Grand Hotel*, and he lived like a lord.

Professor Reese *never* gave so-called "performances," but on special occasions he made himself available to people. He also took delight in surprising people as he had surprised us that day.

Baroness Puttkammer said good-bye, but before she did, she asked Professor Reese if she might prevail upon him to give her advice on a very important matter. It was about her relationship with her son-in-law. Professor Reese declined politely but firmly. Afterward he told us that he did not like the lady at all and that he did not want to have anything to do with her.

After that, we all left, but I took the opportunity to talk with Professor Reese alone for a moment. I asked him if he would give me some advice on a matter that interested me very much. He told me to meet him that evening at the *Volksgarten*, where he would be having dinner with his wife and a few friends. I went there and had the opportunity to speak with Professor Reese alone. He made some comments that made me believe that he was aware of what I wanted to ask him, even though I did not touch upon the subject with a single word. After a short conversation he said to me, "Come to see me at my hotel tomorrow at noon. I won't expect you to pay me, but you must bring one hundred crowns, which I require as payment for the vials that I must use." And then we parted.

That put me in a mood that I cannot describe. On the one hand, this man thrilled me to the core. On the other hand his asking for the hundred crowns "for some vials" was how a charlatan operates.

When I arrived home, I told my daughter Agnes about my strange experience, which troubled her greatly. Eventually, I went to bed but did not find either sleep or rest. As I mulled over the events of the day, my primary feeling was that this Reese was nothing more than an excellent prestidigitator. I would definitely go and meet him and even take the hundred crowns with me, but I was determined not to part with them. During my reflections I also remembered that I had witnessed a performance at the *Ronacher** not long before, where a prestidigitator had surprised me with some very astonishing illusions, but that I had later found plausible explanations for all of them.

That strengthened my feeling that I should not put *too much* trust in Professor Reese. On the other hand, I could not shake off the powerful impression that he had made on me.

Lunchtime came, and I went to the *Grand Hotel* with my hundred crowns. Professor Reese met me in his living room, looked at me, and said, "Mr. Heller, more than anything I must know whether or not you trust me completely."

To that I responded frankly, "Professor, I'm very sorry, but I must confess that I cannot believe that you are able to help me in a matter that I believe to be irreparable."

In response to that, Professor Reese stood up without any agitation whatsoever and said in a friendly but firm manner, "If you do not trust me completely, I can do nothing for you."

As I took my leave, I asked his permission to offer his wife a small gift, to which he agreed, and we parted in a very friendly manner.

That same evening I got together with my son-in-law, Dr. Robert Heller. Our wives were both on vacation at the time. I told him all about the interesting experiences that I had had since the day before. He, too, was inclined to think that it was not a question of charlatanism but something that we simply could not explain. My story had interested him greatly.

Time for supper came, and I suggested that we go to *Hopfner's*. I had not yet visited his new restaurant. It was a strange coincidence that the first person that we saw there was Professor Reese, who was accompanied by his wife and a few American friends. He noticed me a short time later and came over to our table. I introduced my son-in-law to him and we talked for a short while. He declined Robert's request to give him a demonstration of his abilities like the one he had given me and explained that he was going on to Karlsbad very early the next morning.

That concludes my memories of my personal encounters with Professor Reese.

One year later in Vienna, I once again had the opportunity to speak with Mr. Maasbach and Mr. Steiner from New York. When I asked them about Professor Reese, the former answered: "That man is no longer welcome in my house. I invited him for dinner, but he made my wife so nervous that she pleaded with me to avoid him in the future. I haven't seen him since."

Mr. Steiner told me that Professor Reese had come to see him at his office and had been in a very good mood at the time. Right then Mr. Steiner had a business friend from Philadelphia visiting him, and without being asked Professor Reese told him when, where, and in which shop he had bought his suit and tie etc. and how much they had cost. Those comments were so precisely accurate that the poor man from Philadelphia suffered a mild shock and was totally perplexed.

Once again a long period of time passed without my hearing anything about Professor Reese. In 1909 or 1910 I read in a Berlin newspaper that he had caused great excitement all over the city. He had been invited to demonstrate his ability in front of a large number of competent Berlin authorities and permit them to evaluate it. The result had been a bitter argument, an enormous difference of opinion among those experts. While some of them declared him a fraud, others fully believed in his abilities and defended him, ascribing to him an inexplicable talent that allowed him to do unbelievable things.

Even the German Emperor in Berlin received Professor Reese in those days.

This summer I happened to come across an edition of the newspaper *Berliner Tageblatt*, dated the 31st of July 1913. In it there was a lengthy article by the well-known Berlin writer Felix Hollaender describing his recent experience with Professor Reese. Since I had such interesting experiences with him, I do not mind making the effort to reproduce that article here in its entirety. I do it in the hope that either I or someone who reads these lines at a later date might come across a continuation of these interesting stories, or perhaps even an explanation for them.

No. 384
*Berliner Tageblatt**
Thursday, July 31, 1913

The Phenomenon

A record of the strangest events.

By Felix Hollaender

The kind reader is requested not to suspect a belated April Fools Day joke in what I am about to write here. From the outset I am quite aware of the fact that I will be maligned. I can already hear the condescending laughter of my precise scientist friends, and I can see the derisive expressions on their faces. All of that, however, will not keep me from relating events, some of which I experienced myself and some of which were reported to me by completely credible witnesses.
I shall not add any ingredients, nor shall I make any judgments. The dish is already peppered and spiced enough to make the guests' eyes water. In any case, this is what we have all experienced during these July days.
I shall tell the story in the order in which things occurred. I shall name the places and some of the people involved, in order to leave no doubt whatsoever about the authenticity of the events.
At the end of June I arrived at Dr. Apolant's sanatorium in Bad Kissingen at about eight-thirty in the evening. I asked the desk clerk about my room, and in passing I noticed an elderly, short, stout man with a prominent belly. He had a huge square head that was completely bald, framed only in back by a wispy fringe of hair. There was really nothing noteworthy about the man. His snub nose with its tiny round nostrils, his fleshy neck and round face made him look somewhat like a softly growling bulldog. In the dark I could not make out the color of his eyes. I saw only that they were

framed by bushy eyebrows of a dirty blond color. Wisps of hair of the same color grew from his ears. I remember also noticing his large upper lip. It covered his upper teeth so completely that one might have thought that he had no teeth at all.

At first I could not place the man in any category of people, but he caught my attention when I heard him yelling at the desk clerk in a mixture of languages, using German and English expressions in the same breath. "Well, well, well," I thought. "There's a German-American, a cattle trader from over there who has come across the big pond to have his ruined stomach cured." At that moment the desk clerk said in a submissive, humble tone, "Do calm down, Professor."

Just then a servant appeared to show me to my room. I was so puzzled that I did not ask any questions. In this country we have developed a ready-made image of the physiognomy of a *professor*, which we do not like to have to adjust, even if we think that he is a complete ass.

In the dining room I had a table to myself, but mysterious words floated past me from all directions, and I saw meaningful gestures, gleaming eyes that were wide open in astonishment, and animated faces. "They are all talking about Professor Reese," Dr. T., an orthopedist from Berlin, said with a slightly arrogant smile. "Have you met the wondrous gentleman? People here tell amazing stories about him."

After dinner, the director of the Hamburg Opera, Dr. Löwenfeld, came up to me. He seemed to be out of sorts, and his wife was in a disturbed, abnormal state. "There are no ifs or buts about it," he said. "What we've just experienced defies description and could lead a person to cast aside his entire world view." He then told me that he and his wife had just had a conversation with Professor Reese. First Professor Reese had left the room, and on his orders Mrs. Löwenfeld had taken a piece of paper and had written on it her mother's maiden name, which nobody in the house knew. At the same time, Dr. Löwenfeld had written the name of a late teacher of his on a different piece of paper. On a third piece of paper he was to write the name of the preacher who had married him and his wife. On that page he wrote that he could not do so because he had been married at a civil registry. The pages were folded and locked in different drawers. Mr. Reese then came back into the room. Neither Mr. Löwenfeld nor his wife knew which pieces of paper dealt with which questions.

"Take the piece of paper out of this drawer and place it on my forehead like this." A moment passes and then Mrs. Löwenfeld feels an electrical discharge that springs from his forehead across to her elbow. Then - then to her horror he gives the name of the dead teacher, and after that he answers the other two questions perfectly accurately.

A nervous tremor comes over Mrs. Löwenfeld. "What do you see here on my neck?" Professor Reese asks the lady, pointing to a small spot.

"A mole," she answers.

"Correct, and you have a similar one on your left hip."

The Hamburg theater director and his wife feel hot and cold flashes. This small, fleshy man, whose ordinary appearance does not suggest any mysterious talents or powers at first glance, can see through boxes and clothes down to skin and bone.

The orthopedist from Berlin, Dr. T., shrugs his shoulders. The director of the Hamburg Opera, a man with a university degree who is familiar with all sorts of theatrical tricks and cannot be fooled easily, is a perfect witness. Dr. T. shrugs his shoulders.

I [Felix Hollaender] am not yet affected by the giddiness that has come over the others. I trust only what I see with my own eyes and hear with my own ears. I turn to the director of the sanatorium, Dr. Apolant. He says, "It is out of the question that it is a case of fraud. These are mysterious happenings for which we have no explanation."

He tells me that on his first visit Reese circled and sniffed at him as if he were a deer and then declared that he could reveal everything about his life. Dr. Apolant had turned the offer down, but the things that he had experienced here at the sanatorium were simply dumbfounding.

As a physician - and I am sure that he does the same thing with all of the patients in his sanatorium - he asks me to avoid making contact with Reese. He is the scientific type of physician who is gifted with inner calm and prudence, and with a restrained and controlled temperament.

But I [Felix Hollaender] am beginning to feel perplexed. I turn the problem over and over in my mind. After all, Dr. Löwenfeld is a man of the theater. He has the active imagination of a person on the stage. Dr. Apolant, on the other hand, is a cool scientist who sees through the astute eyes of a physician, and who still turns to Hamlet's philosophy on the basis of his observations and says: "There are more things between heaven and earth than our educational wisdom dreams of."

In the evening we sit in the billiard room. One person after another utters his "confessions." One gentleman says, "After Reese told me the strangest things, I argued and said to him, 'All of this is enigmatic and mysterious, and yet there must be an explanation for it. Do you perhaps have x-ray eyes with which you can see through any material thing?' He gave me a piercing glance, and then he answered quite calmly, 'Now I'm going to give you a "pill" to chew on for a while. Fifteen years ago, in such and such a month and on such and such a day, you were sentenced to pay a 400 mark fine for inflicting bodily harm. When reading the verdict the judge warned you, adding that if you were ever convicted a second time you would definitely end up in jail.' Gentlemen, when he told me that, I was beside myself. It was correct to the day and the hour. Fifteen years ago I slapped a man for his anti-Semitic invective and damaged his hearing. I was taken to court, and the outcome was as he described. I never told a single person about that, not even my wife, to whom I have been married for six years."

I [Felix Hollaender] have still not spoken a single word to Reese. I watch him furtively. In the evenings he sits in the game room and enjoys playing cards. He plays skat like a chubby, harmless petit bourgeois. He is really like an adult child. His face quite openly reveals the naïve pleasure that he takes in astonishing us. We avoid each other. He does not take the slightest notice of me, and I follow the physician's advice to avoid any contact with him.

Dr. Apolant tells me a few things about Reese's past. He was born in a small village near the city of Posen. His father was the town clerk and owned a grocery store. The boy's mysterious talent had already begun to manifest itself when he was still a child. It frightened the citizens to the point that they avoided his father's shop. In order not to lose his livelihood completely, the father was forced to send his son away to a boarding school in Posen. The inhabitants of the small village were terrified. They thought that the boy was a magician, the devil incarnate!

"By the way," Dr. Apolant adds, "the man has the most incredible connections. He has been received by the Czar more than once and has been given lavish gifts. The same with the King of Siam, the King of England, and the German Kaiser. The large diamond ring on his finger came from Felix Faure."

Dr. Apolant continues his report: "I've seen American newspapers print several columns of reports about his sessions with the Astors, the Vanderbilts, the Goulds, and the Rockefellers. I'll show you the book sometime."

"Thank you very much, Doctor, but I would hate to leave without having met the man. When you find an opportunity, would you mind asking him if he's ready to meet me?" Dr. Apolant promises that he will do so.

Again there is enormous excitement in the whole sanatorium. A well-known sportsman consulted with Reese about which of his horses would win the next race. "Take me to your stable," Reese answered, and there he pointed to the horse concerned.

The sportsman laughed out loud: "You picked the worst one of my horses."

"Sorry, that one will win the race." And it actually did.

We inmates of the sanatorium have learned from a book that was circulated by Dr. Apolant and contains reports about Reese, that he went to Edison with a letter of introduction from Professor Slaby. Filled with deepest suspicion, Edison conducted some experiments on him, taking the greatest care and using the most accurate methods.

A clipping from the *World* shows Edison and Reese together. The reporter informs his newspaper that Edison said that the man had touched him to the core and appeared to him to be the "Wandering Jew." That description had puzzled Reese and made him angry. He wrote a letter to Edison asking for an explanation. The book contains the clipping with Edison's answer. Edison writes that he by no means intended to hurt Reese's feelings, but he was unable to find a stronger expression for the intense feeling that he had had.

I open to another page and read about Reese's meeting with the famous French doctor Charcot, who is well known as one of the greatest promoters of scientific research in the field of psychology. Charcot tells the journalist from the French newspaper that he felt hot and cold flashes, that fraud was out of the question, and that it was a case of a mysterious phenomenon.

I shall now talk about another event - deliberately and only briefly - that occurred very recently during his last stay in Berlin. One of the world's largest trading companies (I have been asked not to publicize the name) was unable to discover the location of a fraudulent entry in their books that must have been made by one of their employees. Having heard of him, they summoned Reese. He asked for 5% of the sum in question for his fee. They agreed, and without hesitation he went and opened the book to the page that contained the fraudulent entry. At the sanatorium we saw the check from the company in question, one of the largest companies in the world. His fee was 2,500 marks!

There is a long list of other cases that I could quote, but I do not want to weary the reader unduly.

Now I come to my own conversation with the man. He had agreed to talk to me, and our meeting took place one day before my departure. We went outside on the balcony of his room. I was perfectly calm. I intended to observe him coolly and with a clear head. He asked me to write down my questions on small pieces of paper and to fold them up and put them into the various pockets of my suit. When he left the balcony and stepped back inside the room, he said, "On one of the pieces of paper write down the name of the newspaper or periodical that featured the first article that you ever published."

That request confused me a bit. I had to think for a while. Then I remembered that Theodor Wolff, who is now the editor-in-chief of the *Berliner Tageblatt*, had published a periodical entitled *Erste Waffengänge* [First Armed Skirmishes], either just before or just after leaving high school. I was in his class at the *Friedrich Wilhelm Gymnasium* [advanced secondary school] and had the honor of being one of his collaborators. Max Osborn, Dessoir, and others were also spreading their wings in those days and worked with him. I believe that apart from Theodor Wolff and me nobody is aware of that fact.

I also wrote down the name of a dear deceased friend and the maiden names of my mother and my wife, Johanna Baumgärtner. I mixed the scraps of paper and put them into six different pockets before Professor Reese came back out onto the balcony.

But I had also written down a number of very personal things relating to the future, things that I cannot even hint at here. An enormous ability to guess at my past would be required even to touch on any of those questions.

When Reese returned, in his hand he had a piece of paper with Hebrew characters on it. He asked me to cross out some of the hieroglyphs. Then, at his request, I pulled one of the pieces of paper from one of my pockets and put it against his temple.

I looked into his large, light gray eyes. Some of the people in our sanatorium say that ordinarily they are slightly cloudy or milky, but at this point they opened wide, took on a strange gleam, and became transparent and radiant. When I touched his temple, I felt electric shocks run through my body. I could feel his brain working behind his mighty forehead, and I could hear quite clearly some quiet, murmuring sounds that emanated from the inside of his skull. And then he answered all of my questions like some mechanism that functioned with high precision.

For my part, I can only repeat what Charcot said before me: "I had hot and cold flashes." That devil's henchman unlocked the secret drawers of my past existence. I shall have to wait and see if his prophecies come true. After all that I experienced, I am inclined to think that they will.

Dear friends and readers, I forbid you to laugh. A very serious matter is being discussed here. *He* was the one who wrote all matters pertaining to the future on a piece of paper. At one point he stopped and said, "Wait a moment." He then wrote a few lines, and when he had finished he asked, "How many children did your mother have, and which number are you?"

My answer was: "Out of thirteen children I am the eleventh."

He handed me the piece of paper, on which he had written down that fact before I had even told him.

I began asking him questions: "How do these things happen? What processes take place inside you when you do this kind of work?"

He answered, "You know as much as I do about it. I can tell you *absolutely nothing* about it, except perhaps that I become very excited, and that I hear a rhythmic sound behind my forehead each time. It is similar to the ticking of a pocket watch."

"Do you know anything about your own existence?"

"Not the least little bit, Sir! I am completely in the dark about my own family and myself. As if driven by some inner force, I suddenly have to say the most frightful things...

"Somewhere or other I made the acquaintance of an elderly couple from Frankfurt am Main. They told me that their son's jewelry store had been subject to some shocking burglaries of late, and that they had never managed to catch the thieves. I told the old people to their faces that the thief was none other than their daughter-in-law, and that she was cheating on their son and spending the money with her lover!...

"How did I come to that knowledge? I have absolutely no idea. I have to assume that I was born with this sixth sense or whatever you want to call it. Some force that I am unable to resist often makes me say words that are completely foreign and unfamiliar to me, and I do things that, to all appearances, do not make any sense at all. God gave me this gift when He sent me into the world."

"Is there anyone else with faculties that are similar to yours?"

"There are people who follow the same path, so-called 'mind readers.' They usually work in pairs. They have certain instincts, and their blood is not normal. But they are inadequate and primitive and they do not achieve much. On only one occasion have I ever encountered something unfathomable. I discovered a little eleven-year-old American Indian girl who absolutely stunned me. I wanted to be with the little girl and offered her parents, who were dirt poor, forty dollars a week for the rest of their lives, if they would let her stay with me. They refused. They attracted large crowds with her, drank whisky all day, and poisoned the poor creature with it until she died like a little sparrow. That child was a miracle. Perhaps we could have done incredible things together. Who knows?" He said all that very slowly in a tone of voice that made me shiver.

And that is when I discovered that his face had grown very old, and it seemed as if his eyes had seen the things of this world from the very beginning. And then I understood what Edison had meant when he said, "He appeared to be the 'Wandering Jew.'" A genius had found the ultimate, all-encompassing formula for this phenomenon.

After a lengthy silence, I suddenly asked, "Have you heard of Kant, Immanuel Kant?" I repeated the name somewhat nervously.

His look reflected a total lack of comprehension. He had never even heard the name before. "Hmm, and what about Swedenborg?"

At this question a shock passed through his body. "Swedenborg," he said, "passed his gift on to Reb Kifa Eiga, and from him and no other it was passed on to me."

Who was Reb Kifa Eiga?*

That made me think of Swedenborg, and I remembered Kant's little book *Traum eines Geistersehers* [A Spiritualist's Dream], in which he dismisses Swedenborg's miracles coldly and a bit arrogantly. I suspect that Swedenborg will have to be read in a new light…will have to be understood differently. Perhaps many things will have to be revised.

The ultimate "court" has not yet passed judgment on things of a metaphysical nature. Reese's case will keep proper authorities guessing for some time.

ANNOTATIONS

p. 23   "*Leeser*": Grandfather notes: "My grandfather on my father's side was called *Leeser Heller*, in German *Ludwig Heller*. He ran a *Cheder*, a Jewish school. He died in 1816 and is buried in the old cemetery at Teplitz.

p. 24   "*jokes*": As a young boy I was very impressed that my father had a fine and chivalrous first name such as *Balduin*. When I asked him how it came about, he told me that his parents would not even have dreamed of giving the little Jewish boy from a poor family background such a high-sounding name. His intended name was *Beerl*. However, the registry official was in a particularly good mood at that moment and entered *Balduin* in the register books instead of *Beerl*. That name frequently turned out to be an advantage for my father.

"*Schmule*": See the anecdote in the chapter "Character Studies."

"*five gilders*": In the year 1819, when the ten-year-old Balduin received five gilders C. M. (his future base capital) as a consolation, the *Erste Österreichische Spar-Casse* [First Austrian Savings Bank] was founded in Vienna at the personal instigation of Emperor Franz I. To mark the opening of this first large Austrian social institution, the Emperor had savings books, each in the amount of five gilders, distributed to one hundred poor children. (Quoted from: *Wien, am Graben 21*).

That fact gives us a glimpse of the enormous growth of poverty and misery during the previous decades as a result of an extreme rise in prices which was the consequence of the coalition wars against Napoleon, with all their dramatic effects. Just think of the many thousands of dead and wounded, the epidemics that broke out, the bad harvests, the high reparation payments that were imposed, and finally the enormous costs of the Vienna Congress.

This makes it clear why prices increased more than tenfold between 1800 and 1810. In 1808 there was a significant devaluation of currency because the value of banknotes in circulation had reached one billion (ten times what it had been in 1800). Back in 1806 most of the silver coins in circulation had been hoarded. The price for one kilogram of beef had risen from 65 kreutzers (1800) to six gilders (1811). The state faced bankruptcy. There were bread and meat riots and forged currency! Banknotes had to be *devalued to one fifth* of their face value. In 1816 the National Bank was founded in an attempt to restore order to the state's financial affairs. The *Wiener Währung* [W. W., Vienna currency], which had been ruined by unsecured banknotes, was absorbed by *Conventionswährung* or *Conventionsmünze* [C. M., convention currency] at an exchange rate of 250 gilders W.W. to 100 gilders C. M.

When the *First Austrian Savings Bank* was founded, Emperor Franz stated that it was "meant to give factory workers, tradesmen, day laborers, servants, peasants, needy mountain dwellers, the urban poor, and any other hard-working and thrifty people a means of putting aside a small part of their earnings from time to time for use at a later date, as dowry, to help in case of illness, for old age, or to reach any other laudable goal." The deposited capital earned 4% interest. At the time of the Vienna Congress, the following saying made the rounds:

"The Russian Czar makes love for everyone,
The Prussian King thinks for everyone,
The King of Denmark speaks for everyone,
The King of Bavaria drinks for everyone,
The King of Württemberg eats for everyone,
The Austrian Emperor pays for everyone."

p. 26 "*Sholeth*": Grandfather writes the following: "If you want to know what *Sholeth* is, you should either go and ask a very old Jew or read Heine's poems that praise *Sholeth* as noble food of the gods." ("Princess Sabbath," from *Ro-*

   manzero, 3rd book, "Hebrew Melodies") (Ragout of goose with rice or barley and yellow peas).

p. 26 *"Mazes"*: The unleavened Easter bread.

p. 29 *"prayer leader"*: Rabbi David Pick (1836-1878) preached in German and was the first one in Austria to play the organ during Jewish worship. Choirmaster Singer was prayer leader at the same time.

p. 42 *"Glogau's place"*: Father's sister Lotti was married to Elias Glogau (6 children).

   "Teplitz": Spas like Karlsbad (Carlovy Vary) or Marienbad in the Bohemian Ore Mountains are still world renowned today. Teplitz, which could boast of a similar fame until the end of the 19th century, has suffered a different fate since then. Due to its radioactive thermal springs, which brought healing to thousands of guests from all over Europe at the numerous bathing facilities, the quaint old city developed into a delightful summer resort, where the demands of the highest society could be met. It was at its peak in the 19th century (1820-1880), the period that Grandfather describes.

  Nevertheless, the development of the city had been a double or parallel one. On the one hand, the city owed its good reputation to the hard-working and competent citizens who excelled at a number of trades over the centuries. Armorers, needle manufacturers, goldsmiths, and candle makers all had their workshops there. But the majority of the trades were associated with the manufacture of textiles. There were cloth dyers, felt hat makers, and manufacturers of small knitwear and hosiery, the precursors of what later became the knitwear industry. All sorts of spinning and weaving mills opened then and did particularly well during the nascent industrialization.

  On the other hand, the town's history points back to a long tradition as a spa. Its healing springs were known as far back as Roman times and they were rediscovered in the eighth century. The use of the hot (alkaline, saline, sulfured radioactive) springs (28 to 46 degrees Celsius) is recorded again and again in documents from the 12th and 14th centuries onward.

The name *Teplitz* is derived from the Slavic language and means "hot waters."

After the Thirty Years War the Teplitz baths were used not only for high dignitaries, but also to nurse many wounded soldiers. During the 18th century the city was declared "neutral" by the warring rulers, so that nobody could lay siege to it. This meant that officers and soldiers - even from opposing armies - could go there to be cured. (From: *Geschichten eines alten Österreichers*, by Alfons Clary-Aldringen, Ullstein Verlag, 1989).

The local lords of the manor, the Clary-Aldringens, saw to it that the town's reputation grew over the decades. They renovated and embellished the numerous (17) bathing facilities, all of which were under the supervision of excellent physicians and primarily treated skin diseases as well as joint and gynecological problems. In the process those establishments were turned into elegant buildings. At the same time, they swiftly rebuilt the city itself in the classical style following its destruction by a large fire in 1793. Their own palace and the large park were extended and furnished according to the dictates of the taste of that era.

With their strong artistic sense, the open-minded noblemen were also very much concerned about cultural needs. They increased the number of existing schools and founded a theater in their park. It was open to the general public, and concerts and opera productions featuring famous artists were performed there. In 1850, that was a very ambitious project for a small provincial town of 4,000 inhabitants.

But there was no lack of spectators who were hungry for entertainment. Teplitz soon became the favorite meeting place for people of the highest social classes. Emperors, kings, czars, and the most famous families of the aristocracy from all over Europe came together there every year to take their cures or just for a vacation.

Since the Clary-Aldringen family was related to most of those aristocrats, there was vibrant activity in the palace and in the park, where one could encounter such members of the nobility and countless celebrities of the mind and of the arts. For them Teplitz had developed a special magnetism because of its diverse attractions and delightful rural setting.

Naturally, the town's inhabitants did not remain unaffected by the presence of the elegant guests. Anything that those refined visitors might desire had to be readily available. Hospitality, in particular, had to be elevated to a superior standard. Every year there were 8,000 visitors from all over the world. In 1870 the number even rose to 13,000!

In those days the name "Little Paris" was coined for Teplitz. And because meetings of diplomats and congresses of the highest level took place there time and again (1813, 1833, 1835, 1838, 1860, and 1878), it was also called the "European Reception Hall."

The city also contributed by organizing balls, Carnival parades, events, and festivities of all kinds throughout the year to create entertainment. That was also done in order to avoid anything that might arouse the guests' displeasure. In its "ecological" determination, the city also refused to allow any air-polluting industries to be established in the vicinity. Lime pits and brickworks already existed, however, and later an open-pit coal mine was added.

In 1879 a catastrophe of colossal proportions occurred. The hydraulic system that controlled the water supply for the various baths was destroyed by an industrial accident. As a consequence the precious waters disappeared into the ground. They were, however, later successful in channeling the waters of the springs again, but that incident was the primary reason for the steady decline of the city's popularity as a spa from then on.

Toward the end of the 19th century, modern industrial and contemporary political development began in Teplitz, just as it did everywhere else, and Teplitz's heyday was past.

p. 42 "*extended stay*": In the years 1811 and 1812 Beethoven came here to take his cure. His famous meeting in the company of Goethe with the Empress Ludovica and her entourage is said to have happened in the Clary Palace Park.

"*Lange Gasse*": The commerce and the institutions that were essential for the everyday life of the spa, for instance the inns, the pharmacy, and later the post office, were concentrated in *Lange Gasse*. During the first half of the 19th century, many visitors stepped down from their coaches there and received an initial impression of the city. This lively street was then already full of shops. But the more experienced guests knew that the best selection of goods, especially fabrics, was available in the small shops in the Jewish quarter. On *Lange Gasse* itself there were twenty-one buildings on each side, with at least two shops in each.

p. 44 "*Waldstein*": The original form of the name Wallenstein, that of an old aristocratic family. Its most famous representative was Wallenstein, Duke of Friedland, during the Thirty Years War. Later Waldsteins - and Lobkowitz - were among Beethoven's patrons.

p. 46 "*money crisis*": Willing to put some order back into the "chaos of coins" that had been caused by previous wars, Maria Theresia introduced a new currency in 1750. A treaty was signed with Bavaria, agreeing to a new system of coins. The Cologne fine silver mark was to be the equivalent of twenty gilders from then on, where one gilder was the equivalent of half a taler. (The taler was a valuable silver coin whose name was later also used in the English-speaking world and became the dollar.) They called it *Conventionsmünze* [convention coin] because the coin was the product of a treaty in which several states agreed on its equivalent value in precious metal.

Most Southern German states accepted this new treaty on coins. The measure led to an improvement of financial conditions. In order to avoid trimming of the coins, an inscription was engraved around the edge! Small coins made of copper (kreutzer) were also introduced. Apart from the coins, there was also paper money (bank notes) in Austria from 1761 on. However, during all times of crisis it was the metal coins that were hoarded and thus temporarily disappeared from circulation.

p. 47 *"Metternich"*: In 1848 my grandfather was six years old. But even in his old age he remembered the excitement among the populace when the old, much hated Prince Metternich secretly spent one mid-March night in Teplitz during his escape to England. He also clearly remembered the revolutionary events in Prague to the extent that they touched his consciousness as a child.

The Prague Congress on Slavs opened on June 2, 1848. The Czechs demanded the establishment of an independent kingdom consisting of Bohemia, Moravia, and the Austrian part of Silesia. They submitted a draft constitution to Emperor Ferdinand (1835-1848), but he rejected it. That led to a dangerous clash between the Czech nationalists and the Emperor's militia from the 12th to the 17th of June. This so-called "Pentacost uprising" that Grandfather talks about was brutally quashed by the troops of the governor, Prince Windischgrätz.

Similar revolutionary hotspots, however, existed everywhere in the Austrian melting pot of nationalities. One fire ignited after another. The spark came from the French Revolution of 1848. Revolts started in Italy, Hungary, Slovakia, Serbia, Poland, and the Banat [today a part of Romania]. They were frequently directed more against each other than against imperial "authority" - which no longer existed anyway.

The awakened sense of nationalism among the Empire's many ethnic groups was joined - in a world of rapid changes - by other fundamental and aggravating circumstances: the constantly growing industrialization of the economy (the principle of "time is money") caused an irrevocable split in the society. The so-called "better circles" - the aristocracy and the upper middle class - were constantly getting richer and reflected a make-believe idealistic image of virtue and respectability in the Romantic and Biedermeier eras, which, however, "shamefully concealed" another very real aspect of the situation: Impoverished peasants streamed into the factories and were outrageously exploited there the same as other workers, women, and children.

When bad harvests that cause ever higher food prices, devaluation of currency, and epidemics are added to all of that, real starvation occurs to the extent that the unemployed plunder and bakeries are stormed. Soup kitchens have to be established for the poor, and the list goes on. If, on top of that, there is strict police intervention and unpredictable censorship, or in other words, if there is regressive political absolutism, then the ground is fertile for revolution.

Doesn't the old "amusing" nursery rhyme bear witness of this kind of bitter reality:

"...and whatever you buy now costs so much,
the milk and the flour, the butter and such,
and the eggs and the fire are so expensive this year,
and I don't get my wages, I'll run away, do you hear?"

p. 50   *"Purim"*: Celebrates the saving of the Jewish people from annihilation by the Persians. (Book of Esther).

"Hanukkah": Festival of lights.

p. 53   *"Leeser woman"*: See earlier annotation, p. 23.

"covered with white sand": In areas where snakes were common, the custom was to sprinkle the floor inside with pine needles or fine sand to keep the reptiles away, since they were unable to move on such surfaces.

"Buchteln": Yeast rolls filled with plum jam (*"Powidl"*) or ricotta cheese.

p. 58 "*my grandmother's home*": One can admire the historical realistic miniature model of the city of Prague at the *Museum der Hauptstadt Prag*. It is named after its creator, Antonin Langweil, lithographer and miniaturist (1791-1837). Built in the years 1826-1827, it is not just a special curiosity. It also possesses an irreplaceable documentary value. The artist himself called it "Prague, as it was and as it is." This wonderful twenty-square-meter paper model presents the historical center of the city of Prague in extraordinarily lively detail. The three-dimensional color model exhibits over two thousand buildings in the old part of town, the ghetto, and other areas, nestled between the river and areas of higher ground. It shows the graceful façades of the wealthy areas (balconies, gates, window ornaments), picturesque squares with their fountains and monuments, street lights, courtyards, and gardens in loving and scrupulous detail. But even the plainer streets, warehouses, and even stacks of firewood are reproduced very faithfully. (From: "SVEDECKTVI MODELU PRAHY," Schola Ludus Pragensia, 1996).

It shows the Prague of the generation of Rebekka Jeiteles, the city that Grandfather knew as a child and as a young man. The representation shows a section of the densely built-up ghetto with simple houses. (*Zigeunergasse* goes diagonally from top to bottom).

"*Zigeunergasse*": Street named after Salom Salkid Zigeuner, who founded a synagogue in 1613.

p. 61 "*coffee and eggs*": He was eager to abide by the rules of kosher eating, even while traveling.

"*Talmud*": A compilation of Jewish law. It consists of the "Mishna," the doctrine of the oral tradition, and the "Gemora," the commentary to it.

p. 64 "*Pferdebahn*": The horse-drawn railway from Linz to Budweis (Budvar) (1833) was the first one on the European continent. It covered a distance of 130 km. There were three stations along the way, where horses were changed, numerous guard houses, station buildings, and viaducts. It provided regular passenger and freight service. Gently gliding along rails represented enormous progress. The horse-drawn railway was the precursor to the electric streetcar, even in cities.

p. 70 "*companies*": The well-known and long-established Salzburg company of *Joh. Balthaser Neumüller* has had its main branch in the very same building at *Getreidegasse* 2 since it was founded in about 1835. The predecessors of the current owners came from Prague and bought the business in 1925 but maintained its "good name." (Information received during a conversation with the current owners in September of 2000).

The *Junger Company* was founded in 1858 by Georg Junger. He started his own business at *Sigmund-Haffnergasse* 4 after working for several years with *Schön & Neumüller*, a wholesale business in Salzburg. He moved his business to the *Haus beym Steyn*, a traditionally-named building located at *Alter Markt* 11, which he bought in 1883. Assisted first by his brother, later by his sons, he made the company a "household name" among the regional wholesalers in the Austro-Hungarian Empire. Its range of goods included among other things haberdashery, fashion items, and a large, fashion-oriented button department. The business celebrated its 100th anniversary in 1958 but was later closed. (Information from the Salzburg University Library Archives)

The young gentlemen Neumüller and Junger were business acquaintances of the same generation and in the same line of business as J. L. Heller.

p. 72 "*Brünn*" (Brno). Capital of Moravia. In 1857 the city had 60,000 mostly German-speaking inhabitants. It was a lively trade center of international significance with diverse manufacturing industries: linen and cotton mills, knitwear factories, and jute spinning mills. It was an important wool weaving center as early as the Middle Ages. In the 18th century it was the so-called "Moravian Manchester." Mechanical engineering, production of leather goods, chemicals, paper, and wooden products. There were coal mines in the area and an agricultural industry where farm goods were produced, including sugar, fruits, and vegetables.

p. 72   *"taxed at excessive rates"*: Already as early as 1784, Emperor Joseph II had *either completely prohibited* the import from aboad of any *manufactured goods* and a great many *raw materials, or at least imposed taxes of up to 60%* of their value. Among the prohibited items were: cloth, linen, glassware, stoneware, silk, fabrics made of wool and cotton, sugar, coffee, and indigo. Under Franz I the rules on importing foreign goods were made even stricter!

p. 74   *"trade agreement...1854"*: Grandfather writes: "Joining our economy to that of Germany was proposed to us way back when the German Customs Union was founded. It is something that is very much desired today and hopefully will soon be realized. Baron von Gagern represented Germany for quite some time in Vienna for that purpose, but he was forced to return without achieving his goal."

"Total Imports...Austria": Zehn Jahre nach dem Handelsvertrag [Ten Years After the Trade Agreement] by I. Jeiteles (Uncle Ignaz), Vienna, 1864, Zumarski und Dettmarsch. Concerning Uncle Ignaz. See also the chapter "Character Studies."

p. 84   *"school friend Karl Hartmann"*: Son of the owner of the hotel *König von Preußen* [King of Prussia] in Teplitz.

p. 85   *"release fee"*: All through the 19th century, the Emperor and the government tried to reduce state debt, which had reached enormous proportions, by introducing taxes, currency reform, and drastic savings. The latter could only be achieved by cutting back expenses for the army and the navy. During times of peace, since the navy was more important for trade and transportation, the budget for the war ministry was cut back more severely and it was forced to find its "own" financial resources through the release from military service. In 1862, the revenue produced was 13.5 million gilders. (See: Adolf Beer, *Die Finanzen Österreichs im 19. Jh.* [Austria's Finances in the 19th Century]). In 1868, compulsory military service was extended from seven to twelve years!

p. 97 *"Venetia"*: Victorious battle of Custozza and sea battle near Lissa in 1866.

"Beust": Austrian statesman (1809-1886). He was Foreign Minister from 1866 until 1871 and introduced the new constitution and the "settlement" with Hungary in 1867, which put Austria and Hungary on the same level.

p. 100 *"adornment for the city of Vienna"*: According to a "Viennese song" from 1868:
"There are beautiful houses along our city circle, everywhere you look, there are splendid palaces,
Huge shop displays, beautiful lighting, and even a boulevard for horseback riders,
We now have busses and horse-drawn railways for public transportation,
But the good old days, they will never return.
(See: Hilde Spiel, *Glanz und Untergang, Wien 1866-1938* [Splendor and Downfall, Vienna 1866-1938]/DTV).

p. 107 *"match factory"*: Ascher's match factory on the *Spitalberg* was a large business compared with other local ones. In those times of misery it provided a living for approx. fifty women and children. (From the two-volume Teplitz postcard album).

p. 121 *"Hermann Jeiteles"*: see Character Studies, p. 163.

"still flourishing today": Reference to the founding of the important export business in Gablonz in 1882. It was augmented by the factory in Wiesenthal.

p. 129 *"Bubentsch"*: Rural suburb of Prague.

"today": Refers to the end of the 19th and the beginning of the 20th centuries.

p. 138 *"Konrad Heller"*: Pioneer in the field of landscape photography. Book by Friedrich Grassegger: *Konrad Heller, "Wachau um 1900"* (Böhlau: Vienna, 1996).

p. 140 *"fire at the Ringtheater"*: 386 people died in a panic that defied description. The fire brigade rescued eighty-four people by holding up a tarpaulin for people to jump into. After that catastrophe, all theaters were required to have an "iron curtain" installed. Strict fire protection regulations were introduced and the Vienna fire brigade was completely reorganized. Founding of the "Volunteer Rescue Association of Vienna." On that particular evening *The Tales of Hoffmann* by Offenbach was to be performed.

p. 141 *"messenger"*: In those days, the "Vienna City Messengers" were a very useful institution at a time when there were no telephones and hardly any means of public transportation. They were mostly elderly men who were recognizable by their uniform caps and their red-and-white-striped waistcoats. Generally two of them (to be able to chat) sat on little benches at street corners waiting for orders to deliver messages or run errands. In the 1920s one could still see such "street characters."

p. 152 *"stocking underpants"*: knitted long pants that covered the whole leg including the foot.

p. 158 *"Hinterbrühl"*: A picturesque village situated in the Vienna Woods about twenty-five kilometers south of Vienna. Beethoven found inspiration there for some of his compositions. The local railway from Mödling to Hinterbrühl did not open until 1883 and was the first electrical railway in Europe.

p. 161 "*1873*": The year of the world exhibition and the stock market crash.

"*The college*": Vienna 1, Franziskanerplatz 5.

p. 162 "*Dr. Eugenie Schwarzwald*": She continued to develop the school during the years from 1901 to 1938 (until the annexation of Austria by Hitler) in the spirit of its founder. The school included a kindergarten, an elementary and secondary school, and even the first *Frauenoberschule* [women's upper secondary school] in Vienna. This pedagogue and philanthropist, who was much ahead of her time, has recently found appropriate recognition. She died in Switzerland in 1940. Two books have recently been published about her life's work: Hans Dieckmann, *Leben mit provisorischer Genehmigung* [A Life with Temporary Authorization], (Vienna: Guthmann und Peterson) and a collection by Robert Streibl, *Dr. Eugenie Schwarzwald und ihr Kreis* [Dr. Eugenie Schwarzwald and Her Circle], (Vienna: Picus, 1996).

p. 164 "*Kapozvar*": A town in Hungary, now called Comitat Somogy.

p. 170 "*Gaudenzdorf*": Formerly a village, now incorporated into the city of Vienna.

p. 171 "*Rax*": High mountain (2007 m.), Schneeberg, and Semmering, about eighty km. south of Vienna in a wild, romantic landscape. Popular destinations for excursions from Vienna; they offer sports facilities; vacation area.

"*'holy' pictures of saints*": in the mountains, at places where tragic accidents have happened, such naïve, improvised "memorials" invite the passer-by to say a prayer. A simple sheltered wooden cross with an image of a patron saint and a prie-dieu.

p. 173 "*Leopoldstadt*": The second Viennese district, the historic Jewish quarter.

p. 180 "*Selety*": Backward writing of "Jeiteles." His letters to Albert Einstein are contained in Einstein's correspondence. Einstein Archive: Hebrew University, Jerusalem. Franz Josef Jeiteles received his doctorate from the University of Vienna in 1915 at the age of twenty-two. His dissertation was entitled: *Die phaenomenologischen Wurzeln der Psychologie* [The Phenomenological Roots of Psychology]. The young "Selety" was a "freewheeling thinker" who independently pursued the fields of research that were of interest to him. Volume 8 of Einstein's correspondence contains two of Selety's letters from 1917 in German and English (doc. 364, 395), which were published by Princeton University Press in 1998.

p. 182 "*Neue Freie Presse*": Vienna's most intellectual and liberal daily newspaper.

p. 185 "*Yom Kippur*": Reconciliation Day, the most important day of festivity and repentance in the Jewish religion.

p. 193 "*Edlach*": Summer health resort, picturesquely situated seventy-five km. south of Vienna in the Semmering and Schneeberg area.

"*Brioni*": Island in the Adriatic Sea, near Pola (close to Istria, now part of Croatia), area of military-strategic importance.

p. 194-5 "*Otto...blessed*": This passage is a rhyming poem in the original German text.

p. 196 "*Ernst*": Ernst Kanitz, Bachelor of Law, a talented poet, died of polio at the age of twenty-six.

p. 197 "*landscape photography*": See annotation for p. 146.

p. 203 "*Ahlbeck*": Well-known seaside resort on the island of Usedom (West Pomerania) in the Baltic Sea, near Swinemünde.

p. 205 "*Theresienstadt*": Garrison town of the Dual Monarchy in Northern Bohemia. Now Terecin. Concentration camp during the Second World War.

p. 208 "*Belcredi*": Richard Graf Belcredi (1823-1902), politician. Prime Minister from 1865 to 1867. Supported a federal-Austrian and conservative Hungarian line. Resigned in 1867 under opposition from the German National Party. New government under the leadership of Freiherr von Beust.

"*Taaffe*": Eduard Graf Taaffe (1833-1895), statesman. Like his predecessors Belcredi and Beust, he failed because of the nationality question, or better the question of the Slavs.

After the successful "agreement" between Austria and Hungary, which put both countries on the same level (dualism), the Slavic population sought a similar solution (trialism). To that end, Taaffe, who had been Minister of the Interior since 1867, formed a conservative coalition government in 1870. He succeeded in cooperating with the Czechs and made concessions to the Slavs. His ministry was the so-called "Reconciliation Ministry"! But those very concessions caused the German liberals to withdraw from it. Thus the attempted reconciliation of the nationalities in the Empire failed. Nevertheless, Taaffe remained Prime Minister for fourteen years, the longest period for an imperial head of government to keep his post. He coined the term *fortwurschteln*, i.e. to "muddle on."

One of Taaffe's accomplishments was the introduction of *very progressive social welfare legislation that later served as a model for other countries*. Prior to 1884 laws were already in force concerning *the control of sanitation in the workplace, the reduction of working hours to eleven per day, women and children's labor, and work-free Sundays*. In 1888 a very generous "*obligatory health insurance for workers*" was introduced.

In 1893 riots broke out. They were instigated by young Czech rabble-rousers. The causes were not so much language differences as social tensions. Multiple riots, fights, and an anti-German atmosphere provoked a "state of emergency" with the deployment of troops and resulted in arrests. Nevertheless, a reform bill was passed, giving the vote to every citizen above the age of twenty-four, including laborers who were able to read and write or who had at least completed military service. After further commotion in the legislature Taaffe had to resign.

p. 210 "*carelessly written official communiqué*": Probably due to the rise of rumors concerning the high treason of Colonel Redl and the extent and consequences of his "indiscretions" that were discovered at the time.

p. 216 "*Professor Schnitzler*": Surgeon, father of the author Arthur Schnitzler.

p. 219 "*Hirsch*": See page 80.

p. 221 "*Etienne*": Etienne Hirsch, close collaborator of Jean Monet (Father of Europe).

p. 227 "*Jonas Jeitteles*": Jonas Mischel Jeiteles, in: *Jewish Encyclopedia*, Vol. VII, pp. 90-91.

p. 239 "*Ronacher*": Famous Vienna theater café, still exists today.

p. 241 "*Berliner Tageblatt*": Our inquiries regarding the newspaper, article, and author (Felix Hollaender) have not been successful so far (at the time of the German edition in 2001).

p. 249 "*Reb Kifa Eiga*": This mysterious person had not been traced at all in 2001. We are now (2004) in contact with the *Institut für Grenzgebiete der Psychologie und Psychohygiene* [Institute for Border Areas of Psychology and Psycho-Hygiene] (Freiburg), where a specialist (M. Uwe Schellinger) is working on the "Reese" phenomenon. "Reb Kifa Eiga" seems to correspond to the famous Rabbi Akiba Eger, who came from the same region of Posen (Poznan) as Reese himself. A publication on Reese may come out soon.

SIMPLIFIED FAMILY TREES
for the
Jeiteles, Heller, and Foges Families

Prague
From the *Jewish Encyclopedia*
Details in the Annotations

Predecessor of the Jeiteles Family

```
                    Jonas Mischel J. (1735-1806)
              First Jewish doctor to be accredited in Prague
              /                    |                    \
    Baruch J. (1762-1813)          ?              Judah (1773-1838)
       /         \                 |                     |
Israel (Ignaz)   Jakob H. J.   Alois J.          Aaron J. (Justus Frey)
(1783-1843)      (1782-1842)   (1794-1858)            (1799-1878)
Ph.D., h.c.         ∞
                 Rebekka
                 Pick (1790-
                 1857)
```

Jeiteles Family

Umbrella maker in Linz (baptized)

Israel (Ignaz) (1783 - 1843) Ph.D., h.c.

Jakob H. J. (1782 - 1842) ∞ **Rebekka Pick** (1790 - 1857) 9 children

Siblings of Rebekka:
1. Aunt Fanni Pick, 2. Uncle Pick (falsetto),
3. Aunt ? ∞ Michael Goldschmied (jeweler)

Israel (Ignaz)* J. (1811 - 1886) ∞ **Zilie Mayer** 3 children

Sophie J. (1813 - 53) ∞ **Balduin Heller** (1809- ?) 5 children

Marie J. (ca. 1815 - 85) ∞ **Heinrich E. Wiener** 12 children

Joseph J. (1819 - 89) ∞ **Rosa Foges** (ca. 1830-1904) 4 children

Michael J. (ca. 1814 - 70) ∞ **Bondy** 7 children

Hermann J. (1822 - 1909) married twice two daughters

Resi J. ∞ **Moritz Foges** 6 children

Eleonore (Lori) (1841 - 1920?)

Pauline Wiener **Heinrich Heller** (1835 - 1882)

Auguste J. (1851-1911) **J.L. Heller** (1842 - 1921)

Georg J. (1852-1920?) **Rosa Strakosch** (1858 - 1944) Paris; 5 children

Antonie J. (Tony) (1853 - 1937) ∞ **Adolf Schwenk** (d. Oct 1915) 4 children

Max J. (1854 - 1914) ∞ **Jenny Lismann** (d. 1944) 2 children

Klara F. ∞ **Heinrich Schwarz** 5 children emigrated to U.S.A.

*Character Studies
Death year 1944 indicates concentration camp.

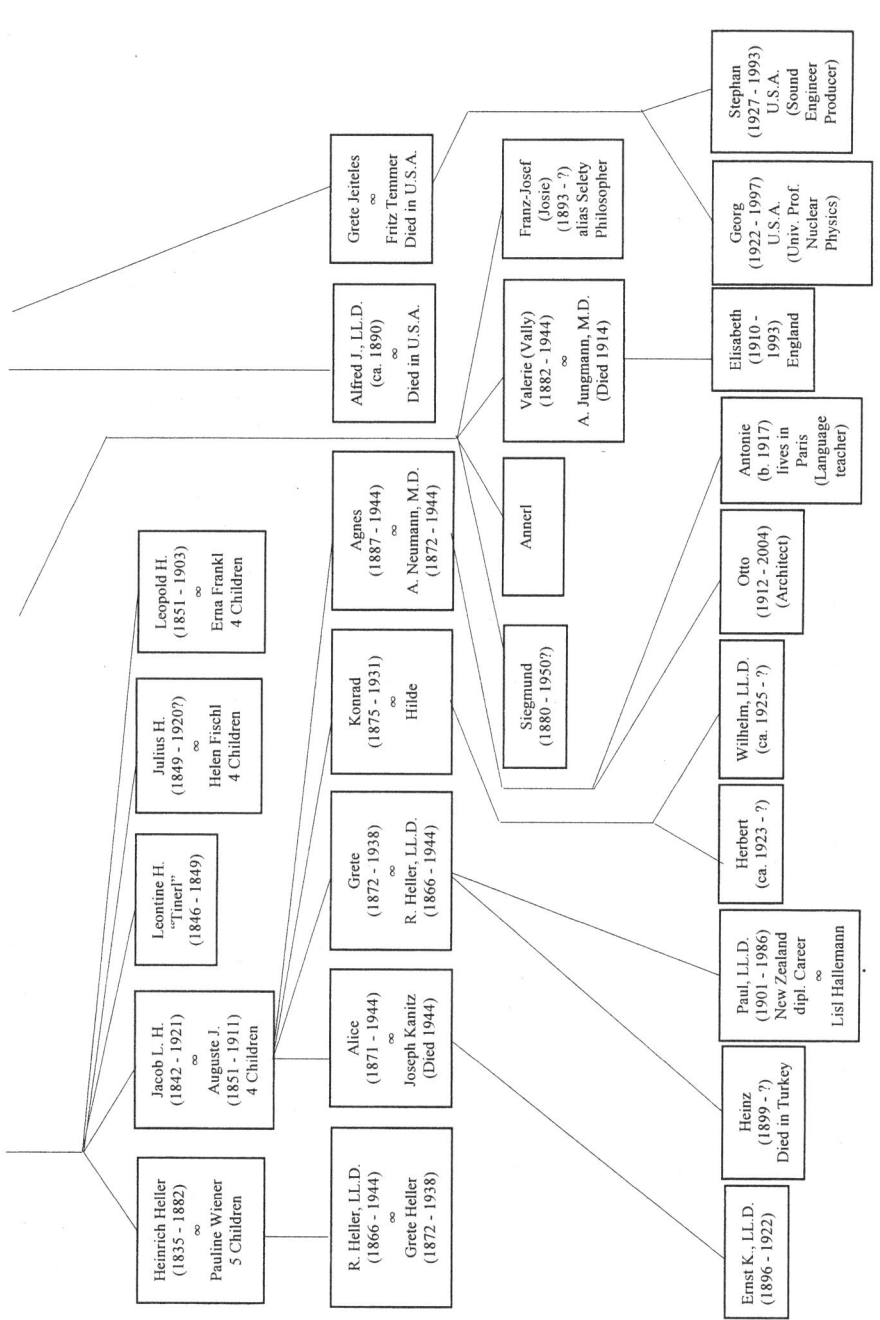

Teplitz
*Character Studies

Heller Family

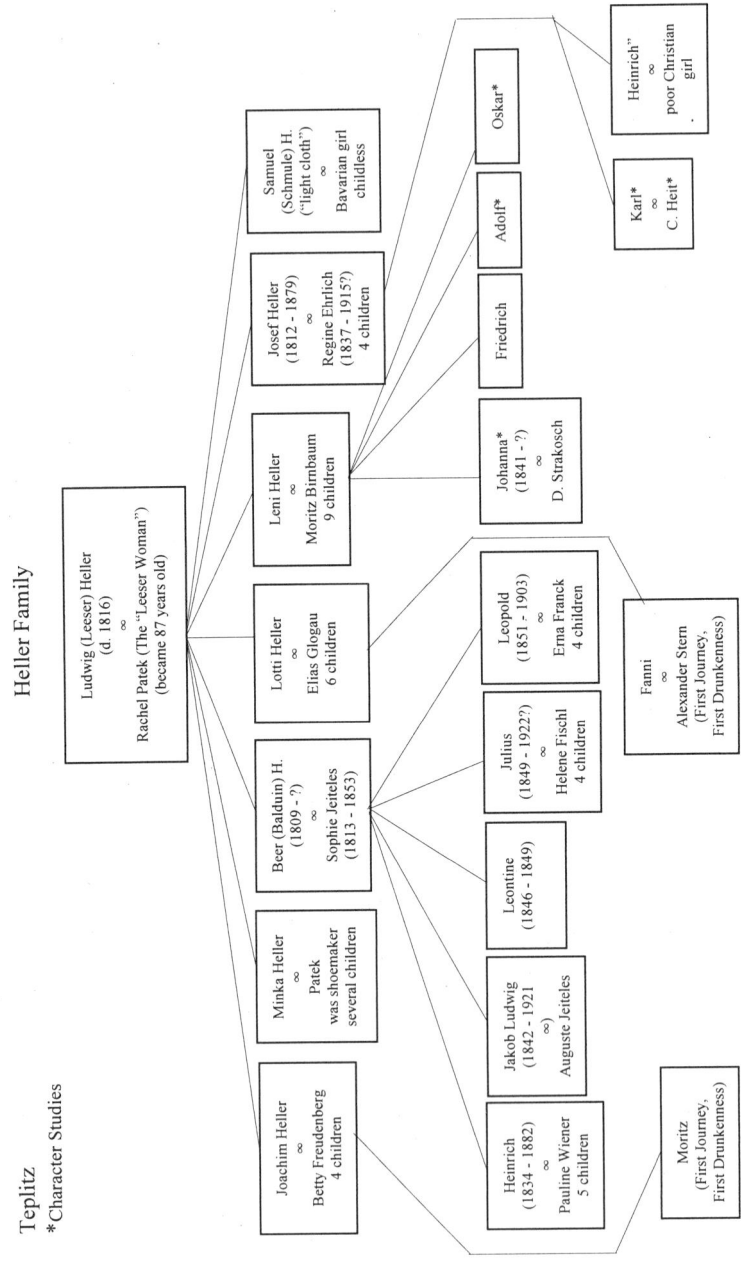

Heller Family

Vienna
Death year 1944 means concentration camp

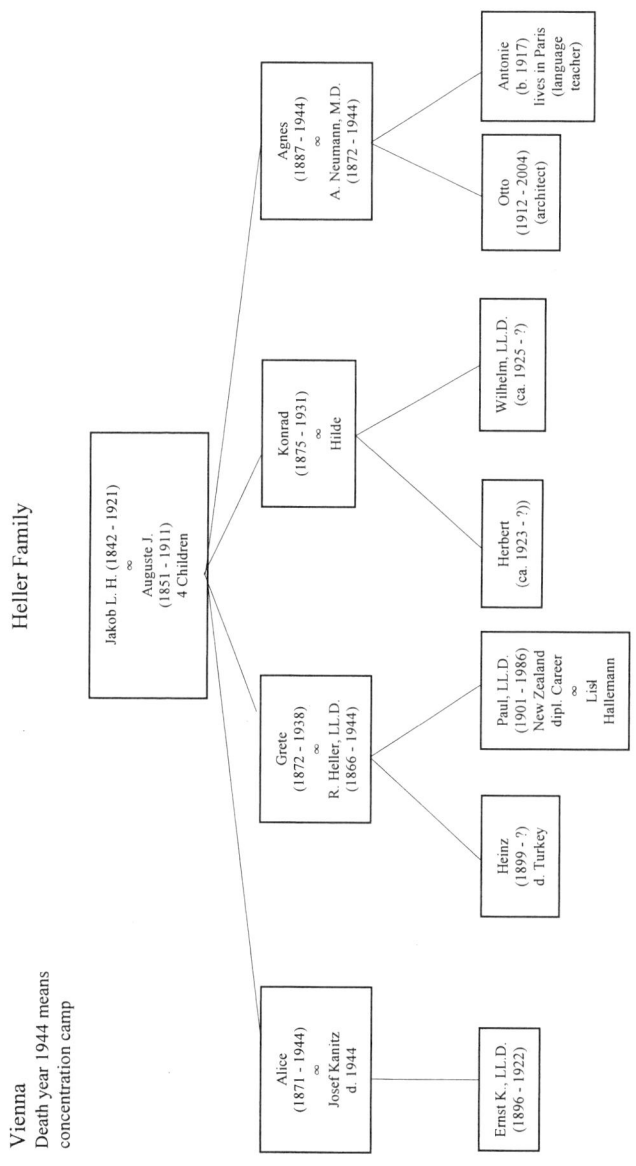

Prague
*Character Studies

Foges Family

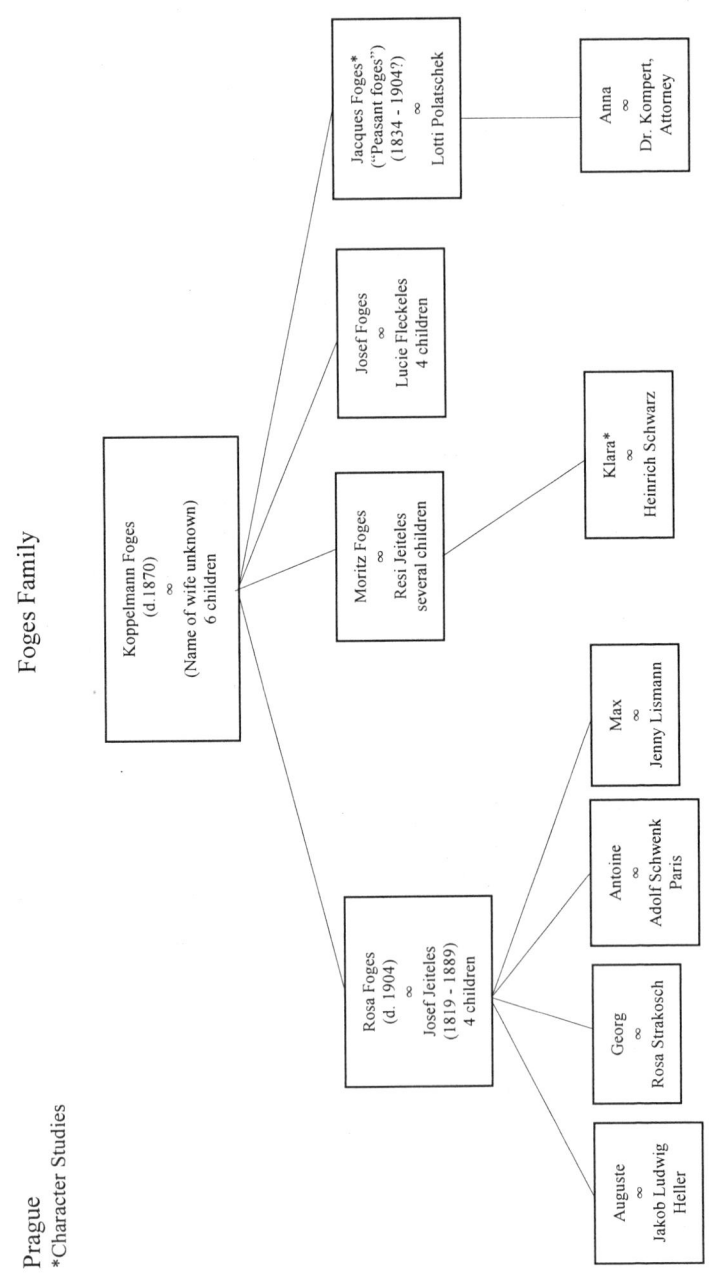

EXCERPTS FROM THE *JEWISH ENCYCLOPEDIA*

Predecessors of the Jeiteles Family

According to the *Jewish Encyclopedia*, this old Prague family was represented by several outstanding personalities in the middle of the eighteenth century.

1. Dr. Jonas Mischel Jeiteles (1735-1806), about whose life Grandfather reports, was accredited as a physician in Prague in 1784 (during the reign of Emperor Joseph II) see p. 232. Two of his sons, Baruch and Judah, were scholars.

2. Baruch Jeiteles (1762-1813) was a scholar of the Talmud and the Hebrew language and a disciple of the liberal philosopher Moses Mendelssohn. He left an extensive collection of works. After the battles of Kulm, Leipzig, and Dresden (1813), in which thousands of wounded soldiers could not be treated in the existing hospitals, he invested his energy in establishing emergency hospitals in Prague. After working tirelessly to find the means to help wounded soldiers *from all armies and of all religions*, he succumbed to a fever epidemic that had begun to rage in all the hospitals.

3. Judah Jeiteles (Prague 1773 - Vienna 1838) dedicated himself to the study of Oriental languages and culture. He wrote the first grammar book for biblical Aramaic in Hebrew (Prague, 1813).

Baruch's son Ignaz and Judah's son Aaron are mentioned in the following generation.

4. Ignaz Jeiteles (Prague 1783 - Vienna 1843). His fields were classical literature and aesthetics. Circumstances forced him to begin a career as a businessman, and he established his professional life in Vienna. He became famous through his frequent contributions to various Austrian and German periodicals. His main achievement, the *Ästhetische Lexikon*

[Aesthetic Lexicon] (Vienna, 1838), earned him an honorary Ph.D. from the University of Jena.

5. Aaron (Andreas) Ludwig Josef Jeiteles (Prague 1799 - Graz 1878). A doctor, poet, and dedicated author. He completed his medical studies in Vienna in 1825 and became head of the Department of Anatomy and Surgery (Vienna, Olmütz). He played an active part in the Revolution of 1848 and became the representative for Olmütz in the revolutionary parliament in Frankfurt am Main. He believed in humanity, justice, and freedom, which gave rise to his pseudonym, "Justus Frey." His collected works fill an entire volume of the *Bibliothek der deutschen Schriftsteller aus Böhmen* [Library of German Authors from Bohemia]. Some of his poems were set to music by Beethoven and other composers.

6. Alois Jeiteles (Brünn 1794-1858). A doctor in Brünn and a cousin of Ignaz and Aaron. He became the chief editor of the official *Brünner Zeitung* [Brno Newspaper] in 1848. Inspired by his contact with Beethoven, Grillparzer, and prominent artists of the *Hoftheater* [Court Theater], he turned to writing. He wrote several plays that were performed on German-language stages everywhere. His poetic cycle *An die ferne Geliebte* [To the Distant Beloved] was set to Music by Beethoven.

From dates, places, and circumstances, it seems more than reasonable to assume that Ignaz Jeiteles was one of the brothers of Jakob Herschmann Jeiteles, which would link us to that family.

ACKNOWLEDGMENTS

I am greatly indebted to all those who played an active part in the production of this work, and to those who gave advice, supported, or encouraged me. First and foremost, my thanks go to my dear friend Ingrid Wagner in Salzburg, who, with her sensitivity, selfless commitment, and unbelievable tenacity, took on the years of devoted work, and with great skill and knowledge produced a complete manuscript of the writings. And to my brother Otto, who, in spite of the great distance, contributed to the choice of texts and found in Sydney the documents that we used from the *Jewish Encyclopedia*. Moreover, I would like to acknowledge Dr. H. Douffet from Freiberg-Dresden, whose friendly invitation and assistance helped me to visit Teplitz and Prague and really started "to get the ball rolling." It has also been very important to me over the years to find in Dr. Albert Lichtblau (University of Salzburg) a person and a specialist who believed in this adventure right from the very beginning, and who gave his recognition again and again through warm words of praise.

Yet should I not also be grateful for the modern technological advancements? This project would not have been conceivable under such difficult conditions without cassette recorders, computers, and fax machines.

Antonie Neumann

This translation has taken form in uncommon conditions, as did the German edition. The collaborators were not only separated geographically between Austria and France, but also between continents.

Translated in Sydney, the present definitive text was originally typed in Paris. We believe in "unexplainable help" and are truly grateful for the very practical support that we received from Mr. Uli Priester, translator (Sydney), whose version, which was rapidly and competently developed, provided the basis for this work. In turn the manuscript was most carefully edited and typed by Jean and Clotilde Grigorieff, friends of my sister in Paris, for whose help we are both most thankful!

It is our deepest hope that Grandfather's memoirs will be received by later generations with the same fond emotions that were ours when we read them for the first time.

Otto Neumann

Teplitz: View from the Castle Square into *Lange Gasse*. Colored engraving. First half of the 19th century (*Teplitz City Museum*)

Jakob Ludwig Heller (1860)

The young couple

Grete						Konrad

Max

Agnes and Alfred
1912

J.L. Heller in the Rathauspark in Vienna, 1913

Otto in a little child's dress, Mother and Grandfather in *Rathauspark* in Vienna

Alfred

BIOGRAPHIES OF THE EDITOR AND TRANSLATOR

Antonie Neumann

Born in 1917, Antonie Neumann spent her early childhood in Vöslau-Gainfarn (Lower Austria). She enjoyed a refined education, including happy, formative years at the well-known Vienna *Schwarzwaldschule*, from which she graduated in 1935. While studying English at the university, she passed the state examination in English in 1937.

Upon receiving an unexpected invitation to spend a year in France as an au-pair girl, in order to learn French she suddenly interrupted her university studies and left Austria at the beginning of February 1938, shortly before Hitler's Anschluss, without any inkling of the dramatic events that would shatter the world a few weeks later.

Alone in a foreign country, suddenly forced to stand on her own two feet, separated from parents that she would never see again, as well as from her older brother Otto, who emigrated to Australia, she spent the years of the Second World War in France in the most difficult and dangerous circumstances. In August of 1942 she miraculously escaped deportation from a French concentration camp to Poland.

She taught English and German in a French private school in the so-called "unoccupied" southern part of France and was appreciated for her methods and results. After the war she pursued that stimulating profession in the environs of Paris. Her aim was to communicate true cultural values to her pupils by illustrating her lessons with music, slide lectures, and authentic material from popular tradition.

As a music lover she participated in a well-known Paris choir that specialized in the works of Bach. She has lived in Paris since 1947, where, in her dedication to arts and crafts, she is a self-taught hand weaver and furniture decorator.

Since her retirement in 1983, she has remained most active in the field of cultural heritage. She gives benevolent lectures, in which her personal collection of slides on architecture, her travels, her arts and crafts, and many other things arouse great interest.

However, during the last eight years she has dedicated most of her time to publishing the handwritten memoirs of her grandfather in German and, together with her brother, in English.

Otto Neumann

Born in 1912 in Vienna, Otto Neumann spent his early childhood in Edlach and Vöslau-Gainfarn (Lower Austria). He enjoyed careful education in an intellectually enlightened family with broad interests. His father was a medical doctor and a contemporary of Dr. Alfred Adler of the Viennese school of psychoanalysis. His mother came from a well-known Jewish family that produced outstanding personalities in the fields of medicine, literature, philosophy, and religious research.

He obtained his secondary education and graduated in 1930 from the *Modernes Gymnasium* [Modern Secondary School] for young men in Baden near Vienna. After enrolling in the architectural program at the technical university, he received his diploma as an engineer in 1935. During his education he spent his summer vacations on building sites in an endeavor to gain practical knowledge of the manual side of all construction trades. That later permitted him to obtain temporary work with several well-known architects in Vienna when the crises of the times created obstacles to finding permanent employment.

That was his situation when Austria was taken over by Hitler. It is not necessary to describe the scenes of horror, the sudden abysmal changes for the worse, the outbreak of hatred and fear in a formerly friendly population, or the situation in which breathing fresh air in a public garden or sitting on a bench was forbidden. It is unnecessary to describe the months of trudging from one foreign embassy to another to "beg" for a visa, the lining up, the endless chicanery to which everybody was subjected, or the danger of simply being on the street when the police decided to comb the area. Nor is it necessary to describe the many other insulting "innovations" for which no words are adequate, nor to speak of his continuous anxiety for his parents and close friends from one day to the next. He has written his memoirs of that unimaginable atmosphere and of his escape from "hell" in a work that will be published in the near future in Australia, the country where he was offered hospitality and even a warm welcome.

Beginning with the moment of his arrival there, he found help, support, friendship, and love. He was taken for what he was and never as an "enemy alien" or a Jew. He built his professional career as an architect in the Australian Housing Commission and was appreciated for his innovative ideas. At the outbreak of the war, he volunteered for the Australian army and was placed in a labor unit that was composed of men of many nationalities, creeds, and colors. It was jokingly known as the R.A.E.A. (Royal Austrian Enemy Aliens).

After spending several years clearing a formerly wild piece of land, he built his house and planted a picturesque garden in an elegant area of Sydney. He gave much of his time to political work in the Labor Party chapter in his district and remained true to the ideals of his youth.

Painting, drawing, and rapid sketching were among his favorite pastimes, along with history, science, and philosophy.

He still felt much sympathy toward his original homeland of Austria and took a heartfelt interest in its fate. He loved to guide Australian friends to the beauties of Austria, but Australia had become the country in which he rediscovered the feeling of "being at home." It was his wish to make our grandfather's writings available to an English-speaking public.

COMMENTARIES

The time for autobiographies has arrived. Interest in authentic life stories seems greater than ever, even greater than well-written works of fiction, because readers begin to recognize that nothing is more fantastic than the complicated reality through which we are forced to make our way. Accounts of everyday life have long since become a source of historic insight, and even historians are beginning to admit that concrete vignettes of an autobiographer's life are often better able to portray what the past was really like.

All of this holds true for the memoirs of Jakob Ludwig Heller, who lived in the Austro-Hungarian Empire during the 19th and into the 20th centuries. The records that he left behind reveal that nostalgic individuals were not far wrong in viewing the Empire and its era as the quintessence of an intact world. Of course things were not as peaceful and happy for everyone in the Danube monarchy, but compared with today's world, Jakob Ludwig Heller's milieu was a true idyll, where marriages endured, family ties were strong, hard work was rewarded, and people rejoiced over simple social gatherings. Upbringing was strict, but caring, the children were well behaved, and earning a living was fun. Long live progress!

The feeling that what he describes is lost forever is magnified further by the fact that he grew up in a Jewish, Central European milieu, where Jews perhaps did not live without tension among neighbors of other faiths, but did live without being persecuted, robbed, and murdered. Not only Jewish readers will regret the loss of that normal way of life.

Near the end of his memoirs, in retrospect the diarist complains about the inexplicable intrusion of lax morals, the disappearance of fixed norms, and the lack of the earlier, ever-present feeling of security and continuity. What would he say today? But what makes the reading of this simple story so rewarding, apart from the historic information, is the intelligent, humorous, warm-hearted man who is encountered on every page. His comments about the First World War are especially touching. Despite his extensive life experience, they betray his naïve belief in Germany and Austria, in the government and the army. He is convinced that the Central Powers fight for a just cause at a time when Karl Kraus is writing *The Last Days of Mankind*. But in those days the great satirist was still quite alone with his opinion. Most of the Jews, even most of the people, probably felt as did Jakob Ludwig Heller. And the waning of those certainties is the greatest tragedy of all, a sign of the insurmountable distance between our world and that of the past.

Professor Egon Schwarz

The memoirs of your grandfather are an interesting account of life in the old Austria and the former Bohemia. They illustrate the important role that the Jews there also played in German history. They show what the collapse of the Imperial and Royal Monarchy and the Nazi crimes against the Jewish population also meant for us Germans. But it is not possible to change history. Only memories remain, not least as a product of the deeds of Jakob Ludwig Heller.

Dr. Heinrich Douffet

BIBLIOGRAPHY

Beer, A. *Die Finanzen Österreichs im 19. Jahrhundert* [The Financial Affairs of Austria in the 19th Century]. Prague: F. Tempsky, 1877.

"Beethoven." In: *Collection Génies et Realités* [Collection of Geniuses and Realities] Paris: Hachette, 1961.

Brusquatti, A. and P. Marginter. *Wien, Am Graben 21* [Vienna, Am Graben 21 (a street address)]. Vienna: Erste Österr. Spar-Casse, 1969.

Clary-Aldringen, A. von. *Geschichten eines alten Österreichers* [Stories of an Old Austrian]. Frankfurt am Main and Berlin: Ullstein Verlag, 1989.

"*Herzliche Grüße aus der Stadt Teplitz* [Cordial Greetings from the City of Teplitz]," "*Herzliche Grüße aus der Umgebung von Teplitz* [Cordial Greetings from the Environs of Teplitz]" [two volumes of picture postcards]. Ed. Antonýn Vengrynský. Teplitz, 1965

Die Chronik Österreichs [The Chronicle of Austria]. Dortmund: Chronik Verlag, 1989.

"Jeiteles." In: *The Jewish Encyclopedia*. Ed. Ididor Singer and Cyrus Adler. New York: Funk & Wagnalls, 1916. Vol. VII., pp. 90-91.

Kügelgen, W. von. *Jugenderinnerungen eines alten Mannes* [An Old Man's Memoirs of His Youth]. Stuttgart: Chr. Belser Verlag, 1900.

Langweil, A. *Svědectví Modelu Prahi* [A Model of Prague - Capital City], Schola Ludus Pragensia, 1996. Muzeum Hlarnicho Města Prahi.

May, Alfred. *Wien in alten Ansichten - Das Werden der Wiener Vedute* [Vienna in Old Depictions - The Development of Viennese Naturalist Painting]. Salzburg: Verlag für Jugend und Volk, Residenzverlag, 1965.

"Reese." In: *Encyclopedia of Occultism and Parapsychology*, 4th ed. Detroit: Gale Research, 1978, p. 1083.